Early Childhood Studies

An Introduction to the Study of Children's Worlds and Children's Lives

Edited by
Jenny Willan, Rod Parker-Rees and Jan Savage

Learning Matters

First published in 2004 by Learning Matters Ltd.

British Library Cataloguing in Publication Data
A CIP record for this book is available from the British Library.

ISBN 1 844450 09 0

Cover and text design by Code 5 Design Associates Ltd
Project management by Deer Park Productions
Typeset by Pantek Arts Ltd, Maidstone, Kent
Printed and bound in Great Britain by Bell & Bain Ltd, Glasgow

Learning Matters Ltd
33 Southernhay East
Exeter EX1 1NX
Tel: 01392 215560
info@learningmatters.co.uk
www.learningmatters.co.uk

Early Childhood Studies

Contents

Contributors

The contributors are all members of the Early Childhood Studies (ECS) team at the University of Plymouth. They all teach on the BA (Hons) in Early Childhood Studies and on the ECS specialist pathway of the BEd degree programme.

Bernie Davis teaches equal opportunities and comparative perspectives in early years. She has done research into the implementation of the Literacy Hour in small rural schools. She worked as a kindergarten teacher in the US and has taught in nursery and reception classes in England. Her current research interests are in forest schools and collaboration among students engaging in small-scale research.

Norman Gabriel, PhD, has many years of teaching experience in Early Childhood Studies. His main area of interest is the sociology of childhood. Inspired by the work of Norbert Elias and Lev Vygotsky, he is investigating the early development of language by young children, and how this development becomes overlaid by cultural and social processes.

Ulrike Gelder, PhD, worked as a Research Associate at the University of Newcastle. Her publications range from young people and sex education to children living in self-employed households. She holds a German childcare qualification and has worked in a wide range of childcare settings in Germany. Her research interests include children and social policy, childcare settings and the relationships that develop between children and their adult carers. She is also interested in cross-national research.

Lesley Griffiths teaches on all aspects of child development. She trained as an early years teacher and worked in a variety of settings. With her husband, she set up a childcare centre which continues to expand and change to meet the needs of children and parents. Her research interest is emotional literacy and she is currently working on an MPhil, looking at indicators of creativity in young children.

Caroline Leeson is teaching on modules with a focus on social policy and social work. Previously she worked as a social worker in mental health, child protection, fostering and adoption. She also managed a family centre in a diverse ethnic community. Currently she is writing her PhD on children's participation in legal decision-making.

Rod Parker-Rees is joint co-ordinator of Early Childhood Studies. He taught three- to five-year-old children in Bristol and conducted research with the National Primary Centre (South West) before joining the University of Plymouth, where he helped to develop the Early Childhood Studies specialist pathway on the BEd and the BA (Hons) degree in ECS.

His research interests are centred on playfulness, communication and the role of young children as active social agents. He is a co-editor of *Early Years: an International Journal of Research and Development*.

Sue Rogers, PhD, is one of the long-standing members of the ECS team. She is an experienced early years teacher. Her research interests lie within early years education, in particular four-year-olds in school and the role of play in early learning. She recently directed a project on children's role play funded by the Economic and Social Research Council.

Jan Savage, PhD, is joint co-ordinator of Early Childhood Studies and helped to develop both the specialist pathway on the BEd and the BA (Hons) degree in ECS. She is interested in promoting an interdisciplinary collaborative approach to continued professional development work in early years, developing links across the sector. She worked for 15 years as a nursery teacher in both London and Devon. Her research interests are young children and those who work with them. She is particularly interested in finding ways of accessing very young children's perspectives.

Jenny Willan teaches on modules with a focus on research methodology. She previously worked in educational research at the University of Cambridge and the National Foundation for Educational Research. She has worked on children's writing, gender studies and teacher action research. Her current interest is in the effects of formal education programmes on boys and girls aged three to six.

Preface

These are exciting times for all of us involved in and responsible for the care and education of our youngest children. New government initiatives, increasing numbers of places in a wide variety of settings, a wealth of challenging research and literature to inform and stimulate, new training opportunities for students and staff and job opportunities demanding knowledge and skills well beyond those envisaged even five years ago are welcome developments in the early childhood field.

At a recent conference I met a lecturer newly appointed to a University in the Midlands to teach on their Early Childhood Studies degree. She was herself a graduate of one of the first multidisciplinary degrees to be offered in this country, and now here she was excited to be what she termed 'a true multiprofessional', teaching on a course demanding just the kind of knowledge which she considered her own degree studies had offered her. This book will be published at just the right time for her. It is just what she and her students and the increasing number of early childhood students across the country will require.

This is an exciting book – working with young children is exciting. It is also extremely challenging and demanding, and students and practitioners require not only a wide range of knowledge and information but also opportunities to reflect and respond if they are to do the job effectively.

This book is written by a group of people I have long admired for their understanding, vision and commitment. The Early Childhood Studies team at the University of Plymouth were well ahead of their time in recognising and responding to the need for multidisciplinary training. I was privileged to act as External Examiner for the University and witnessed at first hand their enthusiasm and commitment to their students, and their deep understanding of young children and their needs.

Students and experienced practitioners will find much to support and challenge in this book. Key themes and practical issues are addressed with equal sensitivity and understanding. I urge you to read, revisit and above all respond to the important messages it contains.

Lesley Abbott

Professor, Early Childhood Education

Manchester Metropolitan University

On behalf of the Early Childhood Studies Team
at the University of Plymouth
we dedicate this volume
to all our students past and present

Jenny Willan, Rod Parker-Rees and Jan Savage
Faculty of Education University of Plymouth
August 2004

Introduction
Rod Parker-Rees

This book has been written by members of the Early Childhood Studies (ECS) team at the University of Plymouth to give readers a taste of the range of issues addressed on our BA (Hons) ECS degree programme. We hope that this collection of chapters reflects the multi-professional and multidisciplinary range and scope of ECS, introducing you to different ways of studying the richness and complexity of children's lives and children's worlds.

We are passionately committed to enabling students to develop their skills as advocates for young children and we are convinced that ECS provides unique opportunities for personal growth and the development of sensitivity to the needs and interests of other people – adults as well as children. While we expect our students to develop skills in working with young children and their families, we also believe that ECS should offer more than voca-tional training. Studying issues which shape children's lives and worlds offers powerful opportunities to develop personal qualities which will enable ECS graduates to make a sig-nificant contribution to improving children's lives and worlds. Developing a critical perspective involves more than just challenging everything (though this is a good start!); it requires a willingness to subject other people's ideas to careful scrutiny, matching them against your own experiences, values, beliefs and principles and noting interesting discrep-ancies. Being critical means being willing to adapt your own views, as well as seeking to influence other people. Developing a personal understanding of complex issues also requires much more than just accumulating knowledge (though, again, this is a good start). Knowledge can only be woven into understanding when the shared frameworks of common knowledge are 'coloured in' with personal significance and the unique richness of personal experience. Understanding requires an ability to move between the cool clarity of generalised theoretical models and the fuzzy, messy detail of particular cases. For example, 'failure' to meet developmental milestones for speech development at the 'normal' age may be indicative of articulatory difficulties but it may also reflect a family context in which other forms of communication make clarity of speech less important.

The study of early childhood presents us with frequent opportunities to stand back and reflect on how our own position relates to that of young children: how would I feel if someone treated me like that? Would I talk like that to another adult? What would it be like if adults could only study alongside others of the same age or if we had no say in what we had to study? How do I feel when I enter a situation in which I don't know anyone and I don't know how I'm supposed to behave?

This introduction cannot hope to represent the full range of ideas addressed in this book but I hope to give you a feel for what you will find in each chapter by showing how the different themes and topics can provide opportunities to learn about yourself as well as about the lives and worlds of young children.

Powerful children: acknowledging the achievements of young children

Part 1 addresses aspects of development with a particular focus on encouraging the reader to reassess the accomplishments of very young children. Because in our first years we learned fast and effortlessly, we can easily assume that what we learned must have been 'child's play', simple and trivial. But think for a moment about how your world would be turned upside down if you were to forget how to control the movements of your body, how to make sense of speech sounds, how to read other people's moods and emotions or even how to adjust your behaviour to different expectations in different contexts. When you imagine the effects of losing what you learned in your first three years in comparison with losing what you have learned in the last ten years, you may begin to appreciate the scale of what infants manage to learn. Observing the way in which children rise to these challenges can be enlightening for adults who have had years (many spent in schooling) to develop whole complexes of attitudes and dispositions which can muddy their own approaches to learning, tackling problems and coping with knock-backs.

In Chapter 1, 'Moving, playing and learning', Rod Parker-Rees explores the relationships between children's developing ability to bring their motor activity under deliberate control, their active, inquisitive and playful exploration of how their actions affect their environment (including other people) and their ability to discover patterns and consistencies in the effects they are able to produce. This is one of the first modules on our BA degree and we encourage students to make their own connections between what they find out about infants' learning and how they think about themselves as learners. As adults we don't tend to find out about the world of ideas by putting things in our mouths, banging them against the floor or throwing them but we can still recognise the importance of active engagement in learning – our equivalents may be active participation in discussions, purposefully looking for connections between new ideas and our own experiences and playful exploration of other ways of thinking about things. The language of ideas is riddled with metaphors drawn from motor activity and it is not difficult to discover the value of poking and prodding at other people's theories, wiggling them loose, taking them apart, rearranging them, noticing anything interesting that happens and then showing other people and seeing how they react. Students also discover that doing things with other people, especially things that involve movement and touch, generates an energy within the group which is much less often achieved when the main activity is talking and listening. Feelings of awkwardness and embarrassment quickly give way to exhilaration, laughter and a strong sense of community which can feed into later, more sedentary, group activities.

In Chapter 2, 'Becoming a person', Lesley Griffiths focuses on understanding and supporting aspects of children's affective development: their construction of a sense of self and their ability to cope with emotions, to make choices and to manage relationships. This focus again provides fertile ground for students to study themselves as they study young children, and some find themselves swept along on an emotional rollercoaster ride as they come to terms with aspects of their own early experiences. Peers as well as tutors can find themselves modelling the 'holding' which allows us to support others, so it is important to discuss ethical issues involved in exposing people (adults or children) to powerful emotional experiences.

Philippe Rochat (2004) has suggested that children's awareness of their own thoughts, beliefs and personalities emerges from their recognition of the differentness of other people's thoughts, beliefs and personalities and this helps to explain the importance of discussion, argument and active, engaged reading in the study of early childhood. By paying careful attention to our own reactions to other people's ideas, jotting down comments in the margins, probing, questioning or offering relevant examples from our own experience, we gradually become more aware of our own understanding of the issues we are studying.

In Chapter 3, 'Developing communication', Rod Parker-Rees argues that careful examination of the earliest stages of infants' communication with other people can help us to recognise that the shared enjoyment of joint attention may be more important than we realise. The 'workaday' model of communication, which focuses on the transfer of information from one brain to another, fails to acknowledge the social importance of the playfulness of conversation. While gossip and idle chat may appear 'unprofessional', this kind of unstructured interaction can be a valuable way of getting to know other people as individuals, with their own interests, perspectives and priorities. Students will experience the difference in 'feel' between tutors who deliver lectures *at* them and those who try to engage with them in conversations, and they can relate this to the feel of different settings where staff either talk *with* parents and children or talk *to* them.

Understanding children's worlds: making the familiar strange

The fact that we have all been children may, at first, appear to give us a good foundation for studying childhood but this familiarity can also make it more difficult for us to notice what is right under our noses. Like the proverbial fish who remains unaware of the existence of water until taken out of it, we can easily just assume that children do what they do because that's just what children do. However, as soon as we begin to introduce some distance between our own experience and the children and childhoods we study, we can realise that what children do is heavily shaped and constrained by what adults want, expect and even need children to do.

In Chapter 4, 'Adults' concepts of childhood', Norman Gabriel reminds us that adults have an interest in childhood which extends well beyond consideration of how best to care for children. Once a contrast is recognised between childhood and adulthood, childhood acquires an important status as a way of defining adulthood: if adults value social polish and civilised manners then childhood is a time of wildness, associated with all that is uncontrolled, passionate, dangerous and exciting; if adults are jaded by the restrictions and artificiality of social conventions then childhood is seen as a time of freedom, innocence and naturalness. The shifts and changes in our attitudes to nature are particularly interesting and remind us of the need to step outside our familiar mindsets when we read accounts of childhood which were written long ago. In 1628, for example, John Robinson, the puritan pastor of a separatist pilgrim church in Holland, railed against the natural qualities of children:

And surely, there is in all children, though not alike, a stubbornness, and stoutness of mind arising from natural pride, which must, in the first place, be broken and beaten down ... This fruit of natural corruption and root of actual rebellion both against God and man must be destroyed.

(Cox, 1995, p.13)

We may associate nature with goodness, purity and wholesomeness but in the seventeenth century, when cold, hunger, wild animals and danger were much closer to everyone's lives, nature had a very different feel about it. Changing attitudes to the contrast between nature and civilisation can be traced in all areas of life; in gardens, for example, as well as in art, literature and advice to parents on how to bring up children. Exploring adults' concepts of childhood can open our eyes to the effects on children of our efforts to define what it is to be grown up and what are the 'childish things' which must be put aside in order to achieve adulthood:

When I was a child, I used to talk as a child, think as a child, reason as a child; when I became a man, I put aside childish things.

(1 Corinthians, 13:11)

In Chapter 5, 'Children and social policy', Ulrike Gelder and Jan Savage trace the strange history of England's policy on admitting children to school at the age of four. This quirk of English policy is used as an example to illustrate the intricate ways in which legal and policy frameworks and family practices are bound up with each other. Careful examination of the relationships between top-down processes, such as the passing of laws and the setting up of administrative structures, and bottom-up processes, such as changes in family structures, attitudes and lifestyles, can help students of ECS to pick their way through the policy landscapes of settings in which they work. How are policies set up? Who is involved in writing, monitoring and revising them? Are they felt as constraints or as supportive frameworks? How confident are practitioners about interpreting policies to suit the particular needs of individual children? Students may also notice connections between their discussions about the nature of policy and the different interpretations of rules in Piagetian and Vygotskian models of development: are rules like laws or are they more like patterns that children discover in the ways people tend to behave?

In Chapter 6, 'Being a child today', Norman Gabriel invites us to use comparisons with the experiences of previous generations of children, our parents and grandparents, as one way to sharpen our awareness of how today's children may experience their childhood. We do not belong to their generation and we sometimes have to work hard to remember that they do not belong to ours. If they do not do the things we fondly imagine we did as children, this may not be a cause for great concern, as they are not growing up in the world we think we remember. Our ability to imagine what it is like to be a child today will always be limited because we can only understand the significance of events and relationships in a child's life in terms of our own knowledge, values and beliefs. Reading autobiographies can help us to see that even a childhood of grinding poverty could offer moments of joy, comfort and exhilaration but even autobiographies are adult fictions which tell us more about the author's present values than about what it felt like to be that remembered, reconstructed child. If, on the other hand, we take time to engage with children, to allow them to let us know what they care about, what they enjoy and what they worry about, we can develop our ability to step outside our own perspective and even to learn to see things in new ways.

In Chapter 7, 'International perspectives on early years education and care', Bernie Davis shows how comparisons with practice in other countries can also help us to notice what we might otherwise take for granted. First-hand experience of other ways of working with children can encourage us to celebrate our differences, rather than mistrust anyone who doesn't work to our rules. Travel and work abroad also provide a powerful metaphor for study. The traveller learns twice: once on arrival in a new place, where many aspects of people's lives and practices seem strange and interesting, and again on returning home, when what had once been too familiar to notice now stands out in comparison with foreign ways. Students who have travelled and visited early years settings in other countries have been forced to recognise gaps in their knowledge about policy and practice in the UK as they struggle to answer their hosts' questions. They have also often been impressed by how green the grass seems to be 'over there'! Like practitioners visiting other settings, who tend to see only what is not on offer in their practice, travellers may need to remind themselves that there may also be features of their practice which their hosts would admire if they were to return the visit.

Whenever we read about other people's ideas and other people's ways of working, whenever we talk with other people and whenever we visit different settings, we have opportunities to bring home souvenirs to decorate our mental mantelpiece but we can also be inspired to rearrange our concepts, to throw out some clutter and even to undertake major redecorations.

Working with children: opening up opportunities

Any study of early childhood must include substantial experience of spending time with children, both working with them in a professional capacity and just enjoying their company. Direct, experiential learning offers special opportunities and challenges, not least because learners must always acknowledge their responsibility for the effects of their actions on the children and they must tiptoe among the eggshells of professional sensitivities – mistakes here have real consequences. But ECS students are rewarded by the energy, vitality and openness of young children which can help them to refresh and nurture 'an inner life invigorated by a connection to the taproot' (Plotz, 2001, p.xvi).

In Chapter 8, 'Observing children', Jenny Willan shows how important it is to acknowledge the environmental factors, the contexts, which influence children's behaviour, and their experiences. While it is sometimes important to take children out of familiar contexts to examine details of their behaviour and development, it is always necessary to remember that what children do, and especially what they *don't* do, in these odd situations may not accurately reflect what they may be able to do in situations where they feel more at ease. You can probably identify with this through your own experience of what happens when you are subjected to questioning under exam conditions! Because it is so easy for adults to take aspects of their contexts for granted, we do need to adopt a purposeful, investigative stance when we attempt to understand what it might be like to be a particular child in a particular situation – we need to observe carefully, to study rather than simply notice. We can also learn from new approaches to studying children that, when they are encouraged and given the time, space and tools to explore and represent what matters to them, they can participate effectively in conversations about improving the quality of their lives and worlds. In Reggio Emilia pre-schools the practice of documentation, involving children, staff and families in recording, representing and revisiting children's developing understanding of an area of interest, offers an excellent model of how the study of children can leak into the fabric of a setting, becoming part of the way of life, for the children as well as for the adults (Katz and Chard, 1996; Forman and Fyfe, 1998).

In Chapter 9, 'The importance of equal opportunities in the early years', Ulrike Gelder reminds us of the value of inclusive thinking. Where the concept of 'integration' could sometimes be interpreted in terms of helping 'different' children to fit in unobtrusively among their 'normal' peers, 'inclusion' acknowledges the need for settings to make such changes as are necessary to allow *all* children to thrive together. The focus on inclusion is driven by changes in provision for children with special educational needs but it fits comfortably within an early years philosophy which insists that every child must be respected as an individual, with individual needs, interests and concerns. Teachers of older children will often throw their hands up in horror at the idea of preparing individual lesson plans for every child in their class but there is no need for this if all children are offered open, flexibly resourced provision and allowed space and time to choose for themselves what will best fit their needs at any time. Providing equal opportunities then means ensuring that the resources on offer do meet the needs of all children, not just those who happen to share the tastes and values of the adults who hold the purse strings. The real value of the concept of inclusion is that it can help us to move beyond tokenistic provision of 'exotic' costumes, cookware and play props towards a genuine celebration of our differences.

In Chapter 10, 'Supporting creativity', Sue Rogers opens up the concept of creativity beyond the plastic-floored 'creative area' and beyond the 'Creative development' area of learning, set out in the *Curriculum Guidance for the Foundation Stage* (QCA/DfEE, 2000). Creativity is a disposition or a habit of mind which comes as part and parcel of our human intelligence, allowing us to make sense of all that we experience. The making of sense, like the making of music, marks or models, is a creative process and one which all children engage in, unless and until they are discouraged, disheartened or prevented. Adults who work with children can value and nurture their creativity or they can channel it into an easy, safe but dull conformity. Adults who are themselves creative will find ways to interpret restrictive policies and rules in ways that allow tendrils of creativity to push their way between the stones, but 'teachers cannot develop the creative abilities of their pupils if their own creative abilities are suppressed' (NACCCE, 1999, p.90).

Working in early years teams: developing empowering communities

Anyone who considers a career working with children because they get on better with children than with grown-ups will soon discover that virtually every possible kind of work will necessarily involve working with adults: parents and families as well as colleagues and professionals from other agencies. Learning how to get on with other adults and how to help them to achieve their full potential is an essential part of any professional training and fortunately we all have plenty of experience of working with others in different kinds of groups and teams, collaborating, submitting to leadership and also, perhaps, leading. We each have a considerable stockpile of both positive and negative examples of factors which affect how people get on, both with each other and with the task in hand. In the early stages of any career our main priority will be to survive being led by others (drawing on our creative ability to interpret what we are expected to do) but sooner or later (and this is alarmingly soon for most early years professionals), we will find ourselves leading other adults as well as children. The experiences we can gain while studying alongside a range of other adults of different ages, with different backgrounds and, possibly with different career interests, as well as our experiences of working in real early years settings, on placements, in a voluntary capacity or in part-time work, can also help us to deepen our understanding of what makes people tick and how to oil the wheels when friction between individuals prevents a team from working smoothly together.

In Chapter 11, 'Leadership in early childhood settings', Jan Savage and Caroline Leeson point out that much of the existing research on effective leadership draws on models derived from studies of businesses or big organisations which have tended to be led by men. In early years settings, on the other hand, the majority of leaders, whether in room, setting or area teams, will be women, whose preferred leadership style may tend to be more collaborative than competitive. This style may prove particularly appropriate for leaders of complex, multiprofessional children's centres, where practitioners from a wide range of backgrounds must be encouraged to support and learn from each other if they are to develop and improve the quality of provision. It can be learnt and practised in any early years context, where children from a wide range of backgrounds must be encouraged to support and learn from each other. This chapter also makes the important point that studies of the role of the leader can only go so far. All leaders are individuals, with unique personal histories and cultures, which cannot fail to influence their style, their decisions and their priorities. Effective early years practitioners and leaders cannot refer to an instruction manual to decide how to respond in a particular situation; they have to acknowledge the individuality of each of the children, parents and colleagues with whom they work.

In Chapter 12, 'Working with colleagues', Caroline Leeson and Lesley Griffiths continue to develop this emphasis on individual differences, reminding us that when we work alongside other people we cannot simply think of them as disembodied and perfectly rational decision-making machines. People have their own interests, needs and concerns and it is unrealistic to expect them simply to switch these off in the course of their work. Effective partnerships and teams require a balance between concern about the task in hand, concern for the needs and interests of individuals and concern for the development of the group. Where the interests of colleagues are given too much priority, children may suffer serious consequences, but an over-zealous attitude of 'we're here for the children not for ourselves' can also prove counterproductive in the long term. Recognising children as colleagues can have far-reaching implications for the way children come to think of their own participation in early years settings just as seeing students as colleagues in communities of learning can transform the ethos of universities and colleges.

Researching practice: developing a critical mindset

One of the aims of any programme of study should be to leave students with a greater awareness of how much more there is still to learn. We have to be careful not to allow such programmes to be reduced to training exercises, aimed at enabling students to collect competences until, when they have enough, they can be considered 'done' and fit to enter a particular area of work. The risk of this training model is that it can leave students feeling that no further study is needed once they have achieved the necessary levels of competence, unless, perhaps, they wish to proceed to the next rung on their career ladder. It is particularly important that people who will be working with young children and their families should actively promote a positive attitude to learning and personal development in all that they do because their example can shape children's learning dispositions at a time when these are especially sensitive to social influences.

In Chapter 13, 'In praise of reflective practice', Caroline Leeson shows how an inquisitive, investigative attitude to all aspects of your own practice can help you to make the continuing development of your professional skills, knowledge and understanding an integral part of your working life. Reflection must always have a strongly personal component, drawing on soft intuitions as well as hard facts, but it can be supported by others. Talking with colleagues about an issue may be a particularly effective way of clarifying your own ideas and collaborative action research, when a group of practitioners agree to meet up to explore an aspect of their practice in a systematic way, has been shown to be one of the most powerful forms of professional development (Edwards, 1999). Most importantly, by modelling enthusiasm for questioning, challenging and probing aspects of what you do, you will be providing a powerful example of positive learning dispositions, not just for the children you work with but for parents and colleagues as well.

In Chapter 14, 'Doing a research project in early childhood studies', Jenny Willan offers a helpful framework for planning, conducting and writing up a small-scale research project. The research project or dissertation can provide opportunities for you to explore an area of personal interest at a depth which will often result in you knowing more about it than most of your peers and, in many cases, more than some of your tutors, too. Developing an area of personal expertise can enable you to make the transition from seeing yourself as a knowledge consumer, dependent on work done by others, to thinking of yourself as a knowledge producer, able to make your own personal contribution to the sum of what is known about the lives and worlds of young children. The process of devising, developing, analysing and presenting your own empirical study can also give you valuable experience of a range of strategies for exploring, testing and refining aspects of your understanding of how things work in early years settings. While you may not regularly conduct similar studies in your working life, you may well find that these strategies prove useful when you need to cope with difficult or unfamiliar situations or when you want to make sense of something that interests or puzzles you.

Conducting your own study can help you to develop a critical mindset, a willingness to question, reflect and continue to learn from all aspects of your work with young children and their families. Chapter 1 explains how young babies' active, physical exploration of their environments enables them to extract much more information than would be available from a passive observation of what just happens to pass before them. These last chapters bring us full circle, showing how you too can benefit from adopting an active, probing, challenging and playful approach. One of the great advantages of studying early childhood is that you will frequently have opportunities to discover connections between what you know about the lives and worlds of young children and what you know about your own life and world. Adopting an active, critical approach to your own learning will enable you to breathe life into what might otherwise feel like dry, dusty, theoretical models and also to find some meaningful structure in what might otherwise feel like chaotically complicated real-world experiences.

Part 1

Powerful Children: Acknowledging the Achievements of Young Children

1 Moving, playing and learning: children's active exploration of their world

Rod Parker-Rees

Introduction

In Early Childhood Studies, we are concerned with offering a challenge to the assumption that the later stages of development are necessarily more important and more interesting than anything that happens earlier in life. By paying careful attention to developmental processes which can easily be taken for granted, because they are so commonplace and because they are so effortlessly achieved, we can show how these 'simple' first steps have an influence which persists throughout our lives.

The aim of this chapter is to outline the central role of active movement in both play and learning. It is widely acknowledged that play provides an important mechanism for children's learning (Moyles, 1994; Bruce, 1996) but the motor activity of babies and young children is still often seen merely as preparation for the more serious, more cerebral, learning which will come later. In the assault on 'Mount Piaget' we may acknowledge the need for preparatory work in the base camps but our eyes are fixed on the cold clear light of formal operational processes which can be achieved only at the summit.

Movement, the controlled activity of our bodies, is at the core of what we are and what we do. Even a process as seemingly straightforward as perception, taking in information from our environment, requires co-ordinated motor activity. Rather than sitting passively waiting for events to pass before us, we actively steer our eyes towards whatever attracts our interest. Our activity extends beyond the immediate requirements of our situation into exploration of our environment, 'movement is the mechanism whereby an organism acquires information about its present and past environment' (Cotterill, 1998, p.339; emphasis in original). We bustle about, poking our fingers into things, leaving no stone unturned and generally gathering up bits and pieces of information which may come in handy later. This active, exploratory probing of the environment is particularly evident in young children's play, down in the foothills of Mount Piaget, but it is also at the heart of such higher level activities as science, research and the arts.

In this chapter, I aim to play lightly over some aspects of the relationships between movement, play and learning with a particular focus on the importance of self-initiated activity in learning at all levels. Beginning with a brief account of the place of movement and play in the structure and early development of the brain, I will go on to explore ways in which the exuberant motor activity of infants allows them to develop patterned and increasingly purposeful movement schemes. I will consider how pretend play can help children to generalise and represent their experiences and enable them to explore the patterns, roles and rules which shape their social lives. Finally, I will argue that thinking about the roles of activity and play in young children's learning may help us to understand more about how we learn as adults.

Your brain is just one part of your body

The importance of what our brains contribute to all aspects of our lives is universally recognised so it is surprising how little most of us know about how this part of our body works. The following brief introduction will focus on the centrality, both in place and function, of areas of the brain which are particularly involved in movement, touch and proprioception (awareness of the position and condition of all parts of the body).

The brain grows, a bit like the head of a cauliflower, up and out from its central stem at the top of the spinal cord. It is not surprising, then, that the oldest parts, both in evolutionary terms and in the development of an individual, will be found nearer to the base, with the latest innovations near the surface.

First, the brain stem, right at the top of the spinal cord, is involved in the control of body functions such as breathing, heart-rate and temperature regulation; the autonomous processes of which we are seldom consciously aware. The brain stem and the cerebellum, or 'little brain', which plays a very important part in co-ordinating movement, together make up what is often described as the 'reptilian brain'.

Above the reptilian brain comes the complex cluster of bits and pieces, described as the limbic system or mammalian brain, which processes emotion states, 'drives', learning from experience and survival functions, including the famous 'four Fs': fighting, feeding, fleeing and reproducing.

Finally we arrive at the brain's surface, the wrinkled, walnut-like, 'grey matter' of the cerebral cortex, which co-ordinates and organises information from the limbic system in order to make sense, learn, represent, predict and plan. The central strip of the cortex, the parietal lobe, is associated with movement, sense of position in space, proprioception and touch – the most primeval and most fully *embodied* forms of awareness. Behind this motor core are areas associated with the processing of other forms of sensory information, first taste and smell, then hearing, and, at the very back of the brain, occupying nearly half of the cortex (in terms of number of neurons), vision (Cotterill, 1998, p.361). This sequence of sensory areas maps the progressive expansion of our perceptual world from the interior world of proprioception to the body space defined by our reach, the larger space from which tastes and smells can reach us, the limits of our hearing and, finally, the vast expanses opened up to us by our sight.

Moving forward from the motor core also takes us from the realm of immediate, direct experience, through areas which prepare and co-ordinate motor activity (including specialised areas for speech movements and for the control of the eyes), to an area which is involved in more intangible, abstract kinds of activity – such as thought, anticipated action, speculation and planning. This part of the brain, the frontal cortex, seems to have developed most recently in our evolution and is last to develop in the individual, with some areas not fully active until early adulthood (Carter, 1999, p.22).

In the cerebral cortex, then, the motor control area lies between the areas which process information about the world beyond our body space (where we are) and areas which process information about our possible futures (where we want to be). The cortex is also divided into two hemispheres, each of which plays a slightly different part in the processing of information. The 'right brain' is associated with holistic, dreamy, emotional, 'female' and 'Eastern' processes, and the 'left brain' is seen as the seat of the analytical, logical, sequential, spatial, linguistic/symbolic, and 'male' processes which tend to be more highly prized in 'Western' cultures, especially in their education systems. Much that is written about brain lateralisation (the division into distinct hemispheres), however, involves gross oversimplification. The two hemispheres are joined by a huge number of connections (the corpus callosum) and most brain processes involve simultaneous activity across a wide range of brain regions. Nevertheless there are real differences between the hemispheres. The left hemisphere, for example, contains proportionally more 'grey matter', the dense network of neurons and the dendrites or branches through which they receive input from their neighbours, while the right has more 'white matter', made up of the myelinated (insulated) longer-range axon connections which carry signals over longer distances. This physiological difference may explain why the left hemisphere is more involved in the processing of fine details while the right hemisphere tends to process multiple forms of information in a more holistic way. Guy Claxton (1994, p.45) explains a possible benefit of brain lateralisation by comparing the right hemisphere to a candle and the left to a torch with a tightly focused beam. Used together, a candle and a torch may be particularly effective since areas of possible interest picked out dimly by the candle can then be examined more closely with the torch. Lateralisation maximises the amount of information processing which can be achieved with given resources by teaming up general, intuitive awareness of what is significant or promising, with active, systematic exploration. The same strategy can be seen in the combination of fuzzy but extensive peripheral vision with a small, central foveal area of the retina which can pick out much more detail.

Tuning, pruning and plasticity

Although our brains have many structural features in common they are also, like other parts of our bodies, unique in the finer details of their organisation. Starting from a broadly similar set of specifications, our brains must tune themselves to the unique demands of a particular body within a particular environment. From before birth and well into childhood, neurons grow a mass of dendrites, or branches, which allow each to connect with tens of thousands of others in a network of great complexity. Young children's brains are much more densely interconnected than adults' brains because the tuning of this network is accomplished by selective reinforcement of some connections and pruning of others. For example, of many possible networks processing control of a particular muscle, some are used frequently, are reinforced and eventually myelinated while others are used less and will be pruned out. This process can be compared to the development of paths and road networks across a landscape: the tracks which come to be used most often are developed into roads or even motorways while unused routes become overgrown and fade away. By actively exploring and adapting to feedback as connections are used, a much more efficient network can be developed than could be produced by any genetic blueprint. Pinker (2002) has argued that the newborn baby's brain is far from being a 'blank slate', entirely dependent on experience to wire up its networks of neurons, but its overabundance of connections does makes it highly 'plastic' or adaptable.

Activity, play and brain development

Connections between the cerebellum, the primeval movement-processing part of our 'reptilian' brains, and the motor areas of the cerebral cortex play a particularly important role in the fine tuning of our brains to our developing bodies. There is a striking correlation between the size of an animal's brain, in proportion to its body mass, and the extent to which it will engage in play activities – animals with bigger brains play more (Iwaniuk *et al.*, 2001). Animals with proportionally bigger brains are generally better able to adapt their behaviour to changes in their environment. Simple animals, like insects and reptiles, have to rely largely on hard-wired or instinctive responses, which may serve them very well, but animals with more elaborate brains can learn how to move, act and react; and play seems to be a particularly effective strategy for this kind of learning.

Play involves exuberant movements (think of gambolling lambs, puppies or kittens) combining elements of different kinds of 'mammalian brain' activities (feeding, aggression, reproduction). The fact that animals expend high levels of energy in play suggests that it must have significant survival value. The levels of energy devoted to the repetitive, exploratory and adventurous movements seen in play may be justified by the training this provides in patterns of correspondence between muscle activity and the resulting effects on how the body moves. How far do I jump if I put this much effort in? What happens if one leg pushes harder than the other? The motor patterns learned and reinforced in this play activity are gradually built into a 'virtual body' in the cerebellum which, across a wide range of species, reaches a peak of synapse formation (making connections between neurons) just as this play activity begins (Bekoff and Byers, 1998).

As the territory of possible movements is explored in play, it is mapped in the neural networks of the cerebellum and, like an explorer's charts, this map can then be used to plan the fine details of muscle activity required to achieve any intended action, even actions which have never been tried before. Unlike a navigator's maps, however, the cerebellum's virtual body can also make allowance for different starting positions, levels of muscle tiredness, stiffness, balance, uneven ground and a whole host of other complicating factors.

Try poking your left index finger into your right ear, passing your arm behind your head. You are unlikely to have had prior experience of this set of movements but, your cerebellum's internal model can still work out what each muscle must do to produce a smooth movement.

Every time the movement model is used it is also updated, refined and, if necessary, corrected as information from the motor cortex about the results of movement is compared with what was intended or expected. The mental model, map or theory stored in the cerebellum is thus used in tandem with the exploratory processes in the cortex; the cerebellum can deal with the fine details of *how* movements will be executed, freeing up the cortex to focus on *what* movements are required.

The cerebellum also plays a crucial role in allowing us to tell the difference between changes in our perceptual world which result from our own activity, e.g. changes in our visual field when we move our eyes, and changes which have nothing to do with what we are doing, e.g. changes in our visual field when something moves in front of us. It can be very important to tell the difference between what we are doing and what is being done to us, as can be simply understood by considering the different responses which you would feel if: a) you were to run your fingers along your leg, or b) you were to receive exactly the same sensory information from your leg, but without the corresponding messages from your hand and fingers! You cannot tickle yourself because your cerebellum knows exactly what your fingers are up to and the sensation they produce is entirely predictable (Blakemore *et al.*, 1998).

The ability to co-ordinate awareness of what you are doing with awareness of how this affects your perceptual world is much more important than these rather frivolous examples may suggest. By mapping our own activity and feeding awareness of this into our processing of sensory information we are able to construct a highly sophisticated awareness of our environment which would be simply unavailable to a passive receiver of environmental inputs (see Activity 1 at the end of this chapter).

The playful exploration of patterns in the relationships between motor activity and the resulting changes in sensory information forms the basis of what Piaget (1952, 1954, 1962) described as the sensorimotor stage of development. Largely through careful observation of his own children, Laurent and Jacqueline, Piaget identified a sequence of stages through which babies passed as they learned to control their active engagement with the world around them. Each 'stage' becomes a source of elements, or schemes, which are combined and co-ordinated in the next stage. While these stages offer a useful, simplified framework for understanding how activity can become increasingly co-ordinated, skilful and purposeful, it is important to remember that any theory or model only achieves its clarity by systematically smoothing out the tangles of individual variation which complicate the picture whenever one moves in for a closer look.

Thelen and Smith (1994) have shown, for example, how the task of developing control over reaching may be quite different for different babies. Gabriel, a very active, flappy baby, had to learn how to damp down his arm movements if he was to exercise sufficient control to bring his hand into contact with a desired object. Hannah, on the other hand, though alert and socially responsive, was much less physically active and her task was to rouse her arm to life. Thelen and Smith make the very important point that the appearance of patterns in development, such as Piaget's substages, may have more to do with the level of detail at which we observe than with the existence of organising structures at work in individual babies:

> Hannah's problem was different from Gabriel's, but it was also the same. She, like Gabriel, had to adjust the energy or forces moving her arm – in her case to make her arm sufficiently stiff or forceful to lift it off her lap ... Their solutions were discovered in

relation to their own situations, carved out of their individual landscapes, and not
prefigured by a synergy known ahead by the brain or the genes.

(Thelen and Smith, 1994, p.260)

The tidying up inherent in any 'ages and stages' model of development can be criticised, but this sort of simplification is an essential part of all theory building or mapping of experience. The selective reinforcement of certain patterns of neural connection resulting from repeated experience is perhaps the most primitive form of this mapping. The precise details of each experience are 'smoothed out' as a more generalised, and more generally useful, pattern or scheme emerges. A brief review of Piaget's account of the substages of sensorimotor development may help to show how babies learn to discover and explore patterns in their own activity (for more detailed accounts see Sutherland, 1992, pp.8–12; Keenan, 2002, pp.121–5; or Smith *et al.*, 2003, pp.393–8).

Piaget's schemes

Reflexive schemes: 0–1 month

Piaget used the word 'scheme' to refer to a pattern of physical or mental action which could be repeated in different contexts. The first schemes, Piaget argued, are reflexive – automatic responses to stimuli (e.g. 'rooting' or turning to suck an object when touched with it on the cheek, or grasping when touched on the palm). As babies suck and grasp different objects, their sucking and grasping schemes are extended and differentiated and their world is organised into distinct kinds of experience: grasping a handful of hair is both like and unlike grasping a finger or a handful of cloth.

Primary circular reactions: 1–4 months

Circular reactions are patterns of movement which the baby is able to control and reproduce. After accidentally bringing a hand up to her face and sucking her fingers she eventually learns how to *make* her fingers move to her mouth. The combination of motor commands needed to move her arm, hand and mouth is developed into a motor scheme which is consolidated and generalised by frequent repetition, enjoyment and playfulness. Babies really appear to delight in the 'joy of being a cause' (Cooley, 1902, p.196) as they find that they are able to affect their sensory experience in predictable ways by controlling their movement. Babies can now respond differently to different stimuli (e.g. to a nipple, a teat or a finger) because different stimuli 'trigger' different motor schemes.

Secondary circular reactions: 4–9 months

When babies learn to sit up, their attention moves out beyond the bounds of their own bodies to objects within reach of their new means of exploration, their hands. A chance discovery that an object can be made to do something interesting (rattle, squeak, roll, etc.) leads to deliberate attempts to repeat the action. Movements are now performed not just for their own sake but also in order to make things happen. Actions can also be combined, producing more co-ordinated activity (the rattle is grasped and shaken). The special activity prompted by different objects may provide the first form of non-verbal categorisation (*this* is the thing I rattle, *that* is the thing I cuddle). Elinor Goldschmied's work with 'treasure baskets' (Goldschmied and Hughes, 1986), offering sitting infants baskets of varied and attractive objects to manipulate and explore, recognises the developmental importance of this interaction between the infant's body and a wide range of different kinds of object.

Co-ordination of secondary circular reactions: 9–12 months

From about eight or nine months of age, as most babies are beginning to crawl, they are also learning to combine earlier action patterns in novel ways (e.g. combining a scheme for moving an object with a scheme for grasping another which the baby wants). Action now looks much more purposeful as the cerebellum's virtual body map is well developed and movement is smoother and more automatic, allowing the now mobile infant to focus more on the goals generated in her cortex than on what she must do to achieve them (as an experienced driver changes gear without needing to think about the separate movements involved). The organisation of fluid, multidimensional activity into a linear sequence of planned steps, the action equivalent of combining words into sentences, greatly expands the baby's movement repertoire and may also provide foundations for the development of language which soon follows (Bridgeman, 1992).

Tertiary circular reactions: 12–18 months

As babies take to their legs and become toddlers, their worlds continue to expand in many different ways. This is when infants really become 'little scientists' or little explorers, deliberately and playfully varying their actions in order to find out what will happen. Where secondary circular reactions were rather serious, goal-directed, affairs, which occupied all of the infant's attention, tertiary circular reactions are more experimental and exploratory, as toddlers are free to pay more attention to the effects of their activity.

Invention of new means through mental combinations: from about 18 months

By the time they reach the age of about 18 months, or even earlier, children are increasingly able to escape from the limitations of the immediate 'here and now'. The use of words to label objects, events and intentions marks the beginning of an ability to represent ideas internally, and the ability to pretend shows that toddlers can hold in mind both what they are *really* doing and what they are *pretending* to do (Perner, 1991). They can now imitate not only what is happening in front of them but also something that happened earlier and elsewhere. Mental models enable toddlers to envisage or imagine what they *might* do, to explore possible courses of action without actually having to move.

Pretending: playing with patterns of movement

It is important to remember that babies are not expected to work their way through sensorimotor development unaided and alone; even before they are born, babies are surrounded by culturally mediated information emerging from the social activity of people around them. By separating out aspects of their world for special attention in pretend play, children are able to develop their understanding of what objects and events mean, not only to themselves but also to other people. When children pretend, and especially when they engage with others in social pretend play, their attention is focused less on the mechanics of their actions than on the significance of what they are doing.

Pretend play enables children to loosen the ties between the specific motor details of their own activity and their increasingly sophisticated awareness of concepts which can be shared with others. When a child first pretends, for example, to drink from an empty cup, her movements may be very similar to those she would use if she were really drinking. By pretending to drink, she loosens these movements from their previous functional scheme and begins to loosen the concept of 'drinking' from the movements normally associated with it. Once 'drinking' has been freed from its motor scheme it can be used more play-fully, offering a cup to a doll or teddy and eventually having a doll bring her own cup to her own lips. What was once a set of motor instructions for *my* body now becomes a 'type' of movement which *any* body can perform.

Early imitation and pretend play are highly dependent on contextual details. Two- and three-year-old children seem to need the prompt provided by familiar sensory stimuli to fire up patterns of behaviour. So a two- or three-year-old will pretend to talk on a real phone, or on a realistic toy telephone, but as the internal representation of 'talking on the telephone' is strengthened this external sensory input will become less necessary and a four-year-old will chat happily to anything remotely resembling a telephone, or even to an entirely imaginary one.

The ability to conjure up objects, events and ideas in the absence of any of the sensory stimuli formerly or normally associated with them is clearly an essential requirement for the development of imagination. It is also a fundamental requirement for the symbolic forms of representation on which language depends; the word 'cup' does not make us think of cups because of any sensory resemblance to cups we have known and used but because we have learned that this is the noise people around us use when they talk about cups.

Lev Vygotsky observed that 'The world of experience must be greatly simplified and gener-alised before it can be translated into symbols' (Vygotsky, 1968, p.6) and common features of children's play (repetition, fragmentation, exaggeration, rearrangement) seem to help children to take their experiences apart and reduce the bits to core concepts which are free from the contextual complexities of specific instances, as a map is free of the com-plexities of an aerial photograph. This allows children to 'go beyond the information given' (Bruner, 1966), to experiment with recombinations of bits of what they know and thereby to escape from the world of 'here and now' (direct sensory information) into a world of imagination in which anything can happen 'beyond the map'.

In Piaget's account of the stages of children's play (Piaget, 1962), sensorimotor play is fol-lowed by symbolic play, in which language is increasingly important and, much later, when children reach the age of six or seven, by games with rules. For Piaget 'games with rules' are games with a pre-specified and finite set of rules, such as might be printed in a set of instructions, but for Vygotsky (1978) children's play is controlled by rather different rules. For Vygotsky, rules are much more like the patterns children notice in their active explo-ration of their world, particularly the habitual patterns of behaviour which can be found in what people tend to do 'as a rule'. Vygotsky noted that although children's pretend play may appear free and unconstrained, it is in fact even more bound by rules than is their ordinary activity. When a child decides to 'be a doctor', for example, she chooses to constrain her activity within the rules (the role) of what doctors can and can't do. Playful 'dressing up in rules' plays an important part in enabling children to work out the significance of the conventions which shape people's behaviour. When groups of children play together there are additional opportunities for each to notice how the others perform their roles and to challenge and question interpretations which differ from their own. A personal concept of 'mum', for example, can be enriched by a wider awareness that 'mum' may mean something slightly different 'as a rule'; comparing our own mum with the general stereotype can help us to notice features which would otherwise be too familiar to be noticeable.

By voluntarily submitting their activity to the constraints imposed by social roles, children are able to explore aspects of their culture, much as adults are able to use the constraints of, for example, a musical score. A skilled musician can use the protected space defined by the score to explore personal meanings which can be expressed (and discovered) through nuances of interpretation.

Playfulness and interpretation of rules

Like maps and symbols, all forms of cultural rules are necessarily simplified and tidied up so that they can apply across a wide range of different contexts. A playful approach allows us to find our own ways to relate these public structures to the private, more complex networks of understanding which we have abstracted from our own experiences. Stig Broström (1997, p.20) has argued that teachers must be careful to prevent play from becoming 'a mechanical and narrow reproduction of reality', instead encouraging children to see it as: 'a creative activity through which the child changes his or her surroundings, transforms knowledge and understanding, invents and creates new insights through experience'.

Adam Phillips (1998, p.87) has suggested that the way we experience our relationship with all forms of authority can be transformed by a playful willingness to 'dress up' in rules, to accept them as Vygotskian patterns of convention rather than as uniforms which deny the individuality of their wearers: 'To treat an order, or any kind of rule or instruction, as merely suggestive – to turn it into something a little more to one's taste – is radically to revise the nature of authority (obedience would be merely fear of interpretation)'.

Although older children and adults may no longer need to explore their world by physically manipulating objects, they still need to take an active part in their engagement with new experiences, changing and transforming them in their words and in their thoughts until they turn them into something a little more to their own particular taste.

Borrowing and interpreting an existing framework

Tina Bruce (1996, p.8) offers a useful four-part framework for understanding the central, co-ordinating role of play in children's lives. With only very minor transformation, this framework can also be used to map the issues addressed in this chapter. Bruce's 'first-hand experience' acknowledges the importance of self-initiated activity and sensorimotor learning in the tuning of brain and body. Activity 1 below demonstrates the extent to which awareness of what we are doing increases our ability to extract information from our sensory input. Bruce's 'representations' are focused on 'making products' but if they are expanded to also include internal representations (from co-ordinated networks of neurons to motor schemes, concepts, symbols, maps and words) they can represent the many ways in which the complexity of experience has to be simplified, generalised and 'diagrammed' if it is to inform future action. The repetition and variation of behaviour provided by play seem to be particularly effective devices for allowing children to discover (and represent) patterns in their experience. Bruce's 'games: understanding rules' acknowledges the range of rule systems that children can explore in their play but I would prefer to re-title this section 'rules and conventions' to focus more on the ways in which play enables children to explore the significance of social patterns and habits as they dress up in these rules and roles in their social pretend play. At the core of Bruce's framework lies play, the co-ordinating activity which brings together first-hand experience, representations and rules. I am not sure that I would differentiate so clearly between activity, experience and play, but playfulness does provide a powerful mechanism for establishing personally satisfying relationships between one's own direct actions on the world, one's ability to map or represent aspects of experience and one's awareness of the rules and structures which frame one's own and other people's behaviour.

If you have ever tried to find your way along a route which you have only previously travelled as a passenger, you will know how much more information your brain takes in, largely without your awareness, when you are in the driving seat. The active sensorimotor exploration of babies and the social exploration of older children show us how important activity is in early learning, but active engagement remains essential in learning at any age. To know about Bruce's mapping of the relationships between play, exploration, representation and rules is one thing but to understand it requires an active process of interpretation, of playing with it until one finds a way to fit it to one's own first-hand experiences. As Adam Phillips (1998 p.6) has observed, 'the given is inert until it becomes the made'.

ACTIVITY 1

Working with a partner you should each prepare a 'touch puzzle' by cutting a simple shape (e.g. a capital letter or a geometric form such as a square or triangle) out of card (a cereal box is fine) and sticking this onto a larger square of card. Don't let your partner see the shape you have chosen! Now shut your eyes and hold out one hand, palm down, keeping your fingertips absolutely still while your partner moves his/her shape puzzle to and fro under them. You will probably find it very difficult to 'read' the shape using only the passive touch sensations this provides. If, however, your partner now holds the touch puzzle still and allows you (eyes still shut, of course) to run your fingers over the shape for yourself, you should find that an 'image' of the shape will quickly pop into your head as information from your cerebellum about the position and movement of your fingers is combined with information from nerve endings at your fingertips. Now do the decent thing and allow your partner to experience the difference too.

ACTIVITY 2

Begin to collect phrases and idioms which include the word 'play' and which are used to describe aspects of adults' behaviour, for example, 'playing the markets', 'he made a play for her', 'playing the fool', etc. What do these expressions tell you about the range of meanings we ascribe to play?

ACTIVITY 3

Watch out for hidden movement metaphors in the language we use to talk about abstract ideas; for example, 'hold a belief', 'understand', 'follow the steps of an argument', etc. You may be surprised by how dependent we are on movement concepts when we try to explain intangible ideas. Many of the words we use to talk about ideas are borrowed from Latin or Greek and this makes it even easier to miss the movement metaphors they contain. To 'abstract' was originally to 'pull out', 'complicated' once meant 'with folds', and 'explain' meant 'smooth out'.

2 Becoming a person

Lesley Griffiths

Introduction

This chapter will explore some of the complex processes of emotional development in early childhood. We will discuss the early stages of emotional development through which an infant grows towards becoming a fully functioning individual, by examining differing theories of emotional and personal development. Transactional analysis is the core model underpinning this chapter. Alongside, we will make comparisons with other theoretical models and argue a case for students to develop techniques drawn from transactional analysis in their own practice.

The National Research Council Institute of Medicine (2000, p.2) has highlighted the following themes that are very relevant to our work with young children:

- The importance of early life experiences, as well as the inseparable and highly interactive influences of genetics and environment, on the development of the brain and the unfolding of human nature.

- The central role of early relationships as a source of either support and adaptation or risk and dysfunction.

- The powerful capabilities, complex emotions, and essential social skills that develop during the earliest years of life.

- The capacity to increase the odds of favourable developmental outcomes through planned interventions.

We want our future adults to be resilient, and, in adversity, to face the challenge. More information is available to us, showing that early interactions are extremely important in influencing the infant's growth into an emotionally robust or an emotionally vulnerable individual.

> *What happens during the first months and years of life matters a lot, not because this period of development provides an indelible blueprint for adult well-being, but because it sets either a sturdy or fragile stage for what follows … Scientists have shifted their focus to take account of the fact that genetic and environmental influences work together in dynamic ways over the course of development.*
>
> (ibid.)

Becoming a person

What does it mean when we talk about 'becoming a person' and why is it important for each of us to 'become' one? Why are emotions so important in this process?

Human beings are intrinsically social animals. Our living is very closely related to the living of others and our way of life is dependent on us living in groups, sharing and caring for each other. Our learning takes place mainly through social interactions. Learning from one another is a fundamental part of becoming fully human and we all develop expectations of ourselves and others within our particular society and culture as we grow towards adulthood. In order that we become efficient social learners, it is important that we develop strategies that will foster a positive disposition towards all kinds of learning. And it is in the development of these learning dispositions that emotional development is so important.

Imagine a group of people living together but not connecting together, a group that cannot intuitively tell what another member of the group is feeling or thinking. It would be difficult to engage in the shared interactions that are so important to our day-to-day functioning. In a group we can be more effective, more powerful: we can achieve so much more than we can as individuals. As a group there are more of us to care for and about each other, more of us to contribute to the collective planning and execution of tasks. But there are also more opportunities for conflict and more opportunities for high emotion such as fear and anger. In evolutionary terms this would have been about survival and our life may have depended on this emotional arousal of fear and anger. Today, survival in the developed world is less about withstanding nature red in tooth and claw and more about finding our way in a highly complex world of hidden competition and strategic understandings. The need for survival through social interaction is still there but transmuted into something else. The modern world has become ever more sophisticated and thus the need for understanding each other's emotional messages as well as the ones we are sending out becomes even more important if we are to operate together through a shared understanding.

As early childhood practitioners, finding out about our own and others' feelings and emotions can help us to work more effectively with our colleagues and with the young children in our care. Many children grow up in confusingly complex circumstances where close relationships are fragmented or fluid. As practitioners, we need to be aware of strategies which allow us to understand, support and contain the feelings and emotional states of children from their earliest years.

The perception of the infant as completely helpless has been a dominant common-sense view of the developing child. The picture is of an infant living in a family group and supported and nurtured by those close to her – firstly by the mother, supported by the father, and later by an ever-widening circle of others. But in our present society, there is a diversity of groups through which to nurture the developing infant. The needs of the child remain the same, but the provision of care and support is delivered in a variety of ways.

Nature and nurture

There have been many different theories about the development of personality. Debates about how far self-identity is due to *in utero* conditions (National Families Network, electronic source), the genetic programming of the infant, or to social influences on the infant after birth, are ongoing (Shaffer, 1994). As practitioners we tend to take a little from each theory, putting together those parts that make most sense in our own situation to try to build our own understanding of how the infant in our care is struggling to become a person. We are unlikely to view the child as wholly predetermined by genetic make-up; neither would we think, as Locke (1693) did, that the child is a *tabula rasa*, a blank slate, to be written on by adults and teachers and happenstance. Neither are we likely to attribute, for example, the fractiousness of a particular child wholly to the fact that the mother was in an anxious state through her pregnancy. Our own experience as adults, who survived childhood ourselves, makes us cautious about attaching particular significance to every environmental event – we know that not every situation that children find themselves in will have a profound and lasting effect on their nature, personality and emotional make-up. However, taken together, we can make some assessment of how aspects of nature and nurture might have contributed to produce the particular dispositions evident in the emotional make-up of the child in our care.

We need to be cautious about our assessments of what is good or bad for the emotional development of a child. It is not the actual event that is so important, but the sense that the child makes of the event. And that sense will be dependent on many different contextual features, both within and outside the child. For example, an infant may cry when the mother leaves, but may not cry if left alone surrounded by her toys or if left with a familiar adult. What makes the difference? One such event may be of no consequence in the long-term emotional development of the child. However, several similar events evoking the same response and repeated over a period of time will affect the picture that the child builds up of the self in relation to others.

The contexts of the interactions children have within the environment (which includes significant people) are vitally important to the sense they will make of each interaction. For example, geographical mobility may be a different experience for different children, affecting them emotionally in very different ways. A child from a rural family settled for generations in one area may find a move to an industrial area traumatic; a refugee family seeking asylum from a war-torn country would have their emotional resilience severely tested. If in these two families, the experience of being uprooted was persistently repeated, it would have serious repercussions for the child's emerging sense of security and well-being. But if the child was used to a nomadic existence, moving regularly from one place to another, mobility would have little effect on the child's sense of well-being. The key factor is the way in which the event can be managed within the family group and the emotional messages of security and containment that the child can receive from the family. The child makes sense of each event according to the context within which it occurs. Adults are part of that context and their reaction to particular life events will affect the way in which those events are interpreted by the child.

Holistic development

Having learnt about the physical, intellectual, linguistic, emotional and social development of children, it is tempting to think of children's development in terms of *P.I.L.E.S*! But it is only for our own convenience that we think about young children in this way and try to 'box' their personalities into different categories. Children themselves are not so accommodating. Their development is their own and although we may influence it, we do not control it. A particular child's development is rather like making a soup. We may start with a variety of different ingredients, different quantities, leaving some things out and putting other things in, cooking some things first and adding other things raw, allowing different people to choose different cooking methods and so on. The outcomes may be very different but there may also be some similarities. Sometimes what we intended to make turns out very differently from the original recipe. Children's development is like this.

All areas of a young child's development are connected and woven together into a whole. We cannot talk about social development without thinking about emotional development; intellectual development is closely interlinked with physical development; language development is rooted in the emotional bonds we forge, the social interactions we enjoy, the physical sounds we learn to make, the patterns that imprint on our brains. We cannot separate one from the other – and running through everything is emotion.

Child development

So what are the important themes around young children's development? When considering the question of how an infant becomes a person, it is useful to look at past theories, philosophical ideas and general assumptions about emotions and childhood to aid our understanding of current beliefs. There are many differing views on how the bundle of cells in the mother's womb develops to form a fully functioning individual and these views differ according to the underlying beliefs of the time and the culture in which they are held.

Oates (1994) summarises the main points taken by theorists on the nature–nurture spectrum of child development. He shows how Locke saw the infant as a *tabula rasa*, placing most emphasis on the nurture of the infant and taking less account of preformed dispositions or hereditary tendencies. He shows how behaviourists, such as Skinner, extended this view of development by describing how an infant reacts to certain stimuli and establishes patterns of behaviour in response to the reinforcement of reward and punishment. For the behaviourist, the infant will have an inherited characteristic or capacity for a certain pattern of behaviour which is then stimulated or discouraged by corresponding responses from their environment. The infant is seen as reacting to the environment, not being an active agent within it. The emphasis is on the nature or genetic makeup of the infant combined with the influence their environment has upon them.

Oates (1994) points out that others have seen infant development as a reciprocal interaction between the infant and their environment. For example, Kant suggested that infants are active members of their environment and that they construct their own relationship with the world. In this model, infants are seen as having been born with certain mental structures or categories of understanding which, through interaction with the environment, order and organise their experiences so that they are actively involved in organising their own understanding of the world. He shows how this view of the reciprocal nature of the process between the individual and the environment underpins the social learning theories espoused by Bandura. He suggested that infants learn by *observing* and *identifying* with significant others in their lives and make choices about how to relate to the world around them based partly on imitation of admired same-sex role models. He also cites Vygotsky, who suggested that infants build up a view of the world through a social constructionist approach. In Vygotsky's model, children are actively engaged in building a world view through *interaction and negotiation* with the people and culture in which they find themselves. This shifts the emphasis in development from a relatively passive process where individuals are acted upon, to a more active process where individuals are agents of their own development. For a social constructionist, like Vygotsky, development happens through interaction with other people, verbal and non-verbal, where children have joint responsibility in building or constructing their own reality. In this view of development, there is an emphasis on the choices made by each contributor in any social interaction in relation to their negotiation of shared understandings and meanings.

The centrality of emotional development – the psychoanalysts

With developments in neuroscience, we are learning more about the development of the brain and how the emotional state of young children (and adults) can have profound effects on their thinking skills and cognitive development. Goleman (1996) talks about the interconnectedness of the site of primitive feelings (the amygdala) and the site of higher learning (the neocortex).

> *The connections between the amygdala (and related limbic structures) and the neocortex are the hub of the battles or co-operative treaties struck between head and heart, thought and feeling. This circuitry explains why emotion is so crucial to effective thought, both in making wise decisions and in simply allowing us to think clearly.*
>
> (Goleman, 1996, p.27)

Miller *et al.* (1989) provide an overview of the psychoanalysts' views of emotional development through the twentieth century. They suggest that the psychoanalytic approach to infant emotional development began with Freud in the first decade of the twentieth century and that psychoanalysis brings together 'different and developing strands of related ideas about the nature of human personality' (Miller *et al.*, 1989, p.23). They tell us how Freud observed and studied infants in their homes and how his work was continued by other analysts (Klein, Winnicott, Bowlby) and is still being continued at the Tavistock Clinic and other centres today. These analysts studied the relationship between what they identified as the needs of the infant and how those needs were met by the significant people in the child's immediate proximity – usually the parents. Their observations provided a new model of the internal emotional world of the infant. Miller *et al.* (1989) point out how, in particular, Melanie Klein focused on an infant's earliest relationships and how the processes within the infant's mind connected to produce a particular emotional profile and a disposition to behave in certain ways, so that infants accumulate experiences that develop and combine together, affecting both their external behaviour and their internal emotions. The complex nature of this relationship between internal states and external behaviour constitutes a dialogue, with each affecting and being affected by the other. From a psychoanalytic perspective, emotional development is seen as a lifelong dynamic, rooted in earliest childhood but capable of modification forever. The nature of the emotional dialogue between needs and the satisfaction of those needs has implications for every aspect of learning from the first moments of contact between the child and the world:

Klein's view was that the meeting of instinctual needs (within the baby) with an external object (aspects of the mother's care) not only results in a physically satisfying experience, an interest in the external world and a rudimentary social relationship with the mother, but also initiates the beginnings of mental development in the infant.

(Miller *et al.*, 1989, p.25)

Within this model the carer, particularly the mother in the early stages, will to a greater or lesser degree 'contain' the emotions of the infant in their care. 'Containment' is a word that is of interest here. The idea is that a person, usually a trusted adult, can 'hold on to' the emotions of the infant, so that within any situation infants will feel 'safe' and will take from their interactions the message that they are strong and resilient and can persevere in difficult situations. In order for this to happen, the 'holding persons' need to be aware of their own emotional state, to avoid contaminating the emotional state of the infant with their own emotions (easier said than done!). According to psychoanalytic thinking, the sense the infant makes of the world derives from the nature of these interactions with the carer.

Transactional analysis

The roots of transactional analysis lie within psychoanalytic theory and emerged from the work of Eric Berne in the 1950s. It is a model that can usefully apply in practical, day-to-day interactions between people, including adults and children. Originally, transactional analysis was used to identify and change adult *life scripts*, the narratives constructed in childhood which can sometimes impede individual development and satisfaction. Later, transactional analysis theory was identified as a useful way of interpreting child development. The transactional analysis model of early emotional development can be a useful tool for practitioners developing their own emotional awareness, both in their work with young children and with their colleagues.

Transactional analysis is sited within a humanist belief that people have a capacity to develop their own potential. According to transactional analysis, there are four underlying philosophical assumptions to keep in mind when we relate to others:

- People are O.K. and everyone deserves respect.

- All people have the capacity to think, and are therefore responsible for their own feelings, thoughts and behaviour.

- People decide their own destiny and can change their decisions over the course of their lifetime.

- Problems are solvable.

Within the transactional analysis model a person will be working towards *personal autonomy*. The three main components of this are:

- **Awareness** – *the capacity to see, hear, feel, taste and smell things as pure sensual impressions, in the way a new-born infant does.*

- **Spontaneity** – *the capacity to choose from a full range of options in feeling, thinking and behaving.*

- **Intimacy** – *an open sharing of feelings and wants between you and another person.*

(Stewart and Joines, 1987, p.266)

Transactional analysis offers a holistic view of personality development. There are connections between the cognitive, thinking self and the affective, emotional self, as well as the physical, behavioural self who may be 'acting out' situations. The early development of the infant, taken from a transactional analysis perspective, influences how that person develops and acts in future situations. Transactional analysis assumes that human beings are relationship-seeking animals. At a deep level they have psychological hungers for recognition, structure/certainty, and stimulation. In order to fulfil these basic needs infants construct life scripts from the kinds and qualities of the relationships within which they exist.

Emotional development in infancy

Now we have an emerging picture of the infant born into the world, already influenced by the chemical balances of the mother during pregnancy, already predisposed with different dispositions and carrying specific genetic messages about the possible emotional make-up they could develop. In infancy, these messages are either encouraged or extinguished by the environment the child comes into. Healthy emotional development is not just about giving the infant positive emotional messages instead of negative ones; it is about enabling and supporting infants to use the capacities they already have to make sense and to survive. This survival is at first just a basic need for food, warmth and security – the infant's behaviour is directed by drives and reflexes. From as early as three months the infant is able to show true emotional responses – that is when *affect* begins to guide and direct their behaviour. This is when the infant begins to invite help from those around by working in 'synchrony with the care-giving environment, rather than mere need gratification' (Sander, 1975, in Sroufe 1995, p.153). The infant is in a reciprocal relationship with the caregiver and the process involves both thinking and physical contact. The process is both chemical (a release of hormonal messages in both carer and infant), and physical (touch, speech and eye contact). When this first relationship is maintained, infants progress into more sophisticated relationships as they become more mobile. These early relationships influence infants' developing view of themselves. If the experience is positive, they will see themselves as capable, supported and contained with a capacity to adapt to, and use, the environment. If the experience is negative, they will feel incapable, unsupported and not contained and unable to function confidently.

In order to develop a relationship, the interactions of the participants are synchronised and co-ordinated. Tickling games, peek-a-boo and baby talk that engage both carer and child are examples of interactions which build synchronised and co-ordinated relationships.

Once infants develop memory, there are profound implications for emotional development. According to the National Research Council Institute of Medicine (2000), development during this early period is seen to be 'highly robust' and 'highly vulnerable'. It is at this stage that infants can anticipate events and react emotionally to them, and each interaction becomes part of the framework through which they evaluate further events and encounters. If they have formed positive feelings within the caregiving environment then they can remember those emotional and visual images and bring out a positive response (laughing, smiling, gurgling) at the appropriate moment; if they have formed negative feelings they may react with fear or anxiety.

Transactional analysis and fostering healthy emotional development

Below is a very brief guide to transactional analysis. The terms and concepts help us to come to terms with our own life scripts and to understand how to help young children develop a positive life script for themselves. Knowing our own life script may help us to uncover patterns of our own behaviour that provoke both positive and negative effects in others.

Strokes

Strokes are the unit of currency used when people signal recognition of another person within their interactions. To fulfil our own needs, we all need to feel recognised and taken into account by other people. As people build up their relationships, an exchange of strokes, a *transaction*, takes place between them. In this way, people build up a store of strokes (Stewart and Joines, 1987).

For infants these transactions form the basis of personality. The quality of the transactions taking place define how well the infant's needs are met and what sense the infant makes of the relationship – 'human development is shaped by the ongoing interplay among sources of vulnerability and sources of resilience'.

(National Research Council Institute of Medicine, 2000, p.3)

Life scripts

By the time we are seven years old most of us will have constructed life scripts. It is an unconscious process, based on the sense we have made of what happens to us during our early life. As infants we find ways to survive in the hostile world. We need to ensure that our needs are satisfied and in doing so, we set up patterns of behaviour. These patterns are then replayed throughout our lives and we may distort what is happening around us to fit in with the script we established in early childhood. During adolescence we may revise our script and the script we write for ourselves will have a beginning, middle and end. We may not be conscious of the life script we formulated for ourselves as children and yet we will continue to live it out.

To ensure that we maintain the life script we will act in our *child ego* state, ignoring any information that does not fit. This is known as *redefining*. We may also selectively ignore information that contradicts our life script. This is known as *discounting*. The relationships we choose will support the life script that we have written for ourselves.

We replay, in our later life, relationships that we had with our parents when we were children. The players in the relationship will take on the roles of parent, adult and child. The players interact together. This type of relationship is called a *symbiosis*.

The life script that we chose as a child may be painful and self-destructive (depending in part on the quality and type of strokes we received as infants) and yet, unless we work to be aware of it, we will continue to replay this script as adults. However, life scripts can be changed at any time by the participant. In order to do this transactional analysis theory suggests that:

> I have to identify the needs I did not have met as a child. I have to find ways of getting those needs met now, using my grown-up resources instead of relying on the script's 'magical solution'.
>
> (Stewart and Joines,1987, p.115)

This model usefully highlights the important reciprocal processes of emotional development – our own and that of the infants in our care who will be affected by the quality of our interactions with them. We need to be aware of where these responses may be coming from.

Ego states

Ego states originate in childhood. They consist of patterns of thoughts and feelings which are related to a corresponding pattern of behaviour. Each time a particular set of behaviours is performed, the person will experience a particular set of feelings; each time a particular set of feelings occurs, the person will act out a particular set of behaviours.

There are three ego states identified in transactional analysis: the *parent ego state*, consisting of thoughts, behaviours and feelings copied from parent role models; the *adult ego state*, consisting of feelings, thoughts and behaviours connected to responses made in the present and not simply conditional on any previous feelings, thoughts and behaviours that may have taken place as an infant; and the *child ego state*, consisting of feelings, thoughts and behaviours from childhood. The parent and child ego states are rooted in the past, whereas the adult ego state is part of the here and now.

Transactional analysis and early years practice

Transactional analysis provides a framework and language for understanding our interactions and relationships. Within our workplace or our home, through our own emotional awareness, we can have a profound effect on the quality of interactions and communications between the practitioners, parents and carers, and children. Transactional analysis seeks to identify and promote the development of healthy emotions within a social context where the caregiver offers positive, secure interactions leading to the building of a secure relationship.

The important point is that infants need to learn to contain their own emotions and to regulate them through a secure relationship with a carer who contains those emotions for them. Without this secure base, the infant's emotional development could be compromised. Infants are actively involved within the environment, organising their own experiences, they are predisposed to seek out the relationships that they need to survive, to be 'OK', and a secure relationship with a carer provides the secure foundation from which to explore further.

The adult's role is complex. Adults who consciously want to support this early emotional development can only do so after identifying their own life script. They must address their own life script to determine whether they can truly recognise the needs of the infant. Some may be working to further their own life script, some may be discounting or redefining their life script through their relationships. Transactional analysis helps us identify our own life script to enable us to understand the life scripts of others. In the case of infants, transactional analysis enables us to understand the needs of infants and to help them build their own life-affirming scripts.

As practitioners working with infants, we can use the techniques of transactional analysis to review our own influence on the infants in our care. We can also work with children to help them see their own life scripts and encourage the development of the awareness, capabilities and strategies needed to decide their own destiny. We can help them to change their decisions, to solve their own problems, to be in charge of themselves. The language specific to transactional analysis encourages awareness of the emotional journey they are undertaking through life and adds a structural approach to that journey that children and adults travel. Although it deals with individual life scripts, transactional analysis takes a social constructionist view of living and learning.

In summary, transactional analysis views all relationships as reciprocal. The ideal position within a relationship is that both participants are equally OK. However, within the transactions that take place between people, each participant's life script will have an influence and the positions may become unbalanced and lead to difficulties. Some positions will be more nurturing than others. In transactional analysis, participant roles are expressed as follows:

I'm OK you're OK.

I'm OK you're not OK.

I'm not OK you're OK.

I'm not OK you're not OK.

In child–adult interactions this has particular implications. If the adult participant adopts an 'OK' position, then the infant may be forced into a 'not OK' position. This would inform their life script and how they viewed themselves in relation to authority figures. For example, a parent might angrily accuse a child of being useless when they failed to come up to expectation. If this position is reinforced many times over, in future situations the grown infant might seek out relationships that placed them into 'not OK' positions in accordance with their life script. This might be the case with children labelled under-achievers, or whose reports read 'lacks self-esteem, needs to try harder, fears failure'.

In working alongside children, practitioners should address their own emotional position; we need to recognise the 'baggage' we bring along with us, that much is clear. Transactional analysis is just one way among many that might help us to do so.

Conclusion

It is for each person working with young children to make sense of the debates that fluctuate around the way we explain emotional, social and intellectual growth. This chapter has focused on the contribution that healthy emotional growth makes to becoming a person.

Emotional development is a complex process. In order for infants to develop their individual pattern of emotions, they need access to caregivers who are able to offer interactions which are consistent, familiar and predictable. Infants need to feel contained, but not confined, by the caregiver. In turn, the caregiver needs to recognise their own emotional needs and work towards meeting them. As practitioners we need to use our knowledge fully to support and encourage the holistic development of every child in our care.

---

*ACTIVITY **1***

Observe an infant with his or her carer. Record the behaviour of both the infant and the carer. Outline, in terms of transactional analysis theory, possible explanations of the interaction between them.

---

3 Developing communication: enjoying the company of other people

Rod Parker-Rees

Introduction

Any form of work with young children and their families will require highly developed communication skills: engaging with children who cannot or will not speak and promoting effective dialogue between colleagues, between colleagues and families, between adults and children and between children. We need to be able to express ourselves clearly and accurately but we should also enjoy the more playful and unpredictable flow of social conversation with children, parents and other adults with whom we work.

For most literate adults, communication has come to mean something a bit like a postal service. When someone decides to communicate an idea, they package it into words and deliver it, either in speech or writing, to someone else who unwraps the parcel of words to receive the message. This 'discrete state' model of communication (Fogel, 1997) can lead to the idea that we communicate information *to* other people, or even *at* them (like the child's idea of teaching, enacted in the stern instruction of a row of passive dolls and teddies). Some forms of communication, such as the exchange of emails, written correspondence or the publication and reviewing of research findings, may be understood in terms of this kind of information delivery. I hope to argue in this chapter, however, that even these can be understood better if we are willing to learn from research into the earliest forms of communication, which reveals a very different kind of structure. As is often the case in early childhood studies, examining how infants acquire and develop particular skills can help us to reflect on how we use those skills ourselves.

Mapping communication

We should begin by mapping what we mean by communication. Try going through a typical day in your mind, noting all the different forms of communication which you might experience, from touch, gesture and movement through various forms of speech to writing, reading, responding to signs and labels and reacting to programmes on TV. When you have built up and developed this list, adding other forms as they occur to you, you can try arranging the different kinds of communication in a spatial array, with the most intuitive forms (touch, 'sixth sense' and what comes naturally) at the bottom and the most formally structured, rule-bound forms (mathematical formulae, musical notation and other symbol systems that have to be learned) at the top. Working on this with one or two friends should generate some useful arguments about where particular forms should be placed and you will probably find that you need to break some of your categories down: drawing, for example, includes doodling, plans and blueprints, diagrams and countless other forms; and where would you put dance, scent or clothes? We do, after all, choose our clothes and our toiletries to give other people messages about who we are and how we are feeling.

When communication is mapped in this way the resulting structure may appear to represent development, with innate abilities at the bottom and those which require most formal training at the top. You may also notice other shifts in the qualities of communication as you work up the list: from intimate to public; from passionate warmth to cool reason; from involuntary and uncontrollable to deliberate and purposeful. You should also notice that the lower part of your map of communication is more crowded and that more of your communication is represented here than in the higher reaches, although we are so used to thinking only about the visible tip of this iceberg that you may not have captured everything that is going on beneath the surface. Touch, for example, is one of the most primitive forms of communication, appearing early both in phylogeny (development of the species) and ontogeny (development of the individual), but it is also one of the most powerful. Its influence is never displaced by later developing, more systematic languages; even the coolest of formal operational thinkers will still respond strongly to a pat on the back, a hug or a shove.

Communication and concepts of development

If we think of development in terms of escape from our baser animal origins we will tend, like Piaget, to value the civilised orderliness of formal, invented systems such as logic and mathematics. If, on the other hand, we share Rousseau's romantic view of development, as the progressive corruption of our noble, innocent nature by the faff and restrictiveness of cultural codes and rules, we will value the passionate intensity of the more basic forms of communication such as touch, dance and gesture.

We may think of development in terms of erecting a building; firm foundations must first be laid if the structure (built with the help of scaffolding, of course) is to be stable and sound (Fisher, 2002). In this case the earliest stages in the development of communication, learning to engage effectively with other people, must receive special attention if we hope to build high. On the other hand, development can be seen as being less dependent on pre-existing blueprints and more chaotic, emergent and serendipitous. Just as sand falling through a sand-timer will form itself into a tidy heap without the intervention of an architect (gravity and the shape of the grains of sand will do the trick), so a continuing stream of action and experience might result in the emergence of a growing developmental mound. Some later experiences will add to the height of the pile but many will also consolidate it, tumbling down to extend it at the base as well as at its peak. By offering a short account of the earliest stages in the development of communication, down at the bottom of the heap, I hope to show that early, social aspects of communication are not just base preliminaries to the business of becoming civilised and educated, destined to be buried beneath the important parts of the building. In all kinds of communication we need to acknowledge all levels of our engagement, so that we do not, for example, simply expect our colleagues to 'leave their personal problems at the door' and knuckle down to their work, as if our emotional lives could be switched on and off at will.

The human foetus does not develop like a fish, lizard or chick, isolated within a shell. From conception we grow in an intimate, but by no means simple or straightforward, relationship with our mother. Foetal development involves both individual and social processes from the outset, including chemical and immunological conflicts (Inside Science 143, 2001) as well as opportunities for the foetus to tune in to the mother's eating and sleeping patterns, to the structure of her speech and even to her favourite music and the signature tunes of TV programmes which she watches regularly (Hepper, 2003). As we grew inside our mother's womb, we had plenty of time to become accustomed to some of the patterns that shape her life, so that we were born already able to 'sing along' in early forms of communication (Trevarthen, 2003).

At birth, our motor development lagged considerably behind our sensory capabilities, ensuring that we would enjoy the ideal context for refining and tuning our early awareness of patterns in the structure of our social world. Imagine how different the relationship between mother and child would be if the baby's development were fully precocial, like a foal or a lamb. If, within hours of birth, babies were already on their feet and gambolling and frisking around the house, there would obviously be much less opportunity for them to study the details of their mothers' movements, expressions, sounds and rhythms.

Imitation

When Meltzoff and Moore (1977) recorded evidence of very young babies imitating facial expressions, they were intrigued by this evidence of an innate ability to connect perceptual information with patterns of motor control. How can the newborn baby relate the still very blurry and indistinct visual image of a protruding tongue to the combinations of muscle actions required to make its own tongue stick out? And, no less puzzlingly, how might a baby benefit from this precocious ability to imitate facial expressions?

Later research has suggested that babies' brains are equipped, from birth, with 'mirror neurons' (Rizzolati *et al.*, 1996), particular links in the complex web of neural connections which perform precisely this function, linking motor control with sensory perception so that simply observing someone else performing an action will stimulate the equivalent premotor activity in our own brain. You may have noticed that your hands get twitchy as you watch someone struggling with a tricky manipulation, such as a child trying to fit a piece into an inset puzzle or someone having difficulty opening a packet or container.

Imitation is much more than a simple, automatic process of 'monkey see, monkey do'. Other studies have shown that when we observe another person's facial expressions, our premotor response, triggered by our own mirror neurons, produces in us the emotional state that we have learned to associate with these expressions (Motluk, 2001). When you see someone frown, the neurons associated with the earliest stages of producing a frown are stimulated in your own brain and this mirror response triggers a feeling of puzzlement or distress. On the other hand, seeing someone else smile or hearing other people laughing may be enough to lift your spirits.

This built-in ability to empathise, to respond to other people's mental states by responding to their physical expressions, combined with plentiful opportunities to pay close attention to a caregiver's actions, expressions and interactions means that the human baby is well placed to develop intersubjectivity – the ability to make one's own intentions known and to recognise the interests and concerns of other people (Trevarthen, 1979).

After a couple of months of legitimate peripheral participation (Lave and Wenger, 1991), observing others from the outside while recovering from the trauma of delivery (and allowing their mothers to recover), babies show the first clear signs of primary intersubjectivity (Trevarthen, 1979) when they begin to participate actively and intentionally in communicative exchanges.

The dawning of primary intersubjectivity, from about two months, is a very special part of a baby's development, a time when communication is enjoyed for its own sake as a form of communing, even of communion. The full-on, eye-to-eye, soul-to-soul engagement that a baby can offer has led many cultures to see special mystical or spiritual qualities in the young infant. This can be seen in Wordsworth's (1888) romantic image of birth:

> Not in entire forgetfulness,
> And not in utter nakedness,
> But trailing clouds of glory do we come
> From God who is our home:
> Heaven lies about us in our infancy!
> ('Ode on intimations of immortality from recollections of early childhood', lines 63–7)

It can also be seen in the widespread belief that babies remain in touch with the infinite until the bones of their skulls knit together and close off the fontanelle; see, for example the poems, 'Fontanelle' by Ben Downing (2003) and 'The African Spider Cures' by Judy Johnson (2002).

Communication and socialisation

On the spectrum of communication mentioned earlier, this primary intersubjectivity is clearly well down in the intuitive depths where communication is more about establishing and maintaining relationships than about exchanging specific items of information. Robin Dunbar (1998) has argued that language developed out of the social grooming used by other apes to allow members of groups, literally, to 'keep in touch' with each other. As group sizes increased, possibly to provide protection from large predators, providing social strokes through physical contact would have become increasingly impractical and speech emerged as a more efficient alternative, allowing us to engage with up to three others at the same time. Gossip or 'idle chat' preserves this social function and most people would agree that the pleasure to be derived from this kind of interaction has very little to do with the topic of conversation. As in the intimate exchanges characteristic of primary intersubjectivity, the interaction is enjoyed for its own sake, as a way of maintaining and celebrating social contact and trust among a group of friends.

From very early on, babies are aware of a difference between people, who generally adjust their own contributions to those offered by the baby, and objects, which generally do not respond in this contingent way. In a study of babies' memory, Carolyn Rovee-Collier (Rovee-Collier and Hayne, 1987) tied a ribbon to babies' ankles, connecting them to a mobile suspended above their cots so that their kicking would cause the mobile to move. The babies were quick to notice the relationship between their movements and the movements of the mobile and appeared to be delighted by their ability to exercise control at a distance. What I find particularly interesting, however, is that the babies would often smile and coo at the mobile as they played, almost as if its contingent response to their actions persuaded them to see it as an animate playmate.

This sensitivity to contingency has also been demonstrated in a series of studies by Cohn and Tronick (1987) in which babies' reactions to 'live' feedback from their mothers was compared with their response when their mothers adopted a 'still face', deliberately avoiding giving their babies any facial feedback. Three-month-old babies would often turn away from their mother's still face or show signs of distress. Murray and Trevarthen (1985) extended Cohn and Tronick's study, observing two-month-old babies' reactions to a live video link with their mothers, which meant that babies could see their mothers on a TV screen as their mothers responded to a closed-circuit TV image of them, preserving the real-time contingency of the interaction. Murray and Trevarthen then repeated the observations but this time with a delay which meant that the babies saw their mothers' reacting to what they had been doing 30 seconds previously. Even this short delay was enough to disrupt the babies' ability to sustain interaction and again some babies were clearly disturbed by their mothers' failure to respond properly to their efforts at communication. Further evidence of babies' sensitivity to the contingency of their communication partner's responses comes from studies of mothers who suffer from post-natal depression (Murray and Cooper 1997). Depressed mothers are less likely to engage fully with their babies and, as a result, their babies may be less interested in initiating interaction with their mothers.

We may not be consciously aware of the ways in which we respond to other people when we engage in communication with them; indeed we may feel slightly uncomfortable about talking with people who seem to manage their responses to us a bit too deliberately – we don't like to feel we are being manipulated. Nevertheless, even when we communicate with young babies, our interactions are co-regulated (Fogel, 1997) or jointly and simultaneously 'steered' by everyone involved. In the early stages this co-regulation is not symmetrical: adults work quite hard to give babies what they want and babies have limited scope for returning the favour. Babies are, however, armed with a very effective tool for rewarding adults who take the trouble to engage with them in co-regulated, contingent interaction. The intentional smile, when skilfully deployed along with its partner, the sad face, can entrap adults into devoting huge amounts of time to entertaining a baby.

The emotionally intense, highly empathetic 'gooiness' of these early exchanges provides the ideal environment for advancing the baby's awareness of the social rules which shape interactions within a particular culture. The mirror neurons which provided a point of entry into other people's interests and concerns are now supplemented by what Rochat (2004, p.267) has described as the *social mirror*: 'Metaphorically speaking, the adult caretaker orients a mirror that is *magnifying* back to the infant an image of emotional expressions that are greatly magnified'.

Rochat argues that this exaggeration of the baby's expressions in the adult's responses helps to differentiate between the adult's own spontaneous actions and those which reflect back the baby's, much as 'motherese' or 'Baby Talk Register' serves to differentiate between speech which is directed towards the baby and speech for others. But what the adult offers is much more than a mirror, even a magnifying one. By tidying up the baby's actions, gestures, expressions and sounds and returning them in a form which follows the rules of social and cultural conventions, the adult is acting as the baby's social editor. A baby's first draft of a smile comes back in the form of a fluent and exaggerated social smile. Babble is revised to become a sequence of phonemes, the common, public sounds of a particular language. Parents are keen to discover meaning in the sounds produced by their babies and it is no accident that the baby's first words, 'mama', 'papa', 'dada', have been adopted in almost every language as labels for their eager parents.

The process of social editing combines affirmation of the baby's contribution with a gentle induction into the patterns, rules and structures of conventional systems of communication. Babies are extraordinarily good at discovering patterns and distinctions in the relationships between their own actions and the changes in perceptual information which result from these actions (e.g. I shake *this* and I hear *that*). This intuitive gift for learning from experience allows the baby to extract information not only from what adults do and say but also from how they edit the baby's own actions – what is kept, what is left out and what is changed. As adults we do the same when we get to know others by noting the ways in which they transform stories, anecdotes, and, most tellingly, accounts of other people's behaviour.

Improvisation in supportive contexts

In a fascinating study of, jazz, improvisational theatre, conversation, and children's play, Sawyer (2001) has argued that one of the fundamental rules of improvisation, the 'yes, and …' rule, informs effective social interaction in each of these kinds of cultural activity. The 'yes, and …' rule requires that any contribution should be both acknowledged and built on, so that each participant contributes to the emergence of both a shared performance and a satisfying feeling of community. In interactions between babies and their parents, social editing operates in just this way, showing the baby that their contribution has been acknowledged but also adding something to it by returning it in a more culturally regulated form.

After several months of wallowing in this pure form of communication, at about the age of four months, babies tend to turn away from their adult partners, seeming to prefer active exploration of the physical world of manipulable objects to the indolent, lotus-eating luxury of primary intersubjectivity. By this age, babies are developing the muscle control and strength that will allow them to sit up, freeing their hands for exploration of the stuff around them. This development heralds a shift of focus, from a Vygotskian participation in social exchanges to a more Piagetian dedication to exploration and investigation. While social editing may be hugely beneficial for learning about cultural practices, it is less welcome when the focus is on empirical examination of one's physical environment, where what is needed is, quite literally, first-hand experience. In some cultures this transition is marked by turning the baby around to face out towards the world from its mother's lap, where before it had faced in towards her (Martini and Kirkpatrick, 1981). In Western cultures, however, parents may experience a slight sense of loss as their cooing, gurgling partner starts to push them aside in favour of single-handed voyages of discovery. But if children are to take their place in the social processes of conversation they must acquire their own experiences so that they too can contribute ('yes, and …') as well as listen and observe.

In the course of this exploratory period, infants begin to realise that they can influence other people's behaviour by indicating their own intentions. To begin with, gestures such as reaching and pointing may be features of the child's relationship with an object but, as the child notices that her actions can influence the behaviour of other people, the focus of her attention shifts to the person whose behaviour she is trying to control. Reaching for an object, especially if accompanied by appropriately plaintive noises to attract attention, may be enough to cause someone else to bring the object within one's reach, and holding up one's arms may let someone else know that one wants to be picked up. Garcia (2002) and Acredolo *et al.* (2002) have explored ways of extending this natural vocabulary of gestural communication by using a form of hand-signing. When parents use 'baby sign' to support their interaction, babies as young as six months can begin to develop a vocabulary of signs which they can use to let other people know what they want and to understand what people want from them. Many of the gestures used in baby signing resemble the actions they represent so, in Bruner's (1966) terms, they bridge the gap between enactive and iconic modes of representation and prepare the ground for the emergence of the symbolic representation required for language, where the connection between sounds and the ideas they represent is almost entirely arbitrary. Merlin Donald (1991) has argued that the evolution of the human mind involved a transition period, which he calls 'mimetic culture', when people were able to communicate deliberately through action, signing or mime. Donald argues that mimesis would have allowed early people to develop a shared culture of rituals, formalised patterns of movement which would enable communities to share knowledge and, most importantly, to pass knowledge from one generation to the next. What seems to be important, both in baby signing and in this concept of a mimetic culture, is that certain kinds of action are given a special status, set apart from the ordinary processes of dealing with the physical world of objects.

Noticing what others notice

From about the age of nine months, infants show signs of what Trevarthen and Hubley (1978) describe as secondary intersubjectivity. Where primary intersubjectivity was entirely contained within the interaction between the people involved (usually the baby and a parent), secondary intersubjectivity involves three-way relationships between the child, another person and an object or event to which both are paying attention. What seems to be particularly important about these triadic relations is that the child can now pay attention to the meanings which adults attach to objects and events, including intentional communicative gestures such as signs and speech.

When children under the age of nine months are confronted by a surprising situation they will usually stare intently at whatever caused this surprise but children over nine months are more likely to look at a familiar adult, to read their reaction for clues about how this situation should be understood (Gauvain, 2001). This 'social referencing' provides immensely valuable access to the cultural worlds of other people. By communicating with others about objects and events, infants can not only learn about their environment, they can also learn about the meaning other people attach to aspects of their world; what is considered important, dangerous, disgusting, funny, rude, kind or cute. Towards the end of their first year, children are particularly interested in how adults react to what they do, actively exploring ways of using this knowledge. Once a child knows, for example, that approaching something dangerous or disgusting will provoke a strong response, this knowledge can be used very effectively to control an adult's attention. If your mum is pre-occupied, talking on the phone perhaps, and not offering as much attention as you need, all you have to do is toddle over to the bin and begin to rummage. The attention you get may not be exactly what you would like but it may be much better than no attention at all. What this example highlights is that what you do (rummaging in the bin) may be pretty insignificant in comparison to your communicative intentions – fiddling with a plug socket or pulling the cat's tail would probably do just as well. When children begin to use words and later phrases, sentences and stories to communicate, it is as well to remember that what they are saying may be much less important than the levels of communication which lie beneath the surface of their words. When a parent cuddles up with a child to share a book the communication which they both enjoy is much richer than words and pictures could ever convey. The book may provide a useful tool for sharing attention but what it contains may not be as important as the communicative experiences with which it has come to be associated.

Enjoying the company of other people

As you read the following account of what is involved in joint attention, try to relate it to your own experience of the kinds of social interaction which you most enjoy – chatting with friends over a drink or two, having a laugh or perhaps debating an issue about which you feel strongly:

> First, the social partners know that they are attending to something in common. Second, they monitor each other's attention to the target of mutual interest. And, third, they co-ordinate their individual efforts during the interaction using mutual attention as a guide. Interactions involving joint attention help children to learn much about the world around them, including things that are important to pay attention to and how these things are valued by others in their community. Because these interactions are set in the context of interpersonal relationships they are a rich and motivating setting for learning.
>
> (Gauvain, 2001, pp.86–7)

What do you learn, about yourself as well as about your friends, from these interactions and how does the emotional 'feel' of this kind of communication compare with situations which have been deliberately organised to support your learning?

How should an understanding of the social core of the early stages of communication affect the way we think about how we communicate as adults? After years of formal education, where communication often centres on a trade in information, we may have set up artificial distinctions between 'work communication' and 'play communication', between talking and writing to get things done quickly and efficiently and talking simply for the pleasure of other people's company. Nell Noddings has challenged this dissociation between work and play orientations in the context of school settings, arguing that the influences of the social environment on children's development are even more important than measures of how much knowledge they have accumulated:

> *Schools should become places in which teachers and students live together, talk to each other, reason together, take delight in each others' company. Like good parents, teachers should be concerned first and foremost with the kind of people their charges are becoming. My guess is that when schools focus on what really matters in life, the cognitive ends we are now striving toward in such painful and artificial ways will be met as natural culminations of the means we have wisely chosen.*

(Noddings, 1991, p.161)

We should remember that all forms of communication are social processes grounded in the negotiation of common, shared understanding. Even the most detached transmission of information always requires the 'sender' to draw on assumptions about how the 'receiver' can be expected to respond. What will be too obvious to be worth mentioning? What will be familiar, interesting, challenging, confusing or irritating? Negotiating common understanding may be much easier in situations which can be co-regulated by all participants; where responses can be monitored and misunderstandings can be repaired almost before they happen. When this is not possible, when communicating with a child's family by means of an entry in a diary, a newsletter or notices and signs, for example, it is all the more important to draw on available knowledge about how a particular form of words might be (mis)construed. Imagination can allow us to role-play communication in our heads, allowing us to tap into implicit, intuitive knowledge about how particular people can be expected to respond, but only if we have taken the time to get to know these people.

Time invested in 'idle' chat with children, colleagues and parents can allow us to get to know them (and let them get to know us), adding to the store of intuitive awareness which will inform our communication with them in the future. We do not feel the need to keep checklists of what we have learned about people in the course of friendly chat because we trust the automatic processes which allow us to sift out information about their personality, likes, dislikes and interests from the kinds of contributions they make (and don't make). Studying the earliest stages of communication may help us to think carefully about how traditionally cool professional discourses and practices can be warmed up if we are prepared to pay more attention to the human aspects of how we live and work in social communities: 'the main function of conversation is not to get things done but to improve the quality of experience' (Csikszentmihalyi,1992, p.129).

ACTIVITY **1**

How much can video capture?

Make a short video recording of interaction between children under three years old (prefer-ably under two) or between one child and an adult or older child. Make sure you obtain the parents' permission both to make the recording and to share it with a colleague. Two or three minutes will be enough but you will probably need to record much more in order to be able to pick out a short sample which is reasonably 'natural' (an adult encouraging a child to 'perform' will be less interesting). Watch the video carefully and try to record what is happen-ing: a) as a transcript of what is said, and b) with explanatory notes about gestures, body language, mood, etc., to try to capture as much as possible of what was going on. Of course you cannot hope to capture exactly how the participants understood their interaction but you can try to explain what you felt (the difference between being there and just seeing the video). You may find it helpful to present both transcripts in parallel columns, one for each participant, so that you can show how their actions and speech overlap.

Share your observations with a colleague, as follows:

1. *Show your colleague just the bare transcript (no scene setting or explanations). How much sense can your colleague make of what is going on? Are they willing or able to comment on how the participants may have felt about their interaction?*

2. *Now play the video but turn the monitor around or turn down the contrast so that your colleague gets only the soundtrack. What additional information does this provide?*

3. *Now reveal all! Play the video with sound and pictures. How much is added to what your colleague was able to make of the soundtrack?*

4. *You could go on to give your colleague your full transcript (with explanatory notes) and talk about how you 'read' the interaction before playing the video one last time.*

Now switch roles and see what you can make of your colleague's piece of video. This should help you to appreciate how much we rely on non-verbal channels of communication of which, in everyday life, we are scarcely aware. Be prepared to have your interpretation chal-lenged and to challenge your colleague's interpretation of his/her piece of video. How could you determine whose interpretation best fits the limited perspective captured on video?

ACTIVITY **2**

Looking below the surface

Develop the habit of standing back from different kinds of social interaction (lectures, dis-cussions, gossip, arguments) to monitor what is being communicated. What do people express through the way they speak, what they emphasise, what they ignore, facial expressions, posture, etc., and how much of this is picked up by others? You may find that it is easier to note what you feel about what is going on and then try to work out what may have informed that feeling. Be warned that if your friends feel that you are analysing their interaction, they may object!

Part 2

Understanding Children's Worlds: Making the Familiar Strange

4 Adults' concepts of childhood

Norman Gabriel

Introduction

In what ways do adults' concepts of childhood influence our relationships with children? How do our childhood memories of the past affect the way we 'think', behave, and work with adults and children? Memories affect our behaviour and beliefs as adults far more than we even realise. Our memories of having been a child remain a central part of who we think we are and who we think we once were.

Are children 'naturally' good or evil little adults, who have to be moulded by wise and caring adults? If children are defined by their own innate 'nature' or 'natural' needs, then a number of assumptions will be made about childhood in order to distinguish its unique qualities from adulthood. A central concern of this chapter will be the way that different concepts of 'nature' have been used to define what we mean by childhood. These different interpretations of what we mean by 'nature' have led to a variety of concepts of childhood:

> The relationship between children, childhood and nature has existed at a number of different levels. It is as complex as our ideas about nature itself: the state of childhood may be seen as pure, innocent, or original in the sense of primary; children may be analogised with animals or plants, thereby indicating that they are natural objects for scientific and medical investigation; children could be valued as aesthetic objects ... but they could equally be feared for their instinctual, animal-like natures.
>
> (Jordanova, 1989, p.6)

We will explore contemporary concepts of childhood by tracing the historical forces that have helped to shape different constructions of childhood. We will begin by looking at some of the dominant assumptions of romantic childhood in literary and philosophical texts by Rousseau and Wordsworth. The impact of these assumptions about children will be considered by focusing on one very important area: the 'moral' upbringing of children and changing patterns of parental advice which have evolved since the eighteenth century. We will then move on and analyse some of the ideological representations of street children and investigate attitudes toward children in work, so that we can unravel the assumptions that lie behind the concept of the 'romantic child' and the 'innocent child' who is need of adult protection.

Preamble – memories

Time it was, and what a time it was, it was
A time of innocence, a time of confidences
Long ago, it must be, I have a photograph
Preserve your memories, they're all that's left you

(Lyrics from Paul Simon and Arthur Garfunkel, 'Bookends Theme')

Our memories are elusive and cannot be read as direct evidence of what we were like as a child. The child we think we remember may be constructed as much from more recent influences, films or books, as from recollections from years ago. From photograph albums or family stories that we have been told when we were growing up as adults, we try to reconstruct or imagine what our childhood was like, or what we would have liked it to have been. At the personal level we frequently look to our own childhoods as a measure by which comparisons between past and present might be made. Yet very often memories of this period in our lives can become imbued with nostalgia or, where too painful to recall, they are shaped by acceptable norms of childhood and childhood experiences. What can sometimes result is a conflict between our understanding of the concept of childhood, as an idealised time of innocence and protection, and our more individual memories of personal unhappiness (Davidoff *et al.*, 1999).

When, for example, I turn to my own childhood, I initially think of a wonderful time for play and adventure with close friends. But then I stop. I was about four and playing on my bicycle with my best friend Kenneth when he said he could no longer play with me because I was different. I did not understand what he was saying, so I asked what he meant. He told me I was Jewish. I ran home crying, telling my Mum and Dad what had happened. They reassured me that being Jewish was not terrible – I was beginning to learn what it felt like to be different.

Romantic aspects of childhood

Jean-Jacques Rousseau was one of the most important thinkers of the eighteenth century, offering a radical, alternative vision of childhood. He criticised the Christian tradition of original sin, arguing that children are born innocent. Although Rousseau did not believe that children were virtuous in the first 12 years of their life, he advocated a form of 'negative education' that would shelter them from vice. As innocents, children should be left to respond to nature and protected from the risks and prejudices of social institutions. Emile, his ideal boy, was not to learn to read until after he was 12: he must be free to roam outdoors in loose clothing, learning by his own interests and experience in a natural environment. Only in adolescence would Emile be allowed to learn to read and write and to master a craft.

The important part played by the concept of 'Nature' in Rousseau's thought is sometimes seen as a precursor to bourgeois romanticism. However, the dissemination of his fame and ideas should also be understood in relation to the highly detailed rules that regulated the lives of people in his society. We can interpret Rousseau's natural child of innocence as a response to the advancing urban development of French society – the idealisation of nature was used by members of court-aristocratic circles as a counterpoint to the constraints of royal rule and suppression of feeling in court life (see Elias, 1983). As more and more people moved into cities and towns, the child became a symbol that represented 'Nature' and their estrangement from the countryside.

The child as 'natural', 'pure' and 'innocent' functioned as a basis for the late eighteenth- and early nineteenth-century Romantic poets' vision of childhood. The early Romantics – Blake, Wordsworth and Goethe – drew attention to the ideal of childhood as an area of self-knowledge within each individual. Their idea of an interior self with a personal history suggested that we all retain an aspect of our individual pasts in our psyches. For Wordsworth, innocence was deeply rooted in the 'natural' world: the child is a part of his own childhood as remembered by an adult looking back in time. Central to this concept of the child is a sense of oneness with his body and the world that surrounded him in childhood:

> Oh! Many a time have I, a five years Child,
>
> A naked Boy, in one delightful Rill,
>
> A little Mill-race sever'd from his stream,
>
> Made one long bathing of a summer's day,
>
> Bask'd in the sun, and plunged, and bask'd again,
>
> Alternate all a summer's day

(Wordsworth, *The Prelude*, 1, pp.291–300, first published 1805; in Ford, 1982)

Gittins (1998) offers an important interpretation of Wordsworth's poem, one that is crucial for understanding the concept of the 'inner child'. The 'inner child' that remains within the adult becomes the repository of feeling and joyousness. Gittins argues that it is not just the child's joy in nature and his own body that is apparent here, but a drawing on the past from the adult's perspective of childhood. The child is a remembered child, reinterpreted by the adult in an idealised process – he is not only reminiscing about himself as a boy, but making generalisations about childhood innocence and the 'nature' of childhood itself. For adults, this remembered knowledge of the child survived in memory. Memory was central for Wordsworth in relation to his feelings about the loss of childhood:

> … I cannot paint
>
> What then I was …
>
> That time is past
>
> And all its aching joys are no more,
>
> And all its dizzy raptures

(Wordsworth, *Tintern Abbey*, lines 75–6 and 83–5, first published 1798; in Ford, 1982)

According to Gittins (1998), loss, informed by melancholic yearning, is the main theme of this poem. This was the beginning of a trend towards interiorisation, in which adults were more and more looking inwards, as well as backwards in time, to their own personal childhood. Steedman (1995) has also traced this concept of 'interiority of the child' in the nineteenth century. She examines the various representations of Mignon, the homeless orphan (originally portrayed by Goethe in *Wilhelm Meister*) who was dislocated by the adults training her to be an acrobat. Throughout the nineteenth century, this mythical image was a crucial source for intensive adult longing and desire – images of the remembered and imagined child were woven together to create a quest to rescue the lost child.

This idea of rescuing unfortunate children from factories or brothels developed in nineteenth-century England, where there was an expansion of philanthropy as well as an increasing state interest in children's well-being. In 1881, Lord Shaftesbury, a British philanthropist, was asked by a Liverpool clergyman to introduce a bill into Parliament to prevent parental cruelty to children. At first he refused, arguing that the matter was 'of so private, internal and domestic a character as to be beyond the reach of legislation' (quoted in Hendrick, 1997, p.45), but he later supported the bill. In 1889 the Prevention of Cruelty to and Protection of Children Act was passed. Ill treatment and the neglect of children became illegal, and a new offence of creating suffering to children was created.

Religious and medical moralities

In marked contrast to the natural goodness of the 'romantic child' were the traditional beliefs held by members of the Evangelical Movement. Despite their relatively small number, they were very influential through their prolific writings about child-rearing practices. Their beliefs dominated the advisory literature available to parents and children's own reading for nearly two centuries (Newson and Newson, 1974). From this period a severe view of the child emerges, one where socialisation is seen as a battleground where the wills of stubborn children have to be broken, but for their own good. For the Evangelicals, the prospect of heaven or hell was a major source of motivation in their attempts to 'form the minds' of their own children. Each child enters the world as a wilful material force, is impish and harbours a potential evil that can be mobilised if adults allow them to stray from the righteous path that God has provided.

'Break the will, if you would not damn the child' (Wesley, 1872) expressed the ever-present fear of damnation, in an age when most families would have lost at least one child. Janeway's famous and influential 'Token for children' (1830), first published in 1672 and reprinted well into the middle of the nineteenth century, makes the connection between dying and hell quite explicit:

> *Are you willing to go to hell, to be burned with the devil and his angels? ... O! Hell is a terrible place ... Did you ever hear of a little child that died ... and if other children die, why you may be sick and die? ... How do you know but that you may be the next child that may die? ... Now tell me, my pretty dear child, what will you do?*
>
> (quoted in Newson and Newson, 1974, p.57)

From Janeway onwards, the pious and happy deaths of good little boys and girls are compared with the terrible deaths of irreligious children who were assumed to have passed straight to the eternal fire of hell. Children's deaths are continuously described and lingered over in children's books of the eighteenth and nineteenth centuries. For example, the *Child's Companion* of 1829, a well-illustrated little volume of poems and stories, contains 13 deathbed scenes, together with one discourse on death and two poems inspired by gazing on children's graves. In a society in which death is such a familiar occurrence and an authoritarian God has unlimited powers to decide who will be rewarded through Heaven or punished by Hell, children need to be prepared as carefully for death as for life.

Miller (1987) sees similar strict aphorisms on childrearing such as 'spare the rod and spoil the child' or 'you have to be cruel to be kind' as part of a wider discourse on *poisonous pedagogy*. Poisonous pedagogy is the process by which adults rationalise their own needs and re-enact the humiliation they experienced in childhood. This rationalisation disguises adults' own negative feelings and experiences, becoming part of a set of common-sense beliefs about what's good for children and informing the larger debate on childcare and education. Such views can legitimise adult cruelty to children:

In beating their children, they are struggling to regain the power they once lost to their parents ... for the first time, they see the vulnerability of their own earliest years, which they are unable to recall, reflected in their children.

(Miller, 1987, p.16)

According to Newson and Newson (1974), this evangelical concern to eradicate the devil in the child has important links with the medical-hygienist movement which dominated the 1920s and 1930s in Britain. Scientific mothercraft offered parents the hope that babies could be successfully reared provided that medical advice was faithfully followed: the vengeful God of Heaven and Hell was replaced by an equally authoritarian expert. A good example of this authoritarian advice was the *Mothercraft Manual* written by Liddiard (1928). Although this was not a government publication, it was extremely important before the Second World War, and even more significantly became the main vehicle for the principles of Sir Truby King (1937) and his Mothercraft Training Society. Babies needed to conform to adult expectations – in a sense, their wishes were suspect because they could conceal dangerous impulses or a rebellious determination to dominate the mother. Truby King (1937) believed that when mothers were in constant control, a 'good' baby was reared:

The mother who 'can't be so cruel' as to wake her sleeping baby if he happens to be asleep at the appointed feeding-time, fails to realise that a few such wakings would be all she would have to resort to ... The establishment of perfect regularity of habits, initiated by 'feeding and sleeping by the clock', is the ultimate foundation of all-round obedience.

(quoted in Newson and Newson, 1974, pp.60–1)

Moralities of 'natural' development and 'natural' needs

A major shift in child management developed in the 1930s under the influence of psycho-analysts like Susan Isaacs. In her book *The Nursery Years* (1932) she advised parents to observe children in 'natural' play because it was an important part of their development, and recommended that mothers take a more tolerant attitude towards prohibited prac-tices, like thumb-sucking. In a similar vein, the publication of Margaret Ribble's very influential book *The Rights of Infants* (1943) represented a humanitarian response against earlier and harsher infant-feeding regimes. There was a growing acceptance that babies' desires were legitimate: babies and children needed not only their mothers' presence, but also the rocking, cuddling and lap play that had previously been forbidden. To deprive babies of the 'natural' expression of maternal warmth could prevent the development of their social relationships and personalities. Ribble (1943, p.100) insisted on the need for the correct guidance of mothers, and the necessity of separate spheres for both parents: 'Two parents who have achieved maturity and happiness in their respective biological roles are the native right of every child.'

By the 1940s and 1950s the influence of psychoanalytic theories, especially the work of Donald Winnicott and John Bowlby, was changing the advice given to mothers. This was now more closely focused on the nature of the relationship between mother and child, and their need for close contact. In his theory of attachment, Bowlby (1969) argues that every newborn baby arrives in the world with an innate tendency to remain close to his or her primary caretaker. For him, attachment is a system of regulation geared to producing a dynamic equilibrium between the mother–child pair: children can be emotionally or psychologically damaged by even minimal separation from their mothers. Theories of maternal deprivation also helped to support the growth of the child welfare movement. This movement had its origins in the war years as a result of the concern of Medical Officers of Health about the physical and emotional deprivation experienced by children in day nurseries.

Waves of informalisation

If we now turn to today's society, we can see that the continuation of this trend to offer parents more informal advice can be explained by a longer trend, by waves of informalisation that have occurred from the twentieth century onwards. According to Elias (1998), this trend represents a period of movement from an authoritarian to a more egalitarian parent–child relationship where there is a loosening of barriers of authority in relations between children and adults. Newson and Newson (1974) refer to this new trend as 'fun morality' in which the fundamental need of parents is to be happy in parenthood. The advice given to parents has now changed from the strictly authoritarian to the friendly, more persuasive approach: whereas in the 1930s, mothers were given solemn warnings about what would happen to them if they disobeyed the rules, they are now given continual reassurances about what might possibly result from some mistaken actions. Benjamin Spock (1946) is the supreme example of the friendly, conversational approach – paternalistic enough to give confidence and reassurance, but willing to talk to the mother on equal terms.

Significantly, a similar change has occurred in the balance of power in the relations between men and women, as women have become an integral part of the workforce. Men are now expected to become more involved with the care and education of their children, and parents are under pressure to renounce violence as a means of disciplining their children. We can observe these processes, for example, in the current and ongoing debates in Britain about the use of corporal punishment, and smacking in the household. The Children Are Unbeatable! Alliance is currently campaigning to scrap the 1860 legal defence of 'reasonable chastisement' in order to give children the same protection from assault in the home as adults. The British government recently published its Children Bill but it contains no proposals to give children such equal protection. Supporters of the Alliance in Parliament are trying to amend the Children Bill to remove 'reasonable chastisement' from common law and statute. However, this growing sensitivity about the use of violence also will require a higher degree of self-control by parents in family life. Corporal punishment is now banned in all schools and this has had an influence on the ways teachers and pupils relate to one another.

Children at work

Child labour is a subject that still provokes fierce debate and discussion, whether it concerns the exploitation of children in the developed world or the employment of children for a newspaper round. These debates are based upon what is harmful to a working child's development and what the nature of intervention should be, given a range of different social and economic circumstances. According to Woodhead (1998), our concern to protect children can easily become distorted by our modern Western sensibilities, leading to inappropriate responses that can make the problems faced by children worse rather than better. White (1996), for example, mentions the case of child workers in garment factories in Bangladesh being thrown out to satisfy consumer pressures for child-free products. No attention had been given to the importance of work in the economic lives of these children and their families. The result was that the dismissed children continued to work, but in much more risky conditions in the informal and street economy. They had reduced earnings, worse nutrition and poorer health compared with the minority who had retained employment. The children themselves believed that light factory work combined with attending school for two or three hours a week was the best solution to their poverty. A new scheme was eventually introduced in which employers linked re-employment with schooling and future employment.

When we look at the history of child labour, it is difficult to avoid the influence of our own adult experiences of living and working in a modern world. It is tempting for us to ask at what age children started work, as if it were the same as starting school today, or whether they were employed or unemployed in the same way as adults (Heywood, 2001). The climbing boy suffocating up a chimney or the little mill hand working to the relentless pace of a machine have become common representations of the Industrial Revolution. But a more useful way of looking at these representations is to examine the way that street children were portrayed and legislated for from the 1830s onwards. In mid-Victorian society, between 1800 and 1900, children were highly visible on the streets, because they represented such a high proportion of the population: from the line of sight established by adults, children, running, playing, crouched in the gutter, dancing, begging, importuning, are noticeable. According to Cunningham (1991), there were three 'overlapping discourses' concerning street children in the period from 1840 to 1870. First, there were religious attempts to rescue these children and restore them to 'order' through voluntary efforts like the Ragged Schools. Mary Carpenter (1807–77), for example, was a philanthropist who was very active in the movement for the reformation of neglected children. She advocated a kind and loving approach, one where children would be seen as different and requiring special treatment. Second, there were more 'professional' attempts to deal with the problem of juvenile delinquency. Third, there were journalists, writers and social commentators who wrote about and represented such children to various audiences.

One important social commentator was Henry Mayhew, who in December 1850 visited the green markets of London as part of his *Morning Chronicle* series on 'Labour and the poor'. During this month, he met and interviewed the Little Watercress Girl, an eight-year-old who defined herself as a worker. She told Mayhew of her life at home with her mother, her brother and two sisters, and her mother's common-law husband, a scissor-grinder by trade. When Mayhew described her narrative, he placed it within a framework of anonymity and ignorance, yet he took from her a detailed account of family organisation, both at the economic and domestic level. Mayhew's attempts to present the children as utterly strange, remote, filthy beyond belief and products of impoverished home circumstances produced quite different evidence (Steedman, 1995). His adult conceptions of the 'lost' child distorted his interpretation of her own words to such an extent that he underestimated her ability to explain her social and economic conditions.

In the nineteenth and early twentieth centuries, the centrality of children's work was changed by child labour legislation and compulsory education. According to Hendrick (1996), the campaign to prevent young children from working in the factories was one of the first steps in the construction of a universal childhood. As children were increasingly being seen by adults as closer to 'nature', their relationship to work began to be questioned. Because children were considered to be innately innocent, special and vulnerable, they should be sheltered form the adult world. In the debates of the 1830s, 'categories of analysis' were used to distinguish between adulthood and childhood. Working-class families were criticised by the Evangelicals in terms of the 'order of nature': 'In the order of nature parents, and particularly fathers, would labour for the support of their young children' (Cunningham, 1991, p.83). The distinctive 'nature' of childhood meant that children were fundamentally different from adults – child labour in factories was distorting the order of both 'nature' and England.

As children were becoming precious and valuable, they needed to be protected from the harsh world of labour. Adults therefore tried to rescue individual children from the more extreme forms of child labour, such as chimney-sweeping and prostitution, and at the same time, they campaigned for state legislation that would give children protection. For example, journalist W.T. Stead's campaign against child prostitution in the 1880s was characterised by moralistic and highly sensationalist stories of young girls. He proved how easy it was to buy children for sexual purposes by purchasing a 14-year-old girl from her mother and publicising how he had bought and then rescued her. Embodying freedom and joy, children should, he argued, be allowed to remain innocent of adult knowledge in order to develop as individuals through play and education.

Education legislation from the late 1870s onwards had a profound effect on the regulation of child labour and the lives of working-class children. By the end of the twentieth century, by which time free and compulsory universal primary education was established, children were being controlled and watched not just by the growing army of child rescue organisations, but also by officials such as the school nurse. Through its legal authority and daily inspection by school attendance officers, schooling was able to impose a vision on its pupils and their parents. Obedience, punctuality and deference became cardinal virtues in all schools. No longer able to sell their labour, children were taken by schools from a 'state of ignorance' to a disciplined form of behaviour that reinforced dependence and vulnerability. These changes had important financial consequences for the lives of children: they would become much more dependent on adults and sheltered from the adult world – children became economically 'worthless', but emotionally 'priceless' (Zelizer, 1985).

However, this urge to rescue and protect working-class children can also be seen as a result of fear. Children who lived and worked in the streets were regarded as 'out of control' or 'wild' because they had no adult supervision and were not directly dependent on adult protection and surveillance. Two contrasting stereotypes of working-class children were developed to portray them as dangerous. The 'little woman', often very young and having to take responsibility prematurely for younger siblings and domestic work, and the 'street Arab', male, street-based and dangerous (Davin, 1990). According to Gittins (1998), the survival of street children, working-class children earning money on the streets, challenged the growing middle-class conception of the family as an institution where independent men supported 'naturally' dependent women and children.

Conclusions

This chapter has argued that adults have developed powerful concepts of childhood to define the ways in which we think about children. We have highlighted the important concept of 'nature' in tracing the different versions of childhood that have emerged, especially since Rousseau. Emile, his 'innocent' version of childhood that needed to be protected from the corruption of adult society, was later developed by writers and poets in literary representations of a lost childhood, one that could uncover the deeper, more intuitive parts of ourselves concealed under the armour of adulthood.

This 'inner childhood' became a very important touchstone for later scientific and moralistic developments in childrearing practices, because it retained the division between the 'good and 'bad' child. If children were 'naturally' good, then parents would have to develop skills to meet their needs and educate them in their ways. But if they were 'naturally' bad or sinful, then according to the Evangelicals children risked forever being damned. We discussed these changing views about how parents ought to bring up their children by focusing on the shifts that occurred from a more authoritarian view of parenting that concentrates on the needs of parents to control their offspring, to a more relaxed view where scientific theories advocated the importance of responding to babies' requirements, to today, where there has been a gradual erosion of power in relationships between men, women and children. We also used adult representations of 'street children' to discuss the growing middle-class sensitivity that viewed work and childhood as incompatible – dependent on adults, children were expected to play and learn in schools.

But is childhood just a series of adult constructions? It is important to ask some questions about the constructions of childhood, pointing to some of the major limitations in the social constructionist perspective. According to Stainton Rogers and Stainton Rogers (1992), our concepts of the child are created by language and narrative: factual information on children is just as much a story as the more obvious narrative of Peter Pan. Gittins' (1998, p.45) response is crucial here. She asks: but who is telling the story? Why is it being told? And how are certain stories used to determine opportunities for some children, but not others? There is the problem of forgetting real children and the centrality of power relations.

But we can go one step further and suggest that even those researchers who wish to study children's own views and perspectives have lost sight of real children. This is especially troubling given that they seem to be aware of the problem. For example, James *et al.* (1998, p.28) state that, 'Social constructionism does run the risk of abandoning the embodied material child'. How can this happen? The answer may possibly stem from their model. These influential sociologists of childhood have placed at the centre of their analysis a concept of interaction that is dependent on an individual child who 'interacts' and 'negotiates' with adults and children. Perhaps they have forgotten that they were once children themselves:

> *This interaction concept, too, owes its central position in present-day thinking to the perspective of adults who have lost sight of their own and other people's development from a child, who proceed in their reflections about human beings as if they had all been born as adults, and who see themselves from within their armour as single individuals interacting with other adults equally armoured.*

(Elias, 1969, p.143)

For adults and children, the need to work and think about our relationships with each other never ends. For us, this chapter may well be the beginning of a long process.

ACTIVITY 1

Reflecting upon the memories of your own childhood, account for some of the major influences in your development as an adult. In what ways have these influenced your current view of childhood and children? Sharing these views with another person, can you notice any similarities in your stories about your childhood? And can you explain any differences?

5 Children and social policy: a case study of four-year-olds in school

Ulrike Gelder and Jan Savage

Introduction

Young children and their lives are high on the political agenda. Whether this is mainly rhetoric or reflects a real commitment to the welfare of children is something we can examine by looking at social policy. Alcock *et al.* (1998, p.7) define social policy as 'actions aimed at promoting social well-being'. In this chapter we will look at policies (actions by the state) and outcomes (the well-being of children). Our particular focus will be on the policy that encourages schools and parents to admit four-year-olds into reception classes. Any study of the growing admission of young children to reception classes soon shows that there is no straight line from policy to outcome. Hill (2003, p.1) uses the expression 'social policy' primarily to 'define the role of the state in relation to the welfare of its citizens'. This definition points to the complex processes in which both the state and individuals take an active part in the process. It is important to remember that social policies can be driven by objectives other than public well-being, and that other policies, not necessarily identified as social policies, can make a contribution to welfare (Hill, 2003).

To demonstrate the way in which social policies interact with individuals we have taken as our case study the thorny topic of 'four-year-olds in school'. This issue has been around for well over a century and has been discussed and argued in different ways from different perspectives. Current debates rumble on about the efficacy of early entry to formal schooling. Admitting children to school classes before they have reached compulsory school age has been hotly contested by the vast majority (particularly researchers, educationalists and practitioners) and supported by a few (mainly policymakers). As we examine the issue we cannot ignore the part that concepts of 'care' and 'education' have played in informing service provision for four-year-olds in the past and the consequences for practitioners both in the institution of schools and elsewhere. The key question explored in this chapter is whether practice has evolved as a result of political and economic expediency or whether it is based on a belief about ways of best fostering young children's potential.

School starting age

In the UK, children must attend school from the term after their fifth birthday (unless parents have permission from the local authority to educate them 'otherwise'). However, in almost any reception class (sometimes called foundation class) in England and Wales we will also find most of our four-year-olds – children who are at least a year younger than compulsory school age. Why is this so? If we cast our eyes across the Channel we see that a very different picture emerges in other countries. A recent study carried out as part of the International Review of Curriculum and Assessment Frameworks (INCA) project illustrated just how out of step the UK is with patterns established in most of the rest of Europe and beyond (Bertram and Pascal, 2002). The trend elsewhere has been towards six as the age for starting compulsory schooling. Information compiled by the European Commission (2003) shows that out of 29 European Countries:

- 15 have a school starting age of six;

- nine have a school starting age of seven;

- one has a school starting age of four;

- all five-year-olds are in primary schools in only four countries.

What follows is an outline of some of the policy decisions and legislation implemented in the UK over the last century with a focus on what effect this has in practice for four-year-olds. Our timeline will inevitably be selective and focused on moments that seem most salient.

Children and social policy

Children are involved across all fields of social policy (Pinkney, 2000), yet they often remain invisible, seen only as members of a family, dependent on well-meaning adults. When children are included in debates they are seen as objects rather than as subjects of social policy. Hendrick (1994) points out that in social policy discourses children are confined to three distinct roles: as victim, as threat or as investment. Even feminists, who made women visible in social policy analysis (Langan and Ostner, 1991; Lewis, 1992) often appear to have a blind spot concerning children (Skevik, 2003). Although there is a growing body of empirical research that shows children as active in contributing to and in constructing social life (James and Prout, 1997; James *et al.*, 1998; Christensen and James, 2000), children still remain largely invisible. Education and child protection are the exceptions. The language used in education policies suggests that children are seen as an investment, as future adult citizens, as employees and as parents – rarely as 'children' *per se*.

Understanding the relationship between the state and the welfare of citizens

One starting point for understanding the relationship between the state and the welfare of its citizens is to look at how policies are made and implemented. Here the adoption of two perspectives is useful (Hill, 2003). One is the 'top-down' perspective. Are the people who implement the policies doing what they are told? If not, why not? The other is the 'bottom-up' perspective. Do the people who implement the policies think the policies are appropriate? Taking these two perspectives we can see tensions between the policymakers and professionals, between intended outcomes and unintended effects. In our case the outcome, that the majority of four-year-olds in England attend reception classes in mainstream schools, looks like a muddle of conflicting intentions. The strength of this type of analysis is that an understanding of processes and actors helps us to see where the tensions lie and where change may be facilitated or resisted.

The history of reception classes

I have found the children have derived very little benefit from being rapidly instructed in reading and writing, particularly when no attention has been given on the part of the superintendent to form their dispositions and their habits.
(Evidence given to the 1816 Select Committee of the House of Commons; reprinted in Owen, 1927, p.98)

Change the word 'superintendent' to 'practitioner' and that statement could have been written at any time since the year 2000. We begin with the 1870 Education Act and then move on to the early 1900s and 'baby' classes. Then we come to 1967 and the Plowden Report with a focus on 'under fives', 'pre-school' and 'nursery education'. Then we progress to the 1970s and 1980s and Margaret Clark's (1988) influential report summarising a decade of educational research and evidence on under-fives to the DES. A major watershed in 1988 follows, with the major theme being 'concern about four year olds in school'. Note the significant shift here in the use of language. Four-year-olds are now separated out from 'under fives' and indeed are often referred to as not even 'four-year-olds', but as 'rising fives', unlike many other European countries that have tended to regard 3–6 or 3–7 as one coherent phase in childhood.

A decade later, in 1998, 'concern' is still the theme but now very much focused on appropriateness or inappropriateness of experiences offered to four-year-olds and the introduction of 'DLOs' or desirable learning outcomes (SCAA, 1996) and of the voucher system. 'Nursery education' takes on a new meaning and is now used to define any pre-school setting in the private, voluntary and state sector in which parents choose to use their vouchers rather than just referring to nurseries within the state-funded sector. Finally, we ponder current issues almost another decade on, and four years down the line from the introduction of the Curriculum Guidance for the Foundation Stage (QCA/DfEE, 2000).

The 1870 Education Act introduced compulsory education for all children and established the school starting age of five in England and Wales. It is still the same today: education must begin in the term after a child's fifth birthday. Woodhead (1989) describes the choice of this early school starting age as mainly arbitrary. However, even in the 1860s there were debates about the most appropriate age to start formal schooling, and six was often being quoted. Arguments for starting school at the age of five were mainly about protecting very young children from exploitation at work and at home, and also to appease employers, who wanted the school leaving age to be as young as possible – by starting earlier, children would be ready to leave earlier.

In practice very young children have always been a part of life in many schools. At the beginning of the twentieth century, 43 per cent of all three- and four-year-olds attended primary school. This may have protected them from exploitation, but it does not seem to have promoted much high-quality experience. Tizard (1988, p.9) describes a typical 'baby' class in the early 1900s:

> the children sat all day, with brief intervals when they were marched around the yard, arms folded, on tiered benches in classes of at least 60, while attempts were made to teach them letters and numbers.

There was concern about the experiences offered to these very young children. In 1905 education inspectors banned early admission to infant schools in the state system (Early Years Curriculum Group, 1995). The discussion was, however, only about the removal of under-fives from inappropriate settings and not about providing alternative quality educational experiences for them in appropriate settings.

In 1967 Bridget Plowden chaired a major review of primary education including nursery provision (DES, 1967). Very little had been achieved in this area since the 1944 Education Act. Widespread nursery education still remained 'an unfulfilled promise'. The Plowden Report recommended a large expansion of nursery education in the expectation that parents would want places for some three-year-olds and most four-year-olds. The report argued for part-time provision because 'prolonged and early separation from mothers is known to be disadvantageous, but a short absence during the day does not harm the child who is ready for it' (DES, 1967, p.120). However, there was a suggestion that 15 per cent of places should be full-time as 'many mothers will work and their children will, as a result, need places in nurseries' (p.120). Five years later in 1972 in the White Paper 'A framework for expansion', Margaret Thatcher, then Prime Minister, set out plans for an increase in nursery education. Within ten years there would be full- and part-time places in nursery schools or classes for all children aged three or four years whose parents wanted them. Was this achieved in the state sector by 1982? Far from it!

During the 1970s and 1980s the sharp decline in birth rates (aided by the availability to women of hormonal contraception, 'the pill') was felt in primary schools. Admitting four-year-olds to schools filled empty classrooms and kept teachers in employment. State nursery education, even when focused on providing part-time education rather than full-time education and care, was still low down on the spending list. By the mid-1980s there was growing concern about the increasing number of LEAs who were admitting not only their 'rising fives', but all their four-year-olds into their reception classes in September of each year (Barrett, 1986; McCail, 1986). No legislation before or since ever suggested that this was the way to expand nursery provision.

The Rumbold Report (DES, 1990) was another watershed. A committee of inquiry was set up to report on issues that contributed to the quality of educational provision offered to three- and four-year-olds. The report was wide-ranging and included recommendations on co-ordination of services, quality control, curriculum, staffing and training. It was published on Christmas Eve and was never highly publicised by government. Many of the main issues and recommendations for policymakers, local authority providers and practitioners that were included in this report (DES, 1990, pp.30–2) have still not been fully addressed. Interestingly there was no mention of the Rumbold Report in either of the later curriculum documents, SCAA (1996) or QCA/DfEE (2000).

In 1995 educationalists who were part of the Early Years Curriculum Group (representing state, voluntary and private sectors) were vociferously arguing that we should still say 'no' to early entry into school. This was 90 years on from 1905 when education inspectors rejected early admission to infant schools and now the discussion was focused on the inappropriateness of much provision. Dowling (1995) was also arguing that, as increasing numbers of four-year-olds entered reception classes in schools, we should turn our attention away from debates about starting age and begin thinking about the kind of experiences offered to these young children. The question should not be, are four-year-olds ready for school, but are schools ready for four-year-olds? In other words, quality matters. In terms of educational documents, what emerged was SCAA (1996) and the infamous 'desirable learning outcomes' (DLOs). The potential of young children was reduced to a narrow set of outcomes expected by the age of five. Many of us despaired and wondered how many more times and for how many more years we would have to make the case for investment in appropriate high-quality early years provision.

The debate about four-year-olds in school continues. Despite the criticism levelled against the admission to reception classes of young children below compulsory school age, the proportion of three- and four-year-olds in reception classes continue to rise. In 1999, 57 per cent of all four-year-olds attended reception classes. By January 2004 this proportion had risen to 61 per cent; in addition, one per cent of three-year-olds were also in schools (Department for Education and Skills, 2004a). How can this be explained? Let us return to the analytical tools of social policy studies.

Top-down perspective

At first sight the top-down perspective does not seem relevant since there were no policies prescribing the admission of three- and four-year-olds to reception classes. However, if we look at the implementation process of education policies, we see that power and influence on reception classes and attendance reside with elected members of the local authority, the department of the Chief Education Officer, advisers, school governing bodies, head-teachers, departmental heads within schools and class teachers. We should also remember other policies that influence where four-year-olds spend their day. For example, Section 8(2) of the 1944 Education Act sought to extend the provision of nursery schools and classes and although successive governments stated a commitment to free nursery education, they seldom found the necessary resources.

In 1996, the year before New Labour replaced the Conservative government, the Nursery Education Voucher scheme was piloted. Parents could redeem vouchers for part-time places for their four-year-olds in nursery schools, nursery classes or some reception classes. This was at a time when there was less money available to schools. From a financial point of view, offering reception class education rather than nursery provision continued to be attractive. Regulations prescribed a staff–child ratio of 1:13 in nursery classes but did not prescribe a ratio for nursery age children in reception classes. In order to recoup some of the money lost to finance the voucher scheme, primary schools often changed their admission schemes and refused to guarantee places for children who had not attended their own reception class. The piloting of Nursery Education Vouchers reinforced the trend to admit young children to reception classes. This trend has continued and appears irreversible, even though the Nursery Voucher scheme has been abolished (Liu, 2001).

Education and achievement?

One strand of criticism was fuelled by the concern about the educational needs of young children. A series of papers expressing concern about four-year-olds in school was produced in 1986 as a result of a National Association of Headteachers (NAHT) Early Years conference. In January 1988 a major National Foundation for Educational Research (NFER) project was funded to clarify what the educational needs of four-year-olds were, and how such needs could be met in the context of the reception class. Several influential publications were produced (Bennett and Kell, 1989; Cleave and Brown, 1991; Brown and Cleave, 1994).

Government reports continually recommended that four-year-olds should not be in formal education or schooling. For example, *Better Schools* (DES 1985) contains the statement, 'It is unrealistic to expect a teacher to simultaneously provide an appropriate education for younger four year olds and for children of compulsory school age'.

In 1989 a House of Commons Select Committee, set up to look at educational provision for under-fives, recommended that:

> *No further steps should be taken by LEAs towards introducing 3 and 4 year olds into* inappropriate *primary school settings. Policies in LEAs of annual (September) entry for four year olds into schools should be explicitly subject to the availability of appropriate provision and should normally be for part-time places.*
>
> (House of Commons Select Committee Report, 1989 p.8)

It would seem that providing more places for four-year-olds in reception classes ran counter to the educational arguments being expressed. It seemed instead to be driven by falling rolls, empty classrooms in schools, and parental pressure.

One educational argument regarding 'summer born children' was, however beginning to gain currency – these children were only taught in a reception class for one term, putting them at a 'disadvantage' compared with other children who had three terms. Many studies showed differences in performance between the oldest and youngest within a year group, but there was no clear-cut causal link between this and the length of schooling rather than age (West and Varlaam, 1990). Debates about the impact of school entry age on academic achievement had continued to rage. Sharp (2002, p.20) concluded a comprehensive paper on 'when should our children start school' with the following comments:

> *there is a lack of conclusive evidence concerning the benefits of starting school at different ages. The best available evidence suggests that teaching more formal skills early (in school) gives children an initial academic advantage, but that this advantage is not sustained in the longer term. There are some suggestions that an early introduction to a formal curriculum may increase anxiety and have a negative impact on children's self esteem and motivation to learn ... certainly there would appear to be no compelling educational rationale for a statutory school age of five or for the practice of admitting four year olds to school reception classes.*

It can be argued that whatever else, at least the introduction in 2000 of a curriculum framework, Curriculum Guidance for the Foundation Stage (CGFS) (QCA/DfEE, 2000), was more helpful to practitioners than the desirable learning outcomes. The age range 3–5 was now considered to be a coherent phase in terms of the educational experiences that should be offered to children, at least at policy level.

So far, our analysis shows a more complicated relationship between the state and the making of policy, and the welfare of young children. Four-year-olds in reception classes seem to be the outcome of a muddle of several things: of stated intentions unsupported by financial commitment, of different implementation issues at local level, and of complex relationships with other social and educational policies. Before we look at the connection between 'education' and 'care' we need to take a look at the bottom-up perspective.

Bottom-up perspective

As early years practitioners, an important part of our responsibility to young children is to be interpreters of policy. Drummond (2001) argued this point succinctly about the CGFS. She states that the 'QCA document describes a paper curriculum and children do not experience a paper curriculum. They experience a lived curriculum, the quality of which does not depend on glossy documents but on the actions and interactions, debates and decisions of their educators' (p.3).

How are the frameworks being interpreted by policymakers and practitioners? In terms of policymakers, for example, devolution in the United Kingdom has meant a loss of commonality. For example, Wales has taken several important policy decisions since 2000, which differ from those taken in England. Notably, Welsh schools are not expected to teach the Literacy Hour, Key Stage 1 SATs were abolished in 2002, and a new foundation stage for three- to seven-year-olds has been proposed with a core emphasis on 'playing sociably'. It will be interesting to see how these policies are implemented in practice and what it will mean for the muddle surrounding four-year-olds.

What about interpretation by practitioners? Are we achieving a coherent phase for three- to five-year-olds? We hear some schools talking about Foundation Stage 1 (FS1 – nursery) and Foundation Stage 2 (FS2 – reception). A recent report commissioned by the Association of Teachers and Lecturers (ATL) about the impact of the Foundation Stage on reception classes contains some challenging findings for practitioners and policymakers alike.

> *The classroom observations provided evidence that everyday practice in classrooms does not adequately reflect the principles of early childhood education, even as set out by the Guidance document (CGFS). There appears to be a fundamental lack of understanding of the place of the reception year in the education of young children, and what its priorities and principles should be*
>
> (Adams *et al.*, 2004, p.18)

This report is not about blaming teachers, but about recognising the historically ambiguous position of the reception year in which full-time places are offered to children of pre-statutory school age within a school setting. It is argued that the introduction of the Foundation Stage has so far done little to help reduce this ambiguity. The challenge for all of us regarding four-year-olds is still to sort out the 'muddle in the middle'.

Education, care and other policies

The increasing numbers of four-year-olds in reception classes arose as a result of the lack of both an expansion of state nursery provision and a coherent approach to childcare. To working parents, a day in an infant classroom was often seen as preferable – it provided longer hours of childcare (than a two and a half hour session of state nursery education) and it was free. The introduction of Childcare Tax Credits as part of Working Families Tax Credits (now Working Tax Credits[1]) in October 1999 has eased the burden of childcare costs to low- and middle-income families. However, the 30 per cent to be paid by parents can still be a lot for low-income women and may affect the choice and quantity of the childcare they can afford (Rake, 2001). There are also concerns that as markets push prices up to the limits of what parents will pay, the beneficial effect on family finances has been cancelled out by a rise in childcare costs beyond inflation and income rises (Daycare Trust, 2003; Papworth, 2004).

There has always been a political debate around beliefs about the role of government in the lives of children and families, which has often been presented as an 'education' versus 'care' debate. These debates revolve around fundamental questions such as, what do we want for our children? What services and provision are best for families? What constitutes a good childhood? What is the place and status of children in our society? Since the late 1800s there has been an overall consensus that the state has a duty to provide 'education' for all children. Providing 'care' has been seen predominantly as the private responsibility of families.

Education and care generated separate debates for decades. From the perspective of the child this is an artificial and worthless division. Children's needs do not change depending on whether they are in an education or a care institution (Daniel and Ivatts, 1998). Yet dividing providers of early years services into an 'education' sector and 'care' sector and dividing care into part-time and full-time has emphasised the division between mothers who work and mothers who do not work (David, 1993). Successive governments were not interested in universal education and care for all under-fives. Care was clearly seen as the responsibility of families and not the state (except when significant numbers of women were required to work during the two world wars). More daycare nurseries were opened during the early 1940s than ever before, but by 1960 only a third of those opened still remained. Local authorities had the power to establish state nursery schools as a separate part of the education service, from 1918 onwards, but few chose to do so. The campaign for quality provision (nursery education) for very young children had become separated out from discussions about mainstream education.

Currently the state is taking an interest in comprehensive childcare for families whose parents are working. The National Childcare Strategy (DfEE, 1998b) aims to increase the number of childcare places and, in connection with the aim to abolish child poverty (White, 1999), to enable parents to participate in the labour market. This expansion is an

---

[1] At the time of writing the childcare element could offer up to 70 per cent towards the cost of childcare up to a maximum level of £135 per week for one child and £200 per week for two or more children – so parents who have one child in childcare could receive up to a maximum of £94.50 per week and with two or more children in childcare they could receive up to £140 per week.

outcome of planning and co-operation between the private and voluntary sector against a backdrop of state provision. In each local education authority area, Early Years Development and Childcare Partnerships (EYDCPs) are now required to draw up childcare plans at local level to achieve a planned expansion, to provide training and to improve quality. Financial support to providers who offer full-time care is mainly in the form of start-up grants, pump-priming and training (Strategy Unit, 2002). Within the context of high staff turnover, lack of a trained workforce and a lack, in many providers, of entrepreneurial business sense, there are fears about sustainability of childcare places once start-up grants have ended (National Audit Office, 2004). Coherent services catering for the educational and care needs of both children and their families still appear to be some way off.

Whatever view is taken, it would appear that without planned services (not to mention planned coherent services) becoming a reality, the early admission of children to school will continue to evolve in a piecemeal fashion.

Conclusions

The history of four-year-olds in schools presents a stubborn insistence on increasing the proportion of young children in formal education in the face of many critical voices. An examination of this muddle at the centre of policymaking and implementation allows us to identify strengths of current practice and issues for change. Examination of the top-down perspective has shown that the increase in admissions of four-year-olds is not the outcome of proactive policymaking but the unplanned result of a combination of other policies, policy gaps and fallout from local implementation processes. Will our current situation be any different? Since the election of New Labour, has government policy been any more proactive, any more coherently planned in terms of quality care and education for young children and genuine support for their families?

The government may learn from the examination of the challenges encountered when aiming to reach the aims set out in the National Childcare Strategy. For example, a long-term commitment to financial support of childcare providers may make provision sustainable and less expensive to parents. We can learn from successful policies from other countries. Subsidy of childcare costs paid directly to private or voluntary-sector providers allows better business planning and supports sustainability. A study of childminders in Germany and England has shown that even a small, but reliable, subsidy has a big impact on keeping them in business and encouraging them to view the future optimistically (Gelder, 2003).

Education for young children has often been defined in the past in terms of progress towards later attainment and achievement. The education policy of introducing the CGFS can be seen as a positive step towards a more child-friendly approach which does not make an artificial divide between education and care. It does, however, at present depend on Foundation Stage practitioners' skills of interpretation in any setting in which they find themselves. This moves us to the bottom-up perspective. We believe that practitioners have some freedom to use the guidance creatively. It may take some courage to work more flexibly. This in turn can provide better insights into children's needs and learning and these insights can be used to inform policy makers.

We know that it is essential to have a highly educated workforce of people who have a core of highly specialised knowledge, skills and dispositions to work with young children. More early years teachers are now coming out of initial teacher education with the interests of the child firmly at the centre of their understanding of their work and numbers of new early childhood professionals, graduates educated for multiagency work are also increasing. These practitioners should be more able to work together, understand different perspectives, speak a joint language and approach all services in the best interests of children and their families.

We have seen that children can slip easily into the background and become invisible when policies address welfare issues other than education. Childcare has historically only been discussed as a need of working parents. Policies focus on enabling parents to work, driven either by the economy, or by the expenditure incurred by the Exchequer when parents do or do not work. Education has never just been about developing the potential of individual children. Is there any middle ground? Surely it is possible to think of care and education within a positive relationship between trained practitioners, parents and children, benefiting the child here and now, independent of the employment status of his or her parents. Keeping the needs of children firmly in focus may also help to tear down the artificial division between 'education' and 'care', and between teachers and other childcare practitioners. When education and care are genuinely seen as inseparable at all levels, it will matter less whether our four-year-olds are in 'school' or other settings or whether we call the practitioners 'teachers' or 'childcare workers'.

ACTIVITY *1*

In a group of at least three identify a current topic for debate.
- *Allocate each person a different perspective to focus upon, for example, parent/ practitioner/child/policy maker.*
- *Research into the topic, organise your information and develop your argument with both theory and practical examples to back up the perspective you are taking on.*
- *Carry out the debate in role to an audience.*

6 Being a child today

Norman Gabriel

Introduction

How can we understand the dreams and concerns of today's children? This chapter will begin by exploring some of the key problems in trying to develop a child-centred perspective, a perspective that attempts to minimise adult preconceptions of what children should become. It will discuss some of the more recent sociological claims that children should be considered as active 'beings' in here-and-now situations, interacting in the social world. The concept of *generation* will be introduced to understand the social bonds that link children with each other and with adults in today's society, especially in parent–child relationships. To shed light on what it feels like to be a child today, we will draw on historical sources to compare the feelings and aspirations of children from different generations.

We will look at the major obstacles and challenges that children face as they grow up in contemporary British society. 'Life chances' and childhood poverty will be discussed by referring to recent government initiatives such as Sure Start. Can poverty be eradicated in a capitalist society? What are the social boundaries, constructions and institutions which shape the experiences of being a child? We will also examine some of the structural changes to the most important social institutions that children have to navigate: families, pre-school settings and schools. Families are one of the most important settings where children live out their childhoods, develop close relationships with others and discover their identities. In the household, there are opportunities for negotiation and interactive agency in here-and-now activities. But in schools, children can sometimes find it difficult to participate in a future-oriented environment.

Sociological perspectives on childhood

During the 1960s, childhood was seen as a preparation for adulthood: the child was seen as an 'incomplete organism', developing in response to different stimuli. Within the boundaries of childrearing psychology, what was important was finding ways of turning the immature, irrational and incompetent child into a mature, rational and competent adult. These dominant principles at the heart of developmental psychology have recently been referred to by Smart *et al.* (2001) as the 'embryonic model', one where children are considered to be in a state of permanent transition, either within or between stages. Defined as potential persons, they are valued more for their future as adults than for their present lives as children. Such a 'futures' orientation (Cockburn, 1998) tends to place over-riding importance on what children will become when they reach adulthood rather than focusing on their day-to-day lives as children. For example, in the context of divorce and parental conflict, a child may be ordered to have contact with an oppressive parent against his or her wishes because it is presumed that, regardless of the impact in the short term, in the long term the child will benefit.

In the new social studies of childhood that emerged in the 1970s and early 1980s, researchers began to rethink childhood and challenge the view that children were passive recipients. Sociologists of childhood (see, for example, Mayall, 2002) challenged this view by emphasising the present tense of childhood, children's active participation in constructing their own lives and their relationships with family and friends. According to James and Prout (1990), children should be viewed as social actors, as participants in complex relationships with others. In the early years of human life a different framework is needed to understand the institution of childhood: '... children are not formed by natural and social forces but rather they inhabit a world of meaning created by themselves and through their interaction with adults' (James *et al.*, 1998, p.28). The following example is a good illustration of the way in which children define their activities differently from adults:

Five year-old child: When I play with my friends we have lots of fun ... do lots of things ... think about stuff ... and ... well ...

Adult: Do you think you learn anything?

Child: Heaps and heaps – not like about sums and books and things ... um ... like ... well ... like *real* things!

(Moyles, 1994, p.201)

A key aspect in James and Prout's (1990) framework is their commitment to developing a more sensitive awareness of different versions of childhood and children's experiences as they construct their own lives. These authors have criticised the belief that there exists one universal childhood, a 'standard' childhood that is based on the experiences of children in rich countries. They have pointed out that it is biological immaturity rather than childhood that is a universal feature of human groups. To overcome the problems of assuming that children are the same throughout the world, we also need to take into consideration the different cultural contexts of children growing up in developing countries. Childhood is a social construction because of the specific ways in which very young children become socialised in different societies. In this framework, a comparative, cultural analysis enables us to identify a variety of different childhoods in a diversity of contexts.

However, there are difficulties with this child-centred perspective. It raises certain problems for researchers who try to put themselves in the position of children. They may not see children, but an image of themselves as children. Smart *et al.* (2001) argue that adults should not pretend that they can know what children think or want by taking the standpoint of children. Young (1997, p.50) takes a similar line:

Participants in communicative interaction are in a relation of approach. They meet across distance of time and space and can touch, share, overlap their interests. But each brings to the relationship a history and structured positioning that makes them different from one another, with their own shape, trajectory, and configuration of forces.

Generations

Mannheim (1952) was one of the first sociologists to offer a comprehensive study of generations, discussing three levels of generational identification. First, there are *locations* in generations which are based on the biological fact that individuals can share the same year of birth. This chronological level is expressed in our concept of 'age cohort', which refers to a defined population who experience the same significant events. Although Mannheim recognises the influence of biological factors, he argues that these should be placed within social and historical processes. Biological generations may succeed each other every 30 years, but generations are formed in relation to social change. Even though people born in the same period of time in society can be exposed to a similar range of social, historical and political events, their thoughts, feelings and actions will vary according to their class or gender. For example, housing conditions experienced by a working-class child born in Victorian times in Britain were very different from those experienced by a child whose parents were owners of a factory. Second, within these generational locations are mechanisms that can bring about an *actual* generation, for example 'a child of the 1960s', one who participates '... in the characteristic social and intellectual currents of their society and period' (Mannheim, 1952, p.304). And thirdly, a *generational unit* is one where people form a common bond of shared goals and a programme of action; for example, the Impressionist painters in nineteenth-century France.

Mayall (2002) argues that there are two aspects of this concept of generation which can be very helpful in studying childhood. The first aspect is to consider the different processes by which childhood is constructed and modified: in individual relationships between children and adults, in group transactions between teachers and pupils, and in relations between people born at different periods in history. The second aspect examines the extent to which children inhabit a generation, viewing themselves differently from older social groups. The ways in which children think of themselves can be seen as occupying a common generational location, one structured by adult behaviour and interests. This generational location can be used to focus our attention on the relational processes between adulthood and childhood, how adults use their positions of power to define differences between adults and children. Mayall (2002, p.118) provides an example of how decisions for children are influenced by relations of power:

Interviewer: Are there things you look forward to?

Chris: Yes, being 11, in two years, because I'll be older and then I'll get even older and then I can make my own decisions. That's why I want to be older.

Interviewer: What would you like to make decisions about?

Chris: About going out, whenever I want. When I am 17, I'll be able to stay out late, not too late. I'll have to come back around 9, 10. When I'm older, not now.

Mayall (2002) also believes that because of children's powerlessness with adults, they are not able to form a generational unit or common bond to put into practice a programme of activity. However, when given the opportunity children are capable of high levels of joint enterprise. A good example of children organising themselves as a group and on a democratic basis was the establishment of a Children's Parliament in rural Rajasthan in northwest India. The Children's Parliament is unique because children exercise power by persuading adults to accept their view of reality. It emerged from the growth of night schools, a co-operative development between the villagers and the Barefoot College about how to best provide a relevant education that did not alienate children from their surroundings. In the night schools, there was a strong emphasis on environmental education, learning from doing rather than formal classroom instruction. The traditional teacher–pupil relationship was restructured into a joint teaching experience, in which everyone could teach and learn.

Poor children

What are the experiences of today's children throughout the world? Children account for 40 per cent of the world's population, the largest generation of children in history. In 2001, almost 160 million children under five were undernourished (White, 2001). Worldwide, poverty lies at the heart of malnourishment and is a key cause of child mortality. Lack of access to clean water leads to a high death rate among children under five years of age. Globally, 82 in every 1000 under-fives die from preventable diseases, famine, poor-quality water and sanitation, and the consequences of war and political actions (Bellamy, 2002). In a message delivered from the Children's Forum to the Special Session on Children at the United Nations General Assembly, two child delegates made clear their view of the world's children: victims of exploitation and abuse, street children, child soldiers, victims and orphans of HIV/AIDS, children without any access to education and healthcare, children facing economic, cultural, religious and environmental discrimination. At an international level, the world is a very harsh place for many children.

Let us now turn to the national context. What is the level of poverty experienced by children today in British society? Poverty in Britain has a very different profile from that described at the Children's Forum. In the British context, it is defined as those living below 60 per cent of the average income, after housing costs are considered. From 1979 to 1997, the number of children in poverty tripled – one child in three was defined as living in poverty, and Britain had the highest proportion of children in overall poverty of all European countries (Bradbury and Jantti, 1999). As a consequence, the present government made the eradication of child poverty a strategic goal, with a commitment to halve poverty by 2010 and eradicate it within 20 years. A cornerstone of New Labour's policy to tackle child poverty and social inclusion is the Sure Start Programme, with the government investing £1.46 billion to set up 500 Sure Start projects across England by 2004. The programme aims to improve the life chances of children before and after birth, offering services such as family support and advice on parenting. These initiatives are having some success: in a recent Green Paper, *Every Child Matters* (DfES, 2003), the government claims that there are 500,000 fewer children living in households with relatively low income than in 1997, and it is also proposing the creation of Sure Start Children's Centres in each of the 20 per cent most deprived neighbourhoods.

Although levels of poverty are beginning to decline and some individuals or families may benefit, 'solutions' to the problems of poverty offered by government programmes and services are 'illusory' – they are partial solutions to a problem which is based on economic structures. When we look at some of the groups of children who are living in the poorest social circumstances, it is clear that they are born into particular environments. It appears that child poverty is still heavily concentrated in certain types of household, and in particular regions of the country. For example, 48 per cent of poor children are found in families where the youngest child is aged under five (Department for Work and Pensions, 2002). And a quarter of poor children live in a household with one or more disabled children (Office for National Statistics, 1999). Similarly, Hill and Jenkins (2001) identified children from birth to five years as the most likely to be living in chronic poverty. Work conducted by the Social Deprivation Unit, University of Oxford (see Bradshaw, 1993) also suggests that there is a small proportion of wards with very high rates of poverty – Whitfield South in Dundee has the highest proportion of children in poverty with 96.1 per cent, followed by wards in Glasgow and Derry. Social inequalities are constantly being reproduced in our society – ultimately, poverty can only be eradicated by changing social structures (Petrie, 2003).

Although poverty is still persistent in certain households, there is relatively little information about the experiences and attitudes of children living in poverty, and about how this affects children's understanding of the economic world and their value systems and aspirations. However, autobiographical accounts of childhood can offer an insight into the personal hopes and fears of children as they grow up in different societies, a unique record of the most important events which have shaped their lives. These accounts or diaries can be used to bring to the study of childhood a historical perspective, a bridge to link individual history with wider historical periods. Here is a short extract from the childhood of Jack Lanigan, as he remembers his younger years of poverty:

> *'Ave yer any bread left, master?' That was the theme song of hundreds of youngsters of whom my brother Matt and I could be counted. We had our pitches for begging … Besides the heartbreaking cry, 'Ave yer any bread left, master?' there was another common cry at all the 'Fish and Chip' shops, 'Can you spare any scrapings, Sir?' Believe me this was no joke. The kids, myself included, travelled from shop to shop to ensure we had sufficient for the family. We became regular customers as one would say. These scrapings with some bread made a meal.*
>
> (quoted in Burnett, 1994, p.86)

A recent survey by Shropshire and Middleton (1999) set out to explore the attitudes towards money of children from low-income families – the following results are based on an administered questionnaire given out to 435 children aged between 5 and 16 years of age (27 per cent from income-support families, 43 per cent from lone-parent families, and 22 per cent from lone-parent families on income support). Two-fifths of the children worried that their families did not have enough money to live on, and when asked what they would buy if it was their birthday next week, chose items that were significant for being low cost. They had '…learned to accept that they might not get what they wanted for their birthday and to cover up their disappointment' (Joseph Rowntree Foundation, 1999, p.3). It appears that children from low-income backgrounds are likely to be socialised into accepting a continuing cycle of poverty as part of their lives.

Children in families

When I started my degree in social sciences, a major topic for discussion on a first-year course was how we could explain the emergence of the nuclear family from extended family networks. As students, we studied a well-known text by Young and Wilmott (1957) of changing family patterns in Britain. Their study highlighted the weakening of kinship networks as young members of the family moved from working-class communities in Bethnal Green in east London to housing estates in Greenleigh in outer London. The caring arrangements of the extended family were threatened by change as the nuclear family became more dominant:

> In a three-generation family the burden of caring for the young as well, though bound to fall primarily on the mothers, can be lightened by being shared with the grandmothers. The three generations complement each other. Once prise out two of them, and the wives are left without the help of grandmothers, the old without the comfort of children and grandchildren.
>
> (Wilmott and Young, 1957, p.197)

The above quotation is highly representative of the way in which children have been 'fused' with their parents into an 'ideal' family unit. Only passing references are made to children: they are subsumed under the concepts of family, socialisation, and childhood, which are 'moulded together into one piece that cannot be broken into parts for separate consideration' (Alanen, 1992, p.91). One of the important consequences of this marginalisation is that children have rarely been asked to speak about their family lives: it is assumed that their interests and identities are integrated within a single family unit. But family relationships have significantly changed in the last 30 years.

The ideal image of the nuclear family, consisting of a white, heterosexual co-residential married couple with their children who are economically supported by a husband, no longer fits with the rich diversity of ways in which family members live their lives. In the twenty-first century, there is no longer one dominant family form that could provide a model for all others. Family structures are changing through divorce, separations or re-partnering, and evolving in relation to employment patterns, shifting power balances between men and women, and increasing choices in sexual orientation. Nearly a quarter of all children are now living in single-parent families, 91.2 per cent of which are headed by the mother (Office for National Statistics, 2001). The number of one-person households in England has more than doubled over thirty years from 3.0 million in 1971 to 6.2 million in 2001. There is also an increasing trend for younger people, especially men, to live on their own (Office for National Statistics, 2003).

These changes to family structures have encouraged the development of a new way of thinking, one that studies 'children in their families', rather than 'families with children'. Children's perspectives are now taken seriously by researchers, who are exploring what children value about family life, how they negotiate family rules, roles and relationships, and how they engage with their parents, siblings and wider kin (see for example, Brannen and O'Brien, 1996). A research project by Smart *et al.* (2001) explored children's perspectives on the issue of being listened to and participating in family decision-making by carrying out in-depth, conversational interviews with children living under post-divorce/separation arrangements. One aspect of this research examined whether children aspired to participation in decision-making or to making more autonomous choices, and in what circumstances arrangements could be open to renegotiation according to the changing needs of family members. James and his parents, for example, used trial and error to determine what kind of co-parenting arrangement would work best:

> James (9): I thought I'd probably like to spend a bit more time at each house, so I said, 'can I spend a week [instead]?' We talked about it and thought, 'well, a week is a long time, but … then we decided we'd try it and if it didn't work we'd go back to before … We tried it … just as a test … and thought about it and then we went back for a few weeks … and then we decided it might be a good idea
>
> (Neale, 2002, p.462)

Evidence of the importance that children attach to family life, and the significance of family relationships for their well-being and sense of identity, is now increasingly being taken into account by researchers and professionals working with children. Families are the place where twenty-first-century British children can expect to be treated as individuals in their own right (Moore *et al.*, 1996). In today's society, children are no longer invisible, without a voice, but are actively engaged in negotiating their own relationships.

Children in schools

An important starting point for understanding children's opportunities for learning in different settings is to briefly sketch the historical processes which shaped the emergence of schools as a dominant institution in children's lives. This historical context can help us to understand contemporary developments in early childhood education by making us more aware that schooling and the curriculum are shaped by powerful adults who make decisions about the ways children are taught. These decisions, in turn, are influenced by politicians, current and past parents of schoolchildren, and teachers who define and teach the curriculum. Qvortrup (1985) has outlined the processes whereby children have been excluded from work in Western industrialised countries, and placed in schools to carry out their activities as learners, not as workers. This exclusion of children from the workforce and inclusion in schools took place in Britain in the latter half of the nineteenth century, culminating in the Elementary Education Act of 1870, which provided universal elementary education that was soon to become compulsory and free. A state-funded education service was promoted by policymakers as a way to relieve poverty, and to prevent the spread of civil unrest and crime that was perceived by the middle and upper classes to be developing from the large number of children roaming the streets in inner cities (Petrie, 2003).

Once these children entered school, local authority officials and Victorian governments in the latter part of the nineteenth century became increasingly concerned that the children were unable to 'concentrate' and attend lessons, due to under-nourishment and infectious diseases. Concerns for children's health and fears that the next generation would not provide 'fit' soldiers for war eventually led to the introduction of free school meals, medical inspections and treatments. A graphic example of this link between schooling and the military is the following excerpt from an interview with a pupil who was growing up in a Foundling Hospital during the first part of the twentieth century:

We were young soldiers in the making, not that we realised it then … we used to march up to our places. Stop opposite our plate and our mug. Wait for the next thing [bang of the gavel], turn smartly in, bring our hands together in supplication. Next thing was another clap and then we would say grace. Stay in this position till another [bang], and then smartly to the side again, you see … you get over your seat and then sit down. Wait for the next go [bang] and then you could eat.

(Frederick, 87, quoted in Oliver, 2003, p.53)

Alongside this concern for fitness and obedience was the government expectation that investment in children would lead to the development of a disciplined and skilled workforce – scripture, reading, writing and arithmetic were instilled through rote learning. Children were often required to write in a 'fair hand', often by copying poems from the established canon of English literature or from morally uplifting tracts. They had to learn the discipline of parsing sentences in order to learn the syntax of the English language, and had exercises in the comprehension and paraphrasing of high-status texts. It is interesting to compare this emphasis on pupil discipline and the three Rs with contemporary government policy on education and schooling and to ask ourselves whether our children are under less pressure to perform and conform than a previous generation of children.

In the 1990s there were a number of important government initiatives in primary education: implementation of a National Curriculum; national tests in Key Stages 1 and 2 when children are seven and ten; frequent inspection by Ofsted and competition between schools. In 1998, all children in primary schools of compulsory school age were required to be taught a literacy and numeracy hour every day. Young children, from the age of four, are now tested for their Foundation Stage Profile on their recognition of initial sounds in words, letters by both shapes and sounds, and ability to write their names and words independently. Testing has become common and overt – on spellings, times-tables, arithmetic, the 'facts' of history and geography.

This discourse on 'school' subjects has dominated curriculum reform since the Education Reform Act of 1987, and has increasingly 'colonised' pre-school settings (Anning and Edwards, 1999). It is based on a very narrow conception of the curriculum which is inappropriate for young children, because it has led to excessive priority being given to children's academic achievements, and very little to their emotional and social development. Very recently, Drummond (2003) expressed her disappointment that the establishment of the Foundation Stage was not having the positive impact she had expected. Instead, the formal instruction that had characterised reception classes was still evident. She observed that there was a 'daily rhythm of learning intentions and plenary sessions, an overriding emphasis on literacy and numeracy'. Anning and Edwards (1999) also argue that literacy and numerical tasks in print or mathematical notation form are being presented to children far too early – British children are becoming disadvantaged as they are confronted with problems that are 'disembedded', abstracted from their real-world connections. By placing so much emphasis on an early introduction to print and numbers, government policy is preventing children from playfully exploring the relationships between different types of symbolic systems.

There is now research evidence to suggest that the introduction of national assessment tests across the key stages of the National Curriculum is creating stress and anxiety among pupils and contributing to a drop in their self-esteem (see for example, Davies and Brember, 1999). Young children are beginning to disengage from schooling. The following excerpt is taken from a competition that *The Guardian* hosted, asking children about the school they would like (Burke and Grosvenor, 2003):

> *... The school I'd like could do more sensory things, more hands on, more touchy/feely. Everyone has loads of senses. We can feel with different parts of our body, we can see, hear, taste, smell. How many senses does the national curriculum focus on? Sometimes I find life in the classroom boring and sometimes the pace is too fast and I switch off. Well, who wouldn't – day in, day out, literacy hour, numeracy hour, registration. How about smelling hour, tactile hour, music hour and physical activity hour.*
>
> Hugh, 6 (with help from his Mum), Wellington

Spaces in between – listening and learning

Moss and Petrie (2002) have argued for an alternative way of thinking about young children, a move from children's services to children's spaces. This concept of a children's space does not just imply a physical space, in terms of a particular setting or environment for different groups of children, but a social space where meanings are kept open for adults and children, a place for wonder and amazement, curiosity and fun. In this alternative view of childhood, children's questions are taken seriously by pedagogues who are themselves open to listening and learning from children:

> *... Listening to thought is not the spending of time in the production of an autonomous subject, or an autonomous body of knowledge. Rather it is to think beside each other and to explore an open network of obligations that keeps the question of meaning open as a locus for debate. Doing justice to thought means trying to hear that which cannot be said but which tries to make itself heard.*
>
> (based on Readings, 1997, p.165)

In learning encounters, this interpersonal relationship is based on mutuality and reciprocity – children are partners in the co-construction of knowledge with adults and other children. An 'ethics of care' can open up the possibility that children would be treated as unique others, rather than as instruments to be exchanged in predetermined educational outcomes. However, it is also important to consider how the affective or emotional aspects of learning processes that take place in the relations between adults and children change over time. These ethical encounters do not happen outside society, but are historically influenced by the structure of relations between adults and children.

Elias (1994) argues that in a long-term trend beginning from the Middle Ages, there has emerged in European societies a growing psychological and bodily distance between adults and children, one that makes it increasingly difficult to 'dissolve' these differences by more democratic learning relationships. Adults 'grow up' and erect emotional barriers between themselves, their own children and other children. As the degree of self-control exercised by adults has increased, children have had to learn more to become acceptable members of society. Today children have 'in the space of a few years to attain the advanced level of shame and revulsion that has developed over many centuries' (Elias,

1994, p.115). It is therefore wishful thinking to suppose that these barriers can be eradicated between generations, and more realistic to assume that the outer layers can be slowly challenged and overcome in attempts to form new learning partnerships.

Conclusion

In this chapter, we have explored some of the issues that face young children as they are growing up in British society. In pre-school settings, schools and families, children are struggling with a wide array of demands and expectations from adults as parents, carers and teachers. We have argued that rapid changes in institutional structures are pressurising today's children to grow up too fast – to learn to read and write at too early an age, and to be involved in difficult decisions in increasingly complex family arrangements. To understand these changes, we should use sensitive tools of inquiry to listen to children's concerns and worries. But children also need to be viewed as a generation, one whose members all occupy similar locations in terms of their power relations with adults.

However, the use of this concept of 'generation' should not be confined to only the present generation. With careful interpretation, a wider range of historical material can be used to look at the ways in which children from different generations have experienced and interpreted their social circumstances. For example, autobiographical accounts of childhood can offer vivid portrayals of what it was like to be living as a poor child in a different century. Even though these personal reflections are made by adults, they can begin to help us to ask important questions. What are the similarities and differences in the social circumstances of different generations of children? How are these links across generations maintained and reproduced? No more questions, well, just one: what will our grandchildren's children think of us?

ACTIVITY 1

Interview two or three generations of your own family. Identify the major 'turning points' in their own childhood. In what ways is your childhood different? What institutions might have influenced these changes in their lives, and how did these changes affect them?

---

7 International perspectives on early years education and care

Bernie Davis

...every citizen must be a citizen not only of his own country but of the planet. Wherever a person lives, he must live confidently. He must respect all people around irrespective of race, philosophy, nationality or education. We must think of how to develop in a child what was given to him by God. We used to have a pedagogics of violence. I can say it for certain that we also have a pedagogics of violence in our institutions. We must reject it and replace it with the pedagogics of respect, of mutual understanding ... we must start to develop a pedagogics of love towards the child.
(Munira Inoyatova, Head of the Department of Science and Education at the President's Office and Former Minister of Education, Tajikistan 2002)

Introduction

Early years education and care are very much a product of a particular time and place. In the twenty-first century, a young child in a village in Tajikistan will have a very different experience from a young child in Norway. This chapter sets out to look at some of the developments taking place elsewhere in the world, to set our own ethnocentric British provision into a wider context. The chapter draws on research and reports from across the world, as well as reports from students at the University of Plymouth who, as part of their studies, have visited early years settings in other countries.

International perspectives on early childhood

There is a long tradition of international comparative education and care research, funded by bodies such as UNESCO, the World Bank and UNICEF. The aim is to examine the similarities and differences between and among the educational systems and practices of individual countries in order to illuminate particular aspects of provision. The concerns raised by these international surveys of provision are reported by Maslak (2003, p.73):

The World Conference on Education for All (1990) held in Jomtien Thailand, attended by national and international representatives, formulated goals to promote education for all children by the year 2000. The document outlined several areas of concern: (1) early childhood care and education; (2) universal and basic education (3) basic learning and skills programs; (4) learning achievement (5) education of women and girls and the elimination of gender disparities; (6) literacy and continuing education; (7) life skills and values; and (8) education for peace and global understanding.

The World Education Forum met in 2000 and adopted the Dakar Framework for Action, 'Education for All: meeting our collective commitments', which reaffirmed the vision articulated in Thailand ten years earlier and set new targets for 2015 (World Education Forum, 2000).

In addition to the global surveys of education and care, there are comparative studies at European and country level. In recent years a number of organisations (OECD, 2001; Eurydice, 2001; INCA, 2003; European Commission Childcare Network, 1996; Olmsted and Weikart, 1995; Olmsted and Montie, 2001) have provided cross-national information and analyses of early childhood education and care in a number of countries. The reasons for conducting these cross-national studies are to provide information and analysis to support and improve policymaking (OECD, 2001), and to make the implementation of a mobility and the credit transfer system across the European Union viable (Oberhuemer and Ulich, 1997). Although some of the studies may offer conclusions about which social and political contexts may contribute to good quality in early childhood services (e.g. Moss and Petrie, 2002; European Commission, 1996) the objective is not to make judgements about countries with better or worse services, but to analyse the nature of similarities and differences (Bertram and Pascal, 2002). The range of the countries participating in different research projects is generally determined by membership of organisations and by individual countries opting in or out of studies (OECD, 2001; INCA, 2003) or by the political context of the research question (e.g. Oberhuemer and Ulich, 1997; Lindon 2000). Therefore studies may include developed and developing countries on several continents (e.g. Olmsted and Montie, 2001), a range of post-industrial countries on different continents (e.g. OECD, 2001), or only European countries (Lindon, 2000; Oberhuemer and Ulich, 1997). As individual countries have different policies and strategies around early childhood education and care determined by their own cultural, social and political beliefs about children and families, there are some common themes and challenges, at least in developed countries. Early childhood services are developing in the context of ageing populations, declining fertility rates and delayed family formation. However, high female labour force participation is linked to higher completed fertility rates. This suggests that raising children and engaging in paid work can be complementary, rather than alternative activities for women (OECD, 2001). The provision of childcare is seen across the developed world as an important contributory factor for the inclusion of women in the workforce and for economic growth, thus supporting women's access to equal opportunities. At the same time, early childhood services are seen as giving children a better start in their educational life or as contributing to the quality of the lives of young children (Bertram and Pascal, 2002). Not surprisingly these studies describe a wide variety of ways early childhood services are organised (public, private, voluntary), the access parents and children have to these services (e.g. as substitute for parental care or complementary to it) and a considerable diversity of training available to people who wish to work with young children. Most countries have in common a predominantly female early childhood workforce and a commitment to increase the qualification level. Also there seems to be a trend towards a compulsory primary schooling age of six (OECD, 2001). The INCA (International Review of Curriculum and Assessment Frameworks Archive) research shows a trend across countries to establish early years curricula. Most of them address social, emotional and cultural areas as well as literacy and numeracy (Bertram and Pascal, 2002). However, these curricula generally prescribe a supportive or 'scaffolding' role for adults working with young children rather than formal education.

Studies comprising a large number of countries inevitably have to omit some of the detail and this may lead to the indigenous inhabitants feeling that their country is misrepresented (Bradshaw *et al.*, 1993). However, research findings may show new ways of organising services and highlight associated outcomes, for example how many hours children spend in formal childcare (e.g. Olmsted and Montie, 2001). Studies may also reveal some surprises, at least for the Western understanding of parental responsibility. For example, Delhaxhe *et al.* (1995) found that four-year-old children in China and in Thailand spend at least an hour (but often longer) each day entirely unsupervised.

Looking at international studies and reports on early childhood raises many questions for students of early childhood studies – and for all of us! For example, do other cultures have a different view of childhood from the one we have? What is the relationship between the work patterns of adults and the care patterns for children? Do all cultures have a concept of play in relation to children? And what exactly constitutes play in early childhood in other cultures? How do parents balance the demands of work and family? How does poverty affect the opportunities of individuals to access education and care for their young children? What social policies are in place for young children in different countries? How do parents regard their children? Are children an investment for the future, a precious gift or a financial burden?

Education for all?

From our Western perspective, we tend to think of education as a universal right for all our children. But this may not be the case in other countries. Just as formal education was once the preserve of the sons of the rich in our own history, so today across the world, sons and daughters in many countries have different rights and expectations in relation to schooling. The pressure for universal education for boys and girls is still continuing:

> There has been a strong global move towards greater gender parity, particularly at primary level, where the ratio of girls to boys enrolled improved from 88% to 94% between 1990 and 2000. Girls' enrolment has increased faster than boys' and in the three regions where gender inequalities are greatest – sub-Saharan Africa, the Arab States and South and West Asia – disparities have eased substantially.
>
> (UNESCO, 2003)

Sometimes we take our own way of doing things for granted and assume that the way we do things is the way everyone does them. Having a comparative understanding of the early childhood field gives us an opportunity to 'think outside the box'.

For example, May (2001) suggests that comparative approaches invite two different theoretical perspectives: the 'difference view' and the 'import-mirror view'. The 'difference view' looks at solutions to particular issues or problems; for example, the amount of time allocated to physical activity and outdoor education, prompting analysis of similarities and differences. The 'import mirror view' looks at the other country through the assumptions and values that shape the observer's perspective, prompting a re-evaluation of the practice they have studied and experienced at home. For example, we may assume that we have a broad, balanced and adequate curriculum and that within that we give an appropriate amount of time to physical education. This may be challenged by observing an alternative practice in other countries. 'Comparativists' acknowledge similarities and differences without losing sight of the national, social and cultural context (Øyen, 1990) and realise the context-specificity of behaviours and practices. Appreciating and valuing diversity is integral to the study of children, their families and communities and is necessary for developing a quality curriculum for the education and care of young children (Early Childhood Education Forum, 1998).

Models of early childhood education and care

Different views on childhood, childrearing practices and the roles of parents, the goals of education and care and the place of practitioners can be demonstrated through an examination of some of the models of early childhood education and care that exist around the world.

Nepal

In many developing countries there are issues about education that seem alien to Westerners – for example, larger cultural and social structures that make it difficult for girls, and for many boys, to gain access to education in some countries. For instance, in Nepal, some families argue that girls do not need an education. They argue that girls' domestic labour is more valuable than the ability to read and write. They point out that girls marry and move away from home and any long-term investment in their education only benefits another family. Others have fears about their daughters mixing with other family groupings, fears about them mixing with different ethnic or religious groups or fears about them mixing with boys in the same setting (Maslak, 2003). These are the practical issues for Nepali parents and for the Nepali government in their efforts to introduce reform.

Central Asia

Every model of early years education and care is an expression of the cultural and moral expectations and aspirations of parents, educators, government and society. The Early Childhood Studies team at Plymouth is involved in a project, including early years, in

Central Asia. The CARK project (UNICEF, 2002) is an educational reform initiative funded by UNICEF in the Central Asian Republics and Kazakhstan. Rather than making comparisons between the 'West and the rest' and finding 'the rest' wanting, this project is concerned with learning and sharing information about education – education with a global dimension. In the CARK countries, there is a particular interest in 'education for all', and in the elimination of gender disparities. The challenge for everyone involved is to ensure that the particularity of the culture in each country is respected and that practitioners are engaged in dialogue with each other rather than in evangelising the principles enshrined in Eastern and Western philosophies.

England

Each country produces an early years system to suit a particular set of circumstances. In England, the early years Sure Start project (Sure Start, electronic source) is a recent government initiative to provide high-quality education and care for families and children in areas of deprivation. It has grown out of a desire to bring socially excluded, 'marginal' families back into mainstream society. The hope is that through educating parents and providing health, welfare and education facilities on one site, parents will be supported and motivated to abandon their dependency on social benefits and find working roles in their communities. Sure Start is based on the American Head Start Project, a social inclusion model created in the 1960s for early years children. Like Head Start, Sure Start is an attempt to overcome social and economic deprivation by enriching the children's early years experiences and helping them make the most of educational opportunities, as they grow older.

New Zealand

In New Zealand, The Ministry of Education has written an early childhood bicultural curriculum called Te Whariki or Te Whaariki for the English-speaking and Maori populations. This is based on a vision for their children:

> *to grow up as competent and confident learners and communicators, healthy in mind, body and spirit, secure in their sense of belonging and in the knowledge that they make a valued contribution to society.*

(New Zealand Ministry of Education, 1996, p.9)

Whariki means a 'rush mat', a symbol that represents a weaving of an holistic curriculum in response to the learning and development needs of children in their early childhood settings. The curriculum focuses on the individual child as a sophisticated learner with accompanying knowledge, skills and dispositions. It also includes the learning contexts of the home, early childhood settings and the wider community and their roles in providing a base for successful learning. The bicultural nature of the curriculum emphasises the important ways in which children learn from their culture and the social relationships available in their environment.

The curriculum contains the four principles of:

- empowerment – to empower the child to learn and grow;
- holistic development – to show how children learn and grow;
- family and community – as integral to a child's learning;
- relationships – the means through which children learn.

Arising from the principles are the following goals:

- Well-being – the health and well-being of the child are protected and nurtured.
- Belonging – children and their families feel a sense of belonging.
- Contribution – opportunities for learning are equitable and each child's contribution is valued.
- Communication – the languages and symbols of their own and other cultures are promoted and protected.
- Exploration – the child learns through active exploration of the environment.

(New Zealand Ministry of Education, 1996)

The principles and goals are symbolically woven together to form a rush mat or *Whariki* as a framework for the curriculum and providing guidance for children's learning and development.

The patterns that may be woven into the *Whariki* represent the diversity in early childhood education in New Zealand, for example, different cultural perspectives, philosophies, environments and resources found in neighbourhoods and settings. The Te Whariki curriculum has been developed to support lifelong learning in a changing society. It has helped meet the needs of families where women work while their children are young and it has also helped to counter racism and prejudice in a country with increasing cultural diversity.

Italy

Italy has a national commitment to early childhood with the cultural view of children as the collective responsibility of the state. The approach known as Reggio Emilia is named after a region in northern Italy. It evolved after the Second World War with the local parents' desire to provide education for their young children that would help to rebuild and ensure a democratic society (New, 2000). In the 1960s Loris Malaguzzi led the way, providing ideas that have been explored by teachers in early childhood settings in Reggio Emilia and have also inspired educators throughout the world. The approach supports children's intellectual development with a focus on symbolic representation. The children are encouraged to explore their environment and express themselves through all of their 'expressive, communicative and cognitive' languages (Edwards *et al.*, 1998, p.7). This might take the form of words, painting, drawing, puppets, shadow play, movement, sculpture, exploratory or dramatic play and many others.

...The child has

a hundred languages

a hundred hands

a hundred ways of thinking

of playing, of speaking...

(Loris Malaguzzi, quoted in Edwards *et al.*, 1998, p.3)

In each school an *atelierista*, a sort of art advisor, helps the children master art techniques and also helps the adults understand the processes of how children learn through their projects.

Another salient feature of the Reggio Emilia approach is the attitude towards relationships. Rather than the traditional notion of knowledge being imparted from teacher to child, there is the belief that within relationships knowledge is co-constructed. Therefore reciprocity or a mutual give-and-take among children and children, children and adults, adults and adults is fundamental to the learning environment and community. The teachers see the parents as their partners in the education of children. In fact the teachers, children and parents are all considered key players in the evolution of the school. How they interact both shapes and determines how the curriculum unfolds.

Comparative studies in early childhood – student experiences

A good way of gaining an understanding of childcare in an international context is to try and get an insider's perspective. In our module 'Early Childhood: A Comparative Perspective' at the University of Plymouth, we have designed a programme to prepare students to visit early years settings in other countries. The aims of the module are :

- to question ethnocentric beliefs in relation to early childhood education and care;

- to understand the role of context specificity in policy, provision and beliefs about early childhood;

- to witness and engage in a greater range of practices and responses to children, their learning and their care;

- to develop and maintain flexibility and resilience in considering and communicating early childhood issues;

- to foster awareness and understanding of what is communicated through body language, intonation and gesture;

- to gain new insights, both professionally and personally.

Students may spend a week or several months living abroad and working in early years settings to meet these aims. The interest for them is in the detail of what they see and how it supports or contradicts what they know about education and care in Britain. For example, although our students knew that children in other European countries began formal schooling at a later age than in England, it was difficult for them to imagine what the system was like and what three-, four- and five-year-olds actually did all day! Observations by the students highlighted very different approaches to, for example, handwriting. While four-year-olds in England were being encouraged to write their names, students found that in Finland 'they would not even hold a pencil [at this age]' and that in the Czech Republic children of four were given finger and hand exercises to develop fine motor skills long before they attempted formal writing.

Another student was intrigued by the Norwegian innovation of 'family groups'. 'Family groups' were designed to provide an opportunity for children to learn how to communicate and socialise with those they may not have normally chosen for friends. Each family in the class agreed to entertain a group of children once during the year out of school for about two hours. The activities, deliberately low cost, included football, picnics in the forest, mountain climbing, skiing, skating, baking, craftwork, etc. Seen as an important part of inclusion, families of disabled and disadvantaged children also took part. Through these family group experiences, there appeared to be a mutual respect for each other and those around them. The 'disadvantaged' children were not obviously noticeable and this was felt to be a direct result of the children having had a lot of time working together during their formative years and learning to appreciate each other's needs. The idea of family groups has now been adopted in the local school of the student who visited Norway (Tozer, 2003).

Students visiting Norway and Finland were particularly struck by the outdoor education. Outdoor education has an important role in the child's early learning – whatever the weather! Children are taken outside and given the freedom to explore in any way they like. In kindergartens they often have large play areas and will be allowed to climb the mountains that are nearby, as appropriate. Skiing trips, skating and many more activities are organised, along with hiking expeditions for the older kindergarten children. This encourages physical and emotional development in the child, along with all the social skills required in teamwork. In England's current climate of fear and risk, these examples may give impetus to a valuing of young children's outdoor experience as healthy, educational and enjoyable (Tozer, 2003; Downie, 2003).

Students visiting the Czech Republic were particularly struck by differences in attitudes to special educational needs. Special educational needs can be an emotive issue to discuss with Czech educationalists, bound up as it is with their particular history and culture. One student's observation was that an 'integration' approach was being adopted in their education system, meaning the children must adapt to the school. This was compared to an 'inclusion' approach being advocated in Britain at the moment where the intention is that school would be accessible to all children with or without special needs, making education available for all within the mainstream settings. In Norway, special educational needs were viewed in yet another way. One student observed that there seemed to be an overall philosophy of 'accepting the child for who s/he is'. A child with a disability is a priority case for admission to kindergartens and schools. Disadvantaged children and children living with single parents also get priority for kindergarten places. The student compared the Norwegian approach with the admissions criteria in her local school and found a different emphasis. (Tipper, 2003; Tozer, 2003).

Conclusion

We cannot ignore the fact that we are living in an increasingly globalised world. With sophisticated technology available we can become aware of national events or personal stories as they happen on the other side of the world. We can communicate our thoughts, feelings and needs with others in a multitude of ways from a local mobile phone call to video conferencing with students in a far-off country. All these developments bring an awareness of others. At the same time they may teach us about ourselves too. Current research and international programmes bring to light many different ways that early childhood education and care are conceptualised in different societies and how this varies depending on the prevalent culture and the social, political and economic circumstances. An emergence of common themes of interest that have the potential to benefit all, helps to frame questions and give meaning to comparisons that we inevitably make. Our access to information and the possibility of personal involvement can help us to think and respond in thoughtful and constructive ways about other people's practice and also to gain a critical perspective on what we see and do in our own practice. Observing and studying the experiences of children and families in other countries broadens the horizon of our own experience. It can be reassuring that some values, attitudes and practices are similar to our own while also challenging us to look beneath the surface to question why people think and do the things they do. To become aware of the ethnocentric lens through which we view other cultures and their practices can be difficult or startling but also liberating. It is possible to come to understand, for example, why so many of our four-year-olds are in school; but with the stimulation and insights gained from studying other countries' provision, it is possible to imagine that the situation could be different, and that changes might be made. Students today have many opportunities for travel, work and study abroad. The potential for developing collaborative and critical thinking skills, the hallmark of university students, is great as students experience other early childhood education and care provision, discuss what they see with the practitioners and then reflect on comparisons with England. The possibility for personal growth in developing confidence and maturity is also large. Students visiting other countries reported that they learned much more than would have been possible through books alone. They also became aware of themselves as ambassadors for England and the need to be able to speak with knowledge and understanding about the system at home. For these reasons and others, international perspectives increasingly have an important role to play in the study of young children, their families and the provision of early childhood education and care.

> ## ACTIVITY *1*
>
> *An early childhood studies student from abroad will be visiting your course for one week. What visits would you organise for her? What experiences would you recommend to allow her an accurate insight into early years provision? Which other practitioners and stakeholders should she meet? What material would you provide for her to take home? What are the specific issues of early years in your town, local authority and your country? What would you ask her about her own experiences of early years provision in her country? What cultural events or leisure activities would you suggest?*

Part 3

Working with Children: Opening Up Opportunities

8 Observing children: looking into children's lives

Jenny Willan

Introduction

This chapter looks at some of the issues around our day-to-day observations of young children. Professionals involved with children – social workers, carers, parents, doctors, speech therapists, teachers – all make use of observation to gather evidence to make informed decisions about working with the children in their care. For early childhood studies students, learning to become competent observers is crucial. Close observation of children helps to link theory and practice and provides a base from which to challenge current theories and orthodoxies about children's development, behaviour and needs. Part of learning to be a good observer involves learning to stand back, to suspend judgement, to watch and above all to listen. Children have views of their own and part of any professional observation or assessment should be, whenever possible, to hear and take account of the child's own evaluation of the situation.

This chapter shows how observing children is a dynamic undertaking conducted within a context of continuous change – children change, situations change, observers change and theories change.

The importance of context

We encounter children in a variety of contexts and each context will have an influence on the way we see them. Bronfenbrenner (1979) imagines the child living within a series of interconnected contexts. He distinguishes between the *microsystem* of the immediate environment of family or classroom; the *mesosystem*, which links home and school; the *exosystem*, which links the child to the outside worlds, for example the parents' working day; and the *macrosystem* of the larger social and political policies which determines the society in which the child lives. All of these affect children to a greater or lesser degree and influence the way they engage with their world.

We live in a complex web of interrelated dimensions – physical dimensions of time and space, social dimensions of status and place, emotional dimensions of self and others, cognitive dimensions of knowing and not knowing. All these dimensions are subtly and constantly shifting. It is our responsibility as observers of children to be aware of the situational features, including our own presence, appearance and language, which might cause them to behave in one way rather than another: 'The emphasis on the whole and on connections within and across systems can be very useful as one seeks to understand children in context' (Graue and Walsh, 1998:48).

The Department of Health suggests a framework for gathering and analysing information about children and their families (see Figure 1). This framework provides a useful checklist for studying the child in context.

Figure 1 The assessment framework (Department of Health, 2000, p.17)

There are general aspects of context to consider in all observations – time, place, gender, age, physical surroundings, relationship with the observer, emotional state of the child, the kind of activity through which the observation takes place. There are also specific contextual features related to particular observations. For instance, a study of the linguistic development of a group of three-year-olds would mean something very different if the children were the offspring of refugee immigrants rather than the children of native-speaking professionals. It would be essential to set each group in context if we wanted to understand anything meaningful about our observations.

Context can alter what the observer sees. For instance, a social worker may describe a child as quiet and withdrawn, while a parent describes him as noisy and boisterous. We can imagine a child who is an elective mute in adult company but the life and soul of the party with friends. We can contrast the four-year-old in Piaget's experimental situation who appears to be at a 'preoperational' stage with the four-year-old in Margaret Donaldson's more relaxed setting who appears to be at a 'concrete operational' stage. What about the child required to give evidence of abuse – will he give the same evidence in the court video as he gave to his sister in the kitchen? Context can be a defining feature of behaviour and when we are observing children we need to search for all the significant features of the context that might have some bearing on what we are observing.

Values and beliefs in observational studies

Observation is something we all do throughout our daily lives but it is not as straightforward as it might seem – we all have a tendency to see what we are looking for and to look for what we already know. We need to be aware of our own perspective and to learn to take into account the perspectives of others. We often talk and think as if we believe that we 'know' what sort of person someone is, as if their character is set. Yet we have all had the experience of finding ourselves and others changing and adapting according to changing contexts.

In order to make the most honest observations and evaluations that we can, we need to take our own beliefs into account. We need to look inside ourselves with a clear and critical gaze to tease out the links between who we are and the judgements we make. As Bruner wrote (Bruner *et al.*, 1956, p.10) (in the days before feminist sensitivities about language came to the fore!):

> *The categories in terms of which man sorts out and responds to the world around him reflect deeply the culture into which he is born. The language, the way of life, the religion and science of a people; all of these mold the way in which a man experiences the events out of which his own history is fashioned. In this sense, his personal history comes to reflect the traditions and thought-ways of his culture, for the events that make it up are filtered through the categorical systems he has learned.*

This examination of self requires effort and will on the part of the observer. Many of the beliefs and assumptions we hold are deeply rooted in the person and in the culture and in the language and have been gradually laid down within each of us since childhood. Others are an expression of the *zeitgeist* – a general feeling in the air that seems to be current, common-sense, the accepted view. Common sense and personal belief can both be poor underpinnings for professional judgement. Sometimes we need to define our terms with a fine degree of precision. What does it mean to talk about observing a child interacting with her 'teenage mother' in a mother and baby clinic? Do we mean the mother is aged 19 or below? Should we distinguish between unmarried and married teenage mothers? Should we distinguish between mothers who have chosen to be pregnant and mothers who have fallen pregnant by accident? What about teenage mothers in stable relationships? Teenage mothers in supportive families? Teenage mothers with educational aspirations? All of these contextual differences will have a bearing on the way we interpret our observations of 'teenage mothers' and this in turn will have an impact on the way we interpret the interactions between mother and child.

Consider the following questions.

- Are there some children we like more than others? Do we judge the children we like less harshly than the children we don't like?

- When we see a child playing alone, do we see a child who is a *loner*, a child who is 'rejected,' a child who is 'self-sufficient' or do we see a 'rugged individualist'?

- When someone tells us a child comes from 'the leafy suburbs' or from 'a run-down council estate', what effect does that have on our view of the child's potential?

- How do we feel when someone tells a child 'Act your age!'?

- Are we more understanding with children who are the friends of our own children than with children who are strangers to us?

These are the sorts of question that challenge habitual ways of thinking and confront underlying beliefs and values. When we are dealing with children, we have a moral duty to question our assumptions and values about childhood. Knowing the context of our own beliefs and values is a starting point for understanding the points of view of the adults and children around us.

Examining expectations about childhood

The way we were expected to behave as children can have long-term effects on the way that we, as adults, expect the children around us to behave. New parents, for instance, often discover that they are at odds with one another over their expectations about childhood. At the least it can be a source of intense irritation; at worst, it can be a cause of inconsistent parenting and major conflict. Parents may first discover a disjunction in their attitudes when they try to plan their first proper family Christmas or Diwali or Hannukah:

- 'we weren't allowed to open our big present until after lunch!'

- 'we always had to go to church/ temple/ synagogue'.

They may discover it when they hear themselves saying the words their parents said to them:

- 'no TV until after lunch!'

- 'no sweets between meals'

- 'when I was your age...'.

People who have a role in children's lives need to address the issues in their own childhood to try to uncover the links between what they were expected to do by their own parents and how they complied with or subverted that expectation. Different people respond differently to the experience of being a child. For instance, in childhood we were all controlled for our own good by a concerned adult. For some it felt like strong love and bred a sense of security. For others it felt like being thwarted and bred a sense of frustration with authority. For others it provided an example of how to behave once they had grown big enough and powerful enough. Some children enjoy being children; others feel their lack of power keenly and are impatient for childhood to end; others are unhappy or lonely; some feel diminished by the expectations of the adults around them; most feel a mixture of all these emotions.

Everyone has an echo of a childhood past which affects their attitudes to children in the present. Whatever your experience of childhood, you need to take into account the expectations that you have internalised when you are observing and reflecting on the children in your care. You may not have to abandon all your beliefs – but you will have to provide yourself with sound reasons for holding them. This can be a mind-expanding experience – as Socrates said, 'The unexamined life is not worth living!'

Observations and emotions

Observing children is not a neutral process. As we have seen, values, beliefs and expectations are all involved. So too are emotions. Both child and observer come with their own load of emotional baggage. The child being observed or assessed has feelings; so do the parents and carers and educators around him/her – and so of course does the observer. It is important to be aware of the emotional dimension of the observational context and to try to take it into account as part of the whole assessment process.

Not all emotions are easy to express in words. Much of our understanding of others is based on a reading of body language – a gesture, a flicker of the eyes, a facial expression, a stance, a way of moving, a tone of voice. Most children learn to respond to body language before and alongside spoken language and much of our understanding as adults involves reading the hidden messages behind words from the contextual cues provided by the speaker. But it is easy to get it wrong! Knowing the derivation of our own emotional reactions can alert us to our tendency to misapply them in certain situations. Take the sniff, for instance. In some families it denotes derision. In other families it merely indicates a runny nose. Some people have a powerful emotional reaction to the sniff; others barely register it!

Awareness of children's body language and of our own body language and its effects on the children we are observing is important. Some children such as those with visual or hearing impairment or non-verbal learning disorders or autistic spectrum disorders may learn body cues more slowly than their peers and may have difficulty in 'reading' the people around them and reproducing the relevant body language themselves. This can make communication and social relationships problematic and can skew our observations of what is going on.

We sometimes hear exasperated adults say 'Look at me when I'm talking to you!' They may be reading lack of eye contact as defiance or avoidance. But it may be related to something else. Boys are popularly reported to make less eye contact than girls. Some children, particularly those on the autistic spectrum, find eye contact painful (Diamond, 2002). Others avoid eye contact when they feel threatened. Others may avoid it when they feel shy and ill at ease. Work by Doherty-Sneddon (2004) on gaze aversion shows that young children (and adults) may need to break eye contact when they need to access internal representations, because the information from eye contact is too compelling (dazzling) to allow children to access the much dimmer images they are able to conjure up in their own minds such as memories, concepts, imagined scenarios.

As an observer or assessor, our role may be perceived as judgemental and this may set up a reaction in the child under scrutiny. We ourselves may react at an emotional level to the child under observation. To be fair in our observations, we need to take into account our own emotional context and that of the child.

Observation and language

As observers and writers of observational studies and reports, we have a duty to confront the way we employ our language. In communicating our observations to others we will need to choose our words carefully.

Sometimes the purpose of observing children is to come to an assessment or evaluation – of their situation, of their understanding, of their ability, of their behaviour. As a consequence, we may have to categorise them in some way. The words we use can be powerful and emotive – they may even be damaging. Slotting people into tidy boxes, labelling them, summing them up in a few chosen words makes report writing quicker but it may not be helpful. Positive labels may help some children (not all), negative ones help no one. Labels are quick shorthand ways of summarising, but too often they can become substitutes for more sophisticated understandings. There may be equal opportunity issues. If interpretations seem to be based on stereotypical assumptions around sex, special needs, ethnicity, culture or class, then they must be challenged.

Where observational reports are passed around among colleagues and concerned professionals, they can quickly generate set responses and prejudice the way children are seen by others. They may even contribute to a self-fulfilling prophesy when readers of the report adopt a corresponding mindset towards a child. We can ameliorate some of the difficulties inherent in articulating our observations by checking them with the child or a carer or a colleague where this is appropriate. Through our exploration of differences in interpretation, we may come to discern our own values and attitudes and recognise how they affect the way we work. In order to become competent observers, we need to explore, acknowledge and confront our own values, beliefs, emotions and language. Testing our observations against another person's helps us refine our ideas and encourages us to be more objective and to stay alert to our duty of maintaining high standards of fairness.

Examining research perspectives

When we study children, we start from a particular perspective, a theory that underpins the way we ask our questions. This perspective is sometimes referred to as our *paradigm* (Kuhn, 1970). The dominant or *hegemonic* paradigm within which we conduct our study of children can affect the way we impose a pattern or interpretation on what we observe. For example, in 1948 Esther Bick pioneered a system of infant observation at the Tavistock Clinic. The close observation of neonates and infants was a compulsory part of the training for child psychotherapists. Student psychotherapists observed the interaction between mothers and fathers and their new-born babies and continued their observations at weekly intervals for a year. In the observation below, the student psychotherapist is trying to understand the baby's emotions during feeding. Because of the particular psychoanalytic paradigm through which he views the incident, he attaches a very particular significance to the way a baby is sucking – first at his mother's breast and then on his fist:

Observation at 12 weeks

Oliver sucked vigorously at the breast then lay motionless. He jerked his head away from the nipple as if he had forgotten that he had it in his mouth. The jerking hurt the mother and she jokingly said that if he did it again she would give him a 'big cup and a straw'. After feeding, Oliver grabbed one fist with the other and vigorously sucked on his knuckle.

Perhaps nipple and mouth were not felt to be separate, in that he may not have attributed a separate existence to the breast but felt it to be part of himself. Sucking on his knuckle may be evidence that he felt he possessed something like the nipple available whenever he wanted. This related to the devastating rage precipitated when Oliver woke up to find mother not there. Then, despite sucking his knuckle, fingers, and other parts of his body, he could not satisfy himself. It seemed hard for him to tolerate a space or the idea that he was dependent on something outside himself or the thought that he did not possess everything that mother had.

(Miller *et al.*, 1989, p.180)

The way we view children influences the way we study them, and the way we study them influences the observations we make. The inferences we draw from our own observations are subject to a kind of metaphorical framing, depending on our own particular paradigm as observer.

Doing observations

The early years workforce tends to be multiprofessional (play workers, teachers, social workers, medical staff, police welfare officers) and multidisciplinary (education, sociology, psychology, medicine). Students of early childhood, whatever their professional aspirations or discipline, are encouraged to learn techniques associated with systematically observing and studying young children.

There is a wealth of literature about observational techniques, some of which is listed in the further reading at the end of this chapter. There are many aspects of children's lives and development that might reward close observation and we have listed some of them below. This section provides a brief introduction to some of the study techniques students of early years might wish to use.

What to look at

All of these provide fertile ground for observation – you can probably think of many more depending on your own professional interest.

Physical development	Inside and outside play (use of space, boys and girls, preferences)
Communication skills	Gendered play
Emotional well-being	
Intellectual abilities	Activities (educational, play, imitative)
Moral and spiritual development	Learning
Social relationships	Behaviour in different situations
Critical incidents (birth of a new baby, starting school, separating from a parent)	Interaction in peer groups
	Interaction with parents
Comparisons of ages and stages	Interaction with different adults
Types of play (free play, directed play, solitary play, interactive play)	Special needs
	Special settings (hospital, sickroom, dentist, first day at nursery)
Patterns of play (play with materials, role play, imaginative play)	Special situations (tests, unfamiliar settings)

Ethics

Once you have decided what to observe, you need to run through a checklist of questions before proceeding to the next stage.

> Do you need permission to observe?
>
> Are there any risks?
>
> Will your observation raise any ethical issues – anonymity or confidentiality perhaps?

How to be an observer

The observation style you adopt will depend on what aspects of a situation you want to observe. You need to think about how close or distant you want to be from the children you are observing. Different styles suit different situations.

> When and where will you observe?
>
> Will you observe alone, with another adult, with a child, with a professional, with a parent?
>
> Will you observe one child or a group of children?
>
> Will you be part of the observation (participatory observer) working alongside the child and involved in the activity or will you be a discreet observer at a distance?

Techniques for studying children

The next step is to choose an observation technique that fits your purpose – or be creative and come up with novel ways yourself. For example, observation with a child as co-observer is an area that is relatively untried and could be rewarding, raising new issues in the conduct of observations. Currently, there is an emphasis on listening to the child, and an acknowledgement that in the past assessments and evaluations have failed to take on board the views of children about their own predicament.

The following is a selection of tried-and-tested techniques – it is not an exhaustive list but it represents some of the most common approaches from the literature.

Narrative observation

This is a pencil-and-paper exercise providing field notes, a naturalistic record of the features that seem most significant to you at the time. Text message spelling can be useful. Examples might be to observe the arrival behaviour of a child at pre-school or the interaction between a foster carer and child.

Focused or targeted observation

This is targeted on a particular child or activity. Sometimes we need to track a child to follow progress and development over a period of time. The Foundation Stage Profile (QCA, 2003) produced by the Department for Education and Skills is a good example of one way of devising a target child observation. It provides for name and date of birth and gives a comprehensive record of social, physical, emotional and cognitive development across a whole year. You may want to devise your own.

Duration and time sampling observations

These allow you to pick up on how long a particular behaviour or activity lasts or how frequently it occurs. For instance, you may have noticed that a child often seems to be staring into space, or that a mother rarely makes physical contact with her child. It could be useful to keep a record of the frequency and duration of each occurrence of the behaviour.

Interviews

There are three main types of interview – *structured*, *semi-structured* and *unstructured*. Structured interviews are verbally administered questionnaires based on the interviewer's predetermined areas of interest. They may prevent you from following up interesting leads but they are easy to analyse. Semi-structured interviews are based on predetermined questions but allow for follow-up discussion of significant points. Unstructured interviews are very flexible but may be difficult to control since the interviewer and interviewee bear equal responsibility for the direction of the talk.

Video, tape recording, photography

There are issues of permission, confidentiality and storage associated with electronic data recording. There are also plenty of opportunities for technical glitches! Managing the machinery at the same time as conducting interviews and observations can be rather difficult but recorded information can be a useful source for backing up field notes. There are some particular limitations of using recording equipment – clarity of sound recording, the narrow view obtained through a camera lens and the effects of self-consciousness on those recorded. But there are also possibilities not open to other forms of observation, such as replaying material to closely examine verbal and non-verbal interactions, or particular personality traits, or the roles played by individuals within a group.

Checking observations

Any study of children needs to be looked at 'from all sides round' – including, where appropriate, from the child's perspective. Part of the context, as we have seen, is the position and perspective of the professional doing the assessment. It can be difficult to reflect on one's own assumptions and expectations, difficult to step outside one's own views and knowledge and experience, to stand in the shoes of the child being observed.

In observation studies of children, it is advisable to collect data in as many different ways and from as many perspectives as possible. This is sometimes referred to as *triangulation*. Triangulation is a way of checking and cross-checking the validity and reliability of observations. There are several ways of doing this. Sometimes researchers use many data sources – child records, past reports, interviews with other significant adults; sometimes they ask several different people to make observations at the same time; sometimes they use several different methods to get at the same information – individual observation, group observations, interviews, video or audio recording. Using multiple sources allows you to check one source against another to provide richer data and a more reliable assessment.

A parent may be trying to get an infant to sleep through the night; a teacher may be having difficulty settling a child into a reception class; a social worker may be trying to decide whether a child would be better off leaving a difficult family situation – they would all need to be aware of the child, their own standpoint, the context and their own effect on the situation. Instead of saying, 'My child is a poor sleeper', the parent might need to think about feeding patterns and bedtime routines and their own expectations about sleep. Instead of writing a child off as clingy or difficult or shifting the blame to overprotective parents, the teacher might need to think about socialisation difficulties or a learning problem or her own behaviour towards the child. Instead of thinking in terms of problem families, the social worker might need to take into account the material circumstances of the family, what's happening all around them, the risks, the state of mind of the child and of course her own underlying assumptions about 'the best interests of the child'.

Whenever possible, a study or evaluation or assessment of a child should be done with the collaboration of a colleague. Collaboration allows the assessor to try out ideas, to have a sounding board, to listen to different views and responses. Working co-operatively provides support and alleviates the feelings of isolation and inadequacy that can well up where the responsibility for a decision weighs heavily. Collaborative consultation can also help to clarify issues and draw together ideas or suggest areas that need further thought. Whenever possible, always try to get a second opinion – your own may not be sufficient.

Concluding remarks

When we study children, we should try to stand in their shoes. We can't, of course, but we can provide ourselves with a more accurate picture if we refer to the contextual features operating around and within the child under observation. This entails looking at ourselves, hearing the child and taking into account the wider influences of family, culture and society.

ACTIVITY **1**

With a colleague, choose one of the observation methods. Choose a child or group to observe. Obtain permission. Choose a focus that interests you. Now observe. Note down significant details of context, time and place of observation. Record anything that strikes you as significant in relation to your focus. Compare your observations – what was observed, what was said, what factors were most significant. Analyse what you have both written. Are there differences of emphasis? Is it possible to distinguish a particular paradigm at work? Comment on the significance of context, values, emotions and language in your two accounts.

FURTHER READING

Fawcett, M (1966) Learning through child observation. London: Jessica Kingsley.

Graue, ME and Walsh, DJ (1998) Studying children in context; theories, methods and ethics. Thousand Oaks: Sage.

Nicolson, S and Shipstead, SG (1998) Through the looking glass: observations in the early childhood classroom. Upper Saddle River, NJ: Merrill.

Pellegrini, AD (1996) Observing children in their natural worlds: a methodological primer. Hillsdale, NJ: Erlbaum.

Wragg, EC (1999) An introduction to classroom observation. 2nd edition. London: Routledge Falmer.

9 The importance of equal opportunities in the early years

Ulrike Gelder

Introduction

Equality of opportunity, or the lack of it, has an impact on everybodys life. Children, parents and early years practitioners are affected by structures of inclusion and exclusion and play an active part in developing inclusive and anti-discriminatory practice. This chapter unravels some of the complex issues attached to the notion of equal opportunities and the implications for work with young children. Early years practitioners have to be aware of the political and social context within which the demands of equal opportunities develop and of a variety of arguments that are used to support or criticise attempts to define equal opportunities for children and their families. The examples in this chapter are mainly drawn from the 'classical' areas of discrimination: class, ethnicity, gender and ability. This is not a comprehensive list but serves as a starting point. As some forms of undue discrimination are curtailed, new forms emerge. Currently in Britain, for example, unaccompanied asylum-seeking children appear to be falling through the gaps in equality legislation.

The current context

The Children Act 1989 and a number of Education Acts from 1944 onwards emphasise the rights of children in Britain to equal opportunities and protection from unfair discrimination. On an international level such concerns are addressed by the United Nations Convention on the Rights of the Child (1989).

As well as needing to work within this legal framework, early years practitioners are expected to actively promote equality of opportunities and anti-discriminatory practice for all children. The Foundation Stage Curriculum Guidance states that good and effective practice in early years settings is based on the principle that 'no child should be excluded or disadvantaged because of ethnicity, culture or religion, home language, family background, special educational needs, disability, gender or ability' (QCA/DfEE, 2000, p.11).

In addition to concerns about children and equal opportunities, there are concerns for adults' equal opportunities. The Early Years Development and Care Partnerships (EYDCPs) are charged with the responsibility of providing equal opportunities for men, for people with disabilities and for older people who work in childcare settings and to actively encourage their participation.

Equal opportunities and early years employees

Early years practitioners who become employers, for example as proprietors of a private nursery or manager in a Sure Start project, have a duty to implement equal opportunities and anti-discriminatory practice for staff as established in a number of Acts. Most important are the Equal Pay Act 1970 amended 1984, the Race Relations Act 1976, the Race Relations Amendment Act 2000, the Disability Discrimination Act 1995, the Human Rights Act 1998, the Special Educational Needs and Disability Act 2001 and the Statutory Regulations on Religion and Belief from December 2003. Employers encounter the practicalities of equal opportunities when they employ new staff or when conflicts between employees, or employer and employees emerge.

Equal opportunities – creating the ethos

Providing equal opportunities is not just a matter of legislation. It is unlikely that the legal framework can be brought to life without staff in early years having a cognitive and affective commitment to equal opportunities. Equal opportunities for young children are predicated on two main arguments. Firstly, there is a moral obligation to provide children, like everybody else, with equal opportunities. Because children are not in control of their own lives but are dependent on their parents for their social and economic position, it is incumbent upon society to protect their rights and treat them equally. For example, Child Benefit is a universal benefit for all children, rich and poor, and any increases to address poverty will be equally applicable to all children. In contrast, adults' eligibility for benefits may be connected to employment, training or actively seeking work because adults are perceived as being largely in control of their own social and economic position. Secondly, there is the argument that sees children as our future and as the makers of future societies. This argument is connected to a belief that we should aspire to provide children with the social competence to respect other groups and individuals (Siraj-Blatchford, 2001). This approach looks towards the future in its desire for a particular version of a just world that has not yet been reached but that, with suitable nurturing, may be achievable in future generations.

Definitions

Equality of opportunities appeals to our sense of justice, but it is not an easy notion to work with. It lacks a clear definition and is used in different contexts and for a wide range of purposes. Equal opportunities can be based on 'minimalist' or on 'maximalist' principles. The 'minimalist' position aims to create 'level playing fields' for competition, to avoid unjust discrimination; it results in unequal but fair outcomes. For example, providing free nursery education for all four-year-olds could be interpreted as providing the necessary conditions for fair competition in school, leading to fair competition for university places in the future. The 'maximalist' position attempts to rectify both discrimination and disadvantage and aims to create equal outcomes (Alcock *et al.*, 2002; Blakemore, 2003). An extreme way to accomplish this might be through a generous citizen's income, payable to all individuals independent, for example, of age and of labour market participation. The

New Labour government has adopted some characteristics of the 'maximalist' principles in declaring its aim to abolish child poverty through a system of benefits available to all lower-income families with children.

In the field of early childhood studies, the definition of equal opportunities depends on how we see children and their role in society. Early years provision can fulfil a number of functions depending on how narrowly equal opportunities are defined. They may be defined as the duty to prepare children for future competition in the educational system and in the labour market. They may be defined in terms of eliminating the disadvantages experienced by certain groups of children, for example by those from ethnic minorities, by boys or by children with disabilities. Equal opportunities may focus on the provision of an environment free from discrimination, to be enjoyed by children here and now. Projects like Sure Start combine all these aims by providing high-quality pre-school education and play in high-quality buildings situated in areas of disadvantage. In addition it is hoped that elimination of disadvantage for pre-school children may result in long-term benefits for society in terms of reduction in crime and unemployment. Tackling multiple disadvantages early in the lives of children may help break the cycle of social exclusion. The short-term costs will be more than offset by a reduction in the long-term need for social welfare and benefits, by reduced levels of crime, and by an increased level of income tax received by the Exchequer (Glass, 1999).

Challenging discrimination

The legal framework and set of standards pertaining to children and early years provision provide some indication of the kinds of disadvantage and discrimination at work in Britain; for example, gender, ethnicity, physical and mental ability, and perhaps overlapping language and religion. They enshrine the belief that we all have an obligation to challenge sexism, racism and 'ableism' (a term linked to discrimination on the grounds of disability). Gaine (1995) defined racism as 'a pattern of social relations and structures, and a discourse (linguistic defining and positioning) which has specific outcomes operating against less powerful groups defined "racially" ' (p.27). This definition may be adapted to each of the different forms of discrimination by replacing 'racism' with 'sexism', 'ableism' and so on. This exercise can help us to distinguish between children who are more likely to start from a disadvantaged position and those who suffer unfair discrimination. This distinction between disadvantage and discrimination also helps us to keep in mind that patterns and relationships change over time and can be demonstrated through example – for instance, through the idea of 'sexism'. Children in Britain grow up in a society where women and men have equal rights. However, women do not have financial equality with men. In spite of the fact that women have equal voting rights, equal pension rights and equal employment rights, that they are present in large numbers in the labour market, and that fathers are spending more time with their children (Hatten *et al.*, 2003), women in full-time work still earn on average only 75 per cent of men's annual income (Equal Opportunities Commission, 2004). In addition, despite their equal rights, women are seldom represented in powerful positions such as company managers, civil servants and politicians.

Recently girls' examination results at all levels have been higher than boys'. What does this mean? Does it mean that boys are not well served by the present system of schooling? Do we need to redress the balance with some gender-specific strategies (Arnot *et al.*, 1998; Skelton, 2001)? Or does it mean that educational settings are now discriminating against boys? What does it mean for the future? Does it mean that once this generation of pupils has reached the labour market, women will progress faster up career ladders and earn more money than their male contemporaries? Or will gender-specific power relationships continue to cancel out educational achievements?

Working with ambiguous concepts of equal opportunities

An example of ambiguity in interpretation of equality of opportunity is the approach towards children whose first language is not English. Some would argue that these children are disadvantaged in relation to their English peers and, in order to create a 'level playing field', they would benefit from additional English language support. Once young people have achieved an approximately equal command of the English language they are in a better position to compete in school and later in the labour market and in further and higher education. This perspective has led to a demand in some quarters for parents to speak English at home to 'overcome the schizophrenia which bedevils generational relationships' (Blunkett, 2002, p.77). On the other hand, research has shown that bilingual children who are supported in the development of their home language go on to achieve higher standards in English (Cummins, 1984). Children growing up with more than one language and receiving support in developing language skills also achieve more highly in other areas of the curriculum (Brown, 1998). Early years practitioners need to be aware of these issues when they are devising programmes for children whose first language is not English.

What are the wider implications of equal opportunities for early years settings? Providers of care and education for young children are required to observe equal opportunities legislation. However, discrimination takes place in quite subtle ways. It can be difficult to translate theories of equality into actual practice. Siraj-Blatchford (2001) observed that some children are disadvantaged because some early years staff have a poor understanding of children from diverse backgrounds.

For example, the two concepts 'race' and 'ethnicity' are often confused – not only by early years practitioners. The term 'race' rests upon beliefs about the importance of supposed biological differences; these differences are then linked to differences in intelligence and social behaviour. Genetic differences determining skin colour are minimal and do not support 'race' as a scientific argument. Individual differences within a group are much greater than between groups. Some people argue that race is a purely social construct based on observed physical and cultural characteristics of individuals (Banton, 1987). The concept 'ethnicity' moves away from biological explanations and includes the historical, social and cultural context in which people live. An ethnic group is seen as a group of people who hold a sense of identity which may arise from a distinct history, nationality, language, norms, beliefs and traditions. This is expressed in many different ways and is often quite striking at the level of detail. For example, the food we eat, how we prepare it and what counts as good table manners vary enormously. Norms and traditions can be accepted as just 'doing things differently' but sometimes they come into conflict with the law of the host country. For example, the practice of taking child brides is illegal in Britain but may be condoned among certain ethnic groups who live here.

Chris Gaine, a former teacher in a predominantly white school, was interested in how teachers continue to claim that racism is not a problem in their school. He identified a number of reasons why teachers and other professionals do not see racism. They may ignore racism because they may be unwilling to challenge their own prejudices; they may not have been confronted directly with racism themselves; or they may believe that dealing with racism is not their business. They may feel reluctant to approach such a sensitive and potentially explosive issue (Gaine, 1995). This reluctance to confront discrimination may be a problem for practitioners in early years, too.

Creating equality of opportunity in early years settings

One starting point for creating equality of opportunity in early years settings is for practitioners to look more closely at how children relate to each other. Literature on children and equal opportunities provides many examples of children using gender, race, religion, language and the sexual orientation or the economic position of their parents to call children names or to exclude them from their activities (Claire *et al.*, 1993; Brown, 1998). Why do children do this? Some illumination is provided by research into gender. Broadly there are two schools of thought. One explains gender differences in biological terms ('nature'), the other explains it with reference to socialisation ('nurture'). Practitioners who are more convinced by biological explanations, such as different hormone levels or gender-specific brain functions, may be more inclined to accept and accommodate the view that boys do not behave like girls and vice versa. Those who lean towards explanations linked to the socialisation process are interested in how gender roles are constructed and how they change over time and across different contexts. However, others argue that 'nature' and 'nurture' are so interdependent that attempting to disentangle them is unhelpful (Head, 1999). From a very early age, children learn what boys and men do and what girls and women do. It has been suggested that when children display 'gender appropriate' behaviour they are rewarded by adults, who may not be aware that they treat boys and girls differently. At the same time others argue that children are active in constructing their own gender roles, forming their gender identity by acting out behaviour that they perceive to be opposite to that displayed by the opposite sex. This explanation emphasises the fluidity of the concept of gender and of children's attempts to 'try out' roles (Skelton and Hall, 2001).

In the same way that children identify with and construct gender roles, they also learn and construct attitudes towards ethnic groups. Milner (1983) found that by the age of two children notice differences in skin colour and between three and five they come to learn that it is 'better' to be white than black in Britain. This has implications for working in early years – the challenge is to find ways of supporting children's growing sense of self in an atmosphere where everyone is valued.

Children's developing understanding of self and others

What is known about children's development of gender identities may be adapted to other areas of their identity. Children develop an understanding of themselves and of others from a number of key sources: their parents and wider family, their peers, their early childhood settings and their neighbourhoods. The task of early childhood settings is to foster positive attitudes and behaviour by engaging in anti-discriminatory practice and including all children and families. Writing about the effects of racism on young children, Derman-Sparks (1989) states that early childhood educators have a responsibility to prevent and oppose any damage from racism before it becomes established. Many textbooks on early years refer to, or have sections on, equal opportunities. They appeal to the practitioners' duty to implement anti-discriminatory practice (Woods, 1998; Bruce and Meggitt, 1999; Preschool Learning Alliance, 2001) or provide lists on how to become an inclusive setting (Hyder and Kenway, 1995). However, what do we mean by 'inclusive'? What exactly does a multicultural setting look like? Is there a danger, for example, in introducing children to other cultures through studying what might be termed an 'exotic' (romanticised and perhaps even incorrect) version of different cultures (Houlton, 1986)? Is it possible that in our endeavour to include as many different ways of living together as possible, we are distracted from thinking more deeply about the stereotypes we may actually be promoting (Woods *et al.*, 1999)?

Challenging adult stereotypes

To unravel these questions, we need to recognise that we all operate with stereotypes. All adults hold deep-seated ideas about gender, ethnicity, age and so on, and about what constitutes appropriate behaviour within their cultural and/or religious framework. Children pick up both positive and negative attitudes and behaviours. In order to help children to unlearn misconceptions and stereotypical thinking that they may have absorbed (Brown, 1998), early years practitioners need to become aware of their own stereotypical assumptions. Stereotypes are oversimplified generalisations; often, but not always directly, these have negative implications. Take for example the stereotypical assumption that black people are good at sport. For the athletic black child it can be a great source of reassurance and identity. But stereotypes like this can undermine the confidence and feelings of self-worth of black children who are not good at sport. Additionally, it can have negative implications for black children who are steered towards sporting achievement but get less support for academic achievement. The effect on white children could be negative, too.

Inclusion and exclusion

How do we know whether our beliefs, values and practices are based on stereotypes? Asking this question is itself a good starting point. The question forces us to think more widely about the concepts and debates around, for example, sex and gender, race and ethnicity and integration and inclusion. An understanding of the theoretical models which explain differences can be useful. These theoretical frameworks can help us to explore issues of inclusion and exclusion, discrimination and anti-discriminatory work and to examine equal opportunities areas in relation to our own life.

As important as it is to look at the stereotypes individuals hold, it does not mean that the context within which they are formed, accepted and spread is less significant. More effective anti-discriminatory practice can be supported by using the PCS analysis (Thompson, 2001). The 'P' stands for the personal, including prejudice and practice, which is embedded in the cultural, reflected in commonalities, consensus and conformity (the 'C'). The 'C' level also includes the 'comic' or humour. Jokes are powerful in passing on stereotypes and can be very hurtful. Humour is also a potent strategy against oppression. The personal and the cultural are embedded in 'S', the structural, for example existing social divisions and the struggle over it, and 'S' is reflected in legal frameworks. None of these levels by itself can explain existing discrimination or show ways to move towards more acceptable practice.

A good example of how theory informs practice and supports reflexivity is provided by two models of disability which have held sway over the past century. For much of the twentieth century, the cause of a disability was seen as physical and residing within the individual person. This perspective is referred to as the 'medical model'. The medical model understands disability as the outcome of disease, trauma or health condition. Disability is the outcome of a 'tragic event' and there is no cure. Disabled people cannot participate fully in society and are dependent on others. Until the 1970s many children with any form of disability were seen as 'ineducable' and removed from their parental homes to spend their lives in institutions. After the Education Act of 1970 made local education authorities responsible for the education of all children, children with impairments most frequently found themselves in special schools, segregated from mainstream education (Wall, 2003).

In contrast to a focus on the individual, the 'social model' of disability looks at the context within which impairments become disabilities. Disability is seen as a socially created problem. Features in the specific physical environments and in the culture and prevalent attitudes can present barriers to full participation for individuals. For example, it is not the inability to walk but the lack of an affordable wheelchair, and the lack of ramps or lifts that prevent a partially paralysed child from gaining easy access to a school built on different levels. Within the social model the problem of disability demands a political response. This perspective requires the development of social welfare strategies that support autonomy and promote independence.

Segregating children with impairments into institutions was widely criticised. The first move to end this segregation was to 'integrate' children with disabilities into mainstream schools. Integration sometimes takes the form of a special school and a mainstream school sharing premises; sometimes schools offer separate lessons for children with special educational needs but allow for shared break times; sometimes schools offer some shared lessons. These forms of integration of children in mainstream services are all informed by the medical model. The focus is on the individual child: he or she will be assessed by a specialist, the diagnosis will specify expected outcomes and recommend an individually tailored programme. Ainscow (1995) suggested that this definition of integration merely means making a few additional arrangements for individual children with disabilities and has little overall effect on their opportunities for becoming full members of the group.

Since the late 1980s, 'inclusion' has superseded 'integration'. 'Inclusion', based on the social model, focuses on the classroom, looks at teaching and learning factors and aims to create an adaptive, supportive regular classroom which will benefit all children. In the context of school education, inclusion is a 'process of increasing the participation of students in, and reducing their exclusion from, the cultures, curricula and communities in local schools' (Centre for Studies on Inclusive Education, 2002, in Wall, 2003). This definition does not emphasise the active part children with disabilities can play. Farrell (2001, p.7) argues that 'for inclusion to be effective pupils must actively belong to, be welcomed by and participate in a school and community – that is they should be fully included'. So, inclusive education is the outcome of a collaborative approach by the whole school community.

Currently, the government shows a strong commitment to inclusion (DfES, 2001, 2004b). However, from the perspective of children with disabilities and their families there is plenty of room for improvement. A review of service provision for children with disabilities and their families showed that they face a lottery of provision and access, often depending on how hard parents can push; they have to rely on a patchwork of services, which sometimes offer too little, too late (Audit Commission, 2003a).

An inclusive approach may meet resistance from specialists in special schools because they feel their expertise is overlooked. There may be resistance too from teachers and practitioners from mainstream services, because they feel ill-equipped to implement inclusive practice (DfES, 2004b). It appears that there are still tensions between the medical model and the social model of disability.

Conclusion

In terms of 'natural justice', equality of opportunity is like apple pie and motherhood – it appeals to all of us. But equality of opportunity is not an easy concept to work with. It requires a lot of hard thinking on the part of practitioners. And that requires us to abandon common-sense beliefs based on uncritical stereotyping. Critical reflection offers an opportunity to think more widely and to examine our vision of the future for our children. This chapter has traced some of the ways in which we can think critically about equality of opportunity.

Debates around equal opportunities involve arguments about 'nature' and 'nurture'. Although it has been pointed out that 'nature' and 'nurture' are intertwined and that to some extent this relationship cannot be undone, it is still valuable to examine the arguments and decide what is and is not acceptable. To use the minimal genetic differences between people of different skin colour as justification for discrimination is not acceptable, but to explore the medical needs and differences of children with disabilities can positively inform the process of becoming an inclusive day centre or school.

Inclusion and exclusion, discrimination and anti-discriminatory practice are processes taking place on a number of interlinked levels. Equal opportunities can not be achieved by stopping short at the individual level, by blaming cultural differences or by declaring social structures as fixed (Thompson, 2001).

This chapter has used a number of examples of discrimination to draw out common patterns. It can only provide a brief introduction. Early years practitioners play an important role in supporting discussions and practices that allow everyone to be part of creating an inclusive setting: colleagues, children, parents and the community. Equality of opportunity cannot be prescribed through legislation alone and as early years practitioners we have a duty to involve ourselves in the long process of developing satisfactory anti-discriminatory practices.

ACTIVITY *1*

Equal opportunities in your nursery

Imagine that you are a member of staff who has recently been given responsibility for equal opportunities in a day care nursery (0–5) in a predominantly white rural community. What elements would you include in a policy document supporting equal opportunities for the children? What obstacles do you foresee in changing attitudes and incorporating the policy into practice?

---

10 Supporting creativity

Sue Rogers

Your three-year-old asks for paper and paints. You groan. You know she will only bash out a few squiggles before getting bored, leaving you to clear up the mess. But you do it anyway. Sure enough, five minutes later comes a cry of 'finished'. You take a look at the random splodges. 'It's a tree,' the three-year-old says proudly. 'Hmm,' you reply doubtfully, before remembering to add, with as much conviction as you can summon 'it's very good.' Two years further down the line, your child might actually draw a tree that looks vaguely like a tree. This time, your enthusiasm is unforced. You ask: 'What sort of tree is it?,' 'Why did you choose that one?' and continue with: 'I like your choice of colour' as you try to engage in a discussion of the drawing.

As a paradigm for nurturing creativity, this could hardly be worse. But at least it's consistent with the attitudes a child is likely to come up against at primary school. The only art that is valued is the representational. Abstract figures are merely the first, tentative steps to achieving likeness, and those children who never progress beyond the crude schema of matchstick people are the ones with little artistic talent. And the praise gets doled out accordingly.

(Crace, 2003)

Introduction

In recent years, the drive of successive governments to improve basic skills across the population in the UK has led to a severe reduction in the time available in schools for art education, and for approaches to teaching that nurture the imaginative and creative capacities of learners (Craft, 2002; Jeffrey and Woods, 2003). Imagination, that powerful human capacity to manipulate ideas, images and experiences, is too important to be overlooked. Imagination and creativity enable us to create and re-create ourselves and our world in the past, the present and the future. In this chapter, I want to:

- explore what creativity means and how it relates to imagination;

- consider how adults might help children to be creative.

So often, we apply adjectives such as 'creative', 'imaginative', 'artistic' interchangeably and with little thought to what they mean. Take 'creative'. What comes to mind when you think of a creative person? An artist perhaps, working in penury, maybe a little eccentric and 'off beat', troubled by life. There are cases of such artists, whose lives are well documented throughout history, and who set impressive role models of creative and highly productive activity against all the odds. Yet at the same time, such images of the artist, whether musician, painter or writer, are misleading and mask the day-to-day nature of a 'jobbing' artist's life. This may seem like a digression from the notion of 'the creative child' but I want to emphasise at the outset that adopting narrow and reductive conceptions of what creative people, artists or otherwise, do, may shroud a more widespread and democratic appreciation of creativity. Creativity is not to be thought of as the preserve of the few, but something that, given the right conditions, can be developed in anybody – it is the notion that 'all people are capable of creative achievement' (NACCCE, 1999, p.28).

What is creativity?

How might we define creativity in this broader sense? 'Creativity', like other concepts tied to lived experience, such as 'play, culture, performance', is an elusive concept. Its elusiveness is compounded by its particular association with the arts, by the complex nature of creative activity itself, and by the variety of theories that have been developed to explain it (NACCCE, 1999). Rather than attempting a single, congealed definition, I will consult the burgeoning literature on this subject and ask you, the reader, to attempt your own interpretation.

The origins of creativity come from the word 'create' or *creare*, which means literally 'to make a thing which has not been made before; to bring into being' (Barnhart and Barnhart, 1983, in Isenberg and Jalongo, 1997, p.4). This sense of an original product brought into existence persists in some of the most recent contemporary attempts to define creativity. For example, the seminal report *All our futures: creativity culture and education* (NACCCE, 1999) defines creativity as 'Imaginative activity fashioned so as to produce outcomes that are both original and of value' (p.29). The report arrives at this definition by suggesting that the creative processes have four distinctive characteristics:

> First, they always involve thinking or behaving imaginatively. Second, this imaginative activity is purposeful: that is, it is directed to achieve an objective. Third, these processes must generate something original. Fourth, the outcome must be of value in relation to the objective.
>
> (NACCCE, 1999, p.29)

Similarly, Seltzer and Bentley (1999, p.10) argue that 'creativity is the application of knowledge and skills in new ways to achieve a valued goal', suggesting that learners need four key qualities:

- the ability to identify new problems, rather than depending on others to define them;
- the ability to transfer knowledge gained in one context to another in order to solve a problem;
- a belief in learning as an incremental process, in which repeated attempts will eventually lead to success;
- the capacity to focus attention in the pursuit of a goal, or set of goals.

Beetlestone (1998, p.2), defines creativity as:

- a form of learning;
- representation;
- productivity;
- originality;

- thinking creatively/problem-solving;

- creation/nature.

Parnes (1963) suggests that creativity is a thinking process that involves connecting with our previous experience, responding to stimuli and generating at least one unique combination (in Isenberg and Jalongo, 1997).

In chapter 2 of her book on creativity in early years education, Craft (2002) discusses the distinctions that have been made between what she terms 'high' and 'low' creativity: 'high' is the sort of creativity which changes knowledge and our perspectives on the world, and 'low' is the creativity of the ordinary person. She argues that all pupils can be creative. She also highlights another distinction within creativity, where creativity is often defined within specific domains rather than being a process which can be applied more widely across domains of knowledge and skill.

From this, we can see that the creative process involves imaginative activity, the ability to generate a variety of ideas (productivity), problem-solving (application of knowledge and imagination to a given situation) and the ability to produce an outcome of value and worth. Put simply, then, creativity carries with it the idea of action and purpose; it is, in a sense, applied imagination, it is about making connections between experiences, ideas and practice.

From this standpoint, the narrow conception of creativity as something associated mainly with the creative arts (a 'sectoral' definition), and as the province of the few and gifted (an 'elite' definition), is replaced by the belief that all people are capable of creative achievement, provided the conditions are right and provided that they have acquired the relevant knowledge and skills (a 'democratic' definition). As the authors of *All our futures* describe it, there is 'the potential for creative achievement in all fields of human activity; and the capacity for such achievements in the many and not the few' (NACCCE, 1999, p.28).

Why is creativity important?

Creativity seems to be a fundamentally human quality that sets us apart from the rest of the animal kingdom. It is a quality that enables us to solve problems, to create artefacts that may be useful or beautiful or both, and that allows us to communicate the values and practices of our age. Related to this human desire to create is the apparent need to represent our experiences in some way (Duffy, 1998). By representing our ideas in a myriad of ways from painted junk to Lego guns, from sonatas to dead cows, from odes to obelisks, we are able to share our intellectual and emotional worlds. Whatever our age and preoccupations, the deeply personal can become interpersonal and connect us with the shared and common values of the people around us and our society at large.

It has become a commonplace to say that we live in a rapidly changing world. There is a common belief that the pace of change is so rapid that children of today will need to be highly creative, flexible and imaginative in order to survive. Some even argue for creativity on economic grounds, suggesting that an ever-increasing part of economic activity is driven by innovation and knowledge and that if we fail to nurture a generation of creative learners we risk losing our competitive edge (Holden *et al.*, 2003, p.1). Some argue that creativity in education is important because it prepares children with the necessary skills for the future and 'to become creative, innovative, enterprising and capable of leadership to equip them for their future lives as workers and citizens' (DfEE, 1999a, pp.11–12). But portraying creativity in this way, as primarily a vehicle for economic success and preparation for work, is surely not the only or most important reason to nurture it in our educational settings.

This narrowly functional argument for encouraging creativity is disputed. Beetlestone (1998) argues that allowing children to act creatively in the classroom is important, not for some economic goal in the future, but because it can greatly enrich their experience of the curriculum and contribute to their social well-being, thereby nurturing higher levels of productivity and motivation.

This argument for creativity as a source of personal enrichment is supported by Duffy (1998), who writes that society has always needed people who are creative and imaginative since creative and imaginative experiences give us the opportunity to:

- develop the full range of human potential;

- improve our capacity for thought, action and communication;

- nurture our feelings and sensibilities;

- extend our physical and perceptual skills;

- explore values;

- understand our own and others' cultures.

You will remember that our starting point in this chapter was that all human beings have creative potential and that this should be nurtured from an early age. So what qualities might we expect to see in creative people? From her research, Craft (2002, p.6) has drawn out a range of qualities and attributes that characterise creative people:

> *strong motivation, endurance, intellectual curiosity, deep commitment, independence in thought and action, strong desire for self realisation, a strong sense of self, strong self-confidence, openness to impressions from within and without, attracted to complexity and obscurity and a high capacity for emotional involvement in their investigations.*

Two official documents need particular mention here in relation to young children. First, the publication of *All our futures* (NACCCE, 1999) has been an important addition to recent debate on the need to inject more creativity into our schools. Second, the Curriculum Guidance for the Foundation Stage (QCA/DfEE, 2000) has promoted a play-based curriculum for children aged from three to the end of the reception year. Although the Curriculum Guidance for the Foundation Stage refers to imagination and play throughout, creativity appears to be housed within creative development, a discrete area of learning which embraces the expressive arts – music, art and crafts, drama. This, as we have seen, is a rather narrow interpretation of creativity and its relationship to young children's learning. Indeed, Craft (2002) has identified the dangers in this separation of creativity from the rest of children's learning. We can see that rather than promoting the idea that all children can be creative in a variety of ways and across the entire range of experiences available to them, such a narrow conception of creativity may simply serve to perpetuate the view that creativity is principally to do with arts education. Craft also argues that there is now a mismatch in official thinking on creativity and education. On the one hand, the Curriculum Guidance for the Foundation Stage puts creativity into the creative arts sector; on the other hand, the National Curriculum sees creativity as a cross-curricular topic (Craft, 2002). You can probably appreciate how problematic this is if we are to achieve progression and continuity in creative education across the stages of young children's school careers.

Creativity as a concept in its broadest sense needs to be expanded to include an understanding of what it means to human experience, how it contributes to the well-being of individuals and society and how it informs and underpins children's learning.

Creative learning?

What exactly is creative learning? The document *Creative partnerships* (Holden *et al.*, 2003) argues that although creative learning complements and overlaps with arts education, it is different. It cannot be neatly defined in a soundbite, but it can be characterised, described and understood. It is about equipping children and young people with the skills, ability, confidence and attitudes to enable them to innovate: in its broadest sense, to work creatively. Fundamentally it can enable learners 'to transfer knowledge across contexts to create new forms of value' (p.1). But is it helpful to think of 'creativity' as a blanket, catch-all concept irrespective of age? Isenberg and Jalongo (1997) suggest that it is probably more helpful to distinguish between creativity in adults and older children on the one hand, and creativity in young children on the other. However, we should recognise that unless the capacity to be creative is nurtured in us as young children, we are less likely to become creative adults. They argue that because early development provides a foundation for all subsequent development, opportunities for creative learning in those early years are vital.

> *Creativity in young children reflects the raw and essential features of our definition in that while it may lack elements of expertise, experience of the world and work habits that we associate with adult creativity, it emphasises the thought processes that underpin creative activity. These include sensitivity to internal and external stimuli; lack of inhibition; the ability to become completely absorbed in an activity. Because early development provides a foundation for all subsequent development, opportunities lost in the first five years of life are difficult if not impossible to regain.*
>
> (Isenberg and Jalongo, 1997, p.77)

Creativity in early childhood

Holden (1987, in Isenberg and Jalongo, 1998, p.7) suggests that young children appear to excel in three areas that we associate with creativity:

1) *sensitivity to internal and external stimuli;*

2) *lack of inhibition; and*

3) *the ability to become completely absorbed in an activity.*

All these properties contribute to their ability to innovate, both in the world around them and in the world inside their heads. We only have to think of the way small boys innovate with whatever comes to hand, in their desire for gun play! Isenberg and Jalongo (1997) point to the important link between imagination and creative learning. Imagination is the capacity to form mental images or concepts of people, places, things and situations that are not present. Fantasy may be thought of as a subset of imagination. Fantasy uses the imagination to create vivid mental images and combinations of images that bear little similarity to the perceptual world. Fantasy is a 'what if' situation and young children, as we can observe in any play situation, have a particular propensity for imaginative activity and fantasy. Isenberg and Jalongo (1997, p.99) go further and suggest that when children are using their creative abilities they typically:

- *explore, experiment, manipulate; play, ask questions, make guesses, and discuss findings;*

- *use imaginative role playing, language play, story telling, and artwork;*

- *concentrate on a single task for a relatively long period;*

- *try to bring order out of chaos;*

- *do something new with the old and familiar;*

- *use repetition as an opportunity to learn more from an experience rather than becoming bored with it.*

Fostering creativity

The adult role in fostering creativity or inhibiting creativity can be crucial. Many parents and teachers believe that they should not intervene in children's artwork since the whole point of it is concerned with self-expression. Furthermore, they often fear that interference may stifle children's creativity and even cause psychological damage. Franz Cisek (cited in Cox, 1997), known as the 'father of child art', believed that children's artwork is universal and spontaneous and that it can and should develop effortlessly into the creativity of the adult artist. Creativity does not take place in a vacuum – we need to create from something to something and artistic practice reflects the surrounding environment and contexts. Thus young children will draw upon their experiences of the world in their pictures, in their play and in their movement. Adults have a facilitating, enabling role to play in fostering the creative impulses of the children in their care and Fisher (1990), in his work on creative thinking and young children, identifies the features that may make an adult either encouraging or inhibiting. His findings are shown in the table.

Encouraging adult	Inhibiting adult
Allows time	Inattentive
Focuses on child's thinking	Authoritarian
Defers judgement	Pessimistic
Stresses independence	Promotes dependence
Optimistic about outcomes	Critical
Actively listens	Disapproving
Shows real interest	Acts as superior
Assumes it can be done	Makes fun of

Shares the risk	Predetermines response
Challenges child to try out ideas	Rejects new ideas
Is available for help	Lacks interests
Accepts child's decisions	Imposes decisions
Follows child's interests	Limits time
Speculates along with	Maintains fixed routines
Deals as an equal	Devalues suggestions
Sees learning in mistakes	Domineers
Uses open-ended questions	Interrupts
Encourages play	Impatient
Values creative ideas	Cross-examines
	Gives no feedback

(Fisher, 1990, p.38)

Children's ideas about the world are manifest in their creative activity, whether in a drawing, in a model, in music-making, in language games or in their imaginative play. Too much adult intervention can stifle imagination and innovation and simple exploration, as we saw in the extract from *The Guardian* at the beginning of this chapter. Adults in formal settings of nursery or school often, unthinkingly, sanction or censor children's ideas about the world, encouraging what they believe is educationally sound and discouraging what they believe to be 'off task'. They make decisions about what is educationally relevant and useful as they plan creative activities for children. An obvious example of this is the way in which children's role-play provision in early childhood settings is often adult-determined, adult-organised and prescribed. Adults are sometimes surprised to find that children in the beautifully presented and elaborately resourced café or pet shop are not interested in playing within the boundaries of the designated theme provided for them. They often subvert adult agendas (subversion is, arguably, a creative act!) and use the area and props in a way that can be disconcerting for the adult. But if we really want to nurture children's creative capacities in an activity like role-play, we should perhaps allow them to make connections for themselves. Jones and Reynolds (1992) argue that it is better to provide open-ended materials which have the potential to be used in new and imaginative ways if we want children to maintain their creative learning.

CASE STUDY

In one particular classroom, I observed reception children playing in the class Pet Shop over a period of three weeks. The teacher had prepared the children well with stories and visits. She preferred not to take a direct role in the children's play. Typically, children entered the role-play area, breaking into pairs or individuals in unrelated activity, moving objects and chatting. Play which could be related to the Pet Shop was brief and perfunctory.

On one particular occasion, Holly emerged as the leader of the play (which after only a few minutes was visibly disintegrating). There followed a period of tremendous activity while Holly began to construct a kitchen in the Pet Shop – I should perhaps tell the reader at this point that the teacher had moved the kitchen/home equipment out of the role-play area (now the Pet Shop), and although it remained adjacent to the area it had been packed away and was 'out of bounds'.

CASE STUDY *continued*

Holly moved the table, laid it and set about preparing an imaginary meal. The other children quickly joined her and began to adopt family roles. This bout of domestic play lasted for over 15 minutes. The levels of social interaction and language use was more sustained and more complex than in any of the Pet Shop play I had observed. I was curious to know what Holly thought about this play. I asked her to tell me about it. Why had she given up on the Pet Shop idea?

...because ... because the Pet Shop is closed today, and so we are at home having tea...

This was of course an entirely plausible answer. Yet I was struck by her body language which suggested to me that my question had engendered a feeling of guilt, that I had somehow caught her out and discovered her subversion. Without wanting to overstate or misinterpret this brief example of role-play, I am persuaded that the children were not remotely interested in the Pet Shop theme, that it may even have prevented creative role-play activity from taking place had Holly not seized the initiative. And it seems to me that initiative is a central and necessary feature of all creative activity, including role-play. In early childhood, role-play requires children to combine their experiences to generate something new and innovative, to express their ideas and feelings about the world and to create an artefact, albeit in the form of a story with actions. During my many hours behind the video camera in various research projects, I have witnessed many similar examples. Like those TV shows which highlight the 'out-takes', the things that go badly wrong (they are often the best bits!), I have often wondered about these examples of subversive play, play which doesn't fit the theme, but which may be of relevance and meaning to children and which often shows them at their most creative.

Fostering a creative learning environment – the Reggio Emilia approach

The Reggio Emilia approach to early years education in northern Italy emphasises the joint endeavour between adults and children and children and children in creating an open environment of trust and wonder in which creativity is allowed to flourish naturally. Reciprocity and negotiation form part of the philosophical underpinning of Reggio Emilia and adults and children learn that collaboration is a powerful experience. The movement successfully promotes creativity by encouraging children's representational and expressive skills through a 'hundred languages' – the myriad ways in which children express themselves in a wide variety of media such as art, movement, language and music. Loris Malaguzzi, founder of the project, valued highly the benefits of a child-centred approach to learning. More recently, academics and educators from across the world have studied Malaguzzi's philosophy and visited the pre-schools to see for themselves how his ideas are played out in practice. One such research visitor, Leslie Abbott, notes several features of the Reggio Emilia pre-schools which make them particularly conducive to creative learning. She is particularly struck by the immediacy of the environment, in terms of the light and organisation of space and she gives the following description:

Distinctive in all the ... preschools is the piazza: the central meeting place where children from all around the school share their play and conversations together. The tetrahedron with the mirrored interior is often to be found there, with children sitting or standing inside it with their friends, looking at themselves, and many versions of themselves ... mirrors proliferate in all the centres in keeping with the central philosophy of 'seeing oneself' and of constructing one's identity. Another distinctive feature of the Reggio preschools is the atelier, the art studio, where children work with the atelierista ... the qualified artist who is a member of the staff.

(Nutbrown and Abbott in Abbott and Nutbrown, 2001, p.2)

Abbott reports that children's work adorns the buildings, showing the evolution of projects undertaken by groups of children and quotes Malaguzzi's words 'We place enormous value on the role of the environment as a motivating and animating force in creating spaces for relations, options, and emotional and cognitive situations that produce a sense of well-being and security' (Malaguzzi in Abbott and Nutbrown, 2001, p.3). Another visiting researcher, Katz (in Abbott and Nutbrown, 2001) noted that 'no evidence was seen of all the children subjected to instruction at the same time, of having to create the same pictures or other art products – a common sight in our schools...' (p.11). By contrast to what we might find in many UK settings, children in the Reggio schools were able to carry out their own plans with confidence, and to take time to pursue their interests. Moreover, the adults also had unfailing confidence in the children's ability to succeed.

The case for creativity in the early years

The drive to prepare children for the literacy and numeracy hours in school has put a heavy emphasis on very young children developing the cognitive skills associated with reading, writing and number. Instead of actively exploring their world in whatever way and through whatever medium suits them best, young children in the UK have been encouraged to master the limited skills involved in learning to read and write. To end this chapter, we would like to present a few observations from the website 'The Campaign for Drawing', on the importance of drawing as a medium for children's expression.

Ken Baynes, visiting professor at Loughborough University, has made a study of how children draw, by recording their work on an interactive whiteboard. 'It's a far more complex activity than it first appears,' he says.

Angela Anning, Professor of Early Childhood Education at Leeds University, believes our attitudes to drawing have a negative impact on children when they begin school:

'If you deprive children of a capability they've learned out of school ... they come to feel as if there's something wrong at home – that they shouldn't be drawing. It also shuts down an important means of communication. In their early years, children are exposed to a huge variety of stimuli, many of which, such as posters and TV, are extremely visual. So they start understanding imagery and learn to express ideas in graphical form in their pre-school years. Yet as soon as they get to school, the primary means of communication gets narrowed down to writing and listening. These are the only skills that are valued, and drawing quickly becomes marginalised.'

Eileen Adams, Education Officer at the Campaign for Drawing says:

'Drawing is a not just a form of expression, it is a form of perception, a way of understanding the world. Just as the pre-verbal babbles of infants are their way of making sense of the world and communicating that understanding, so the same is true of early drawings. Children draw to make sense of their world and to develop their thinking: it's not just an artistic or recreational activity, it's also an intellectual one. Ideas that are either unformed or only partly formed at the beginning gradually take shape and develop through the process of drawing. The visual imagery that children acquire through drawing is vital to their later understanding of subjects such as geography and maths. Without an ability to map components or make sense of symbols, children's development in these areas is likely to be severely restricted.'

Giving more status to creativity in its widest sense, and more narrowly to the creative arts, would open the doors to learning for many more of our children and young people in nurseries and schools. It is well documented that children learn in many different ways; at present the system works against those who learn kinaesthetically and visually and favours those who learn best through language and text. A system which encouraged and fostered creativity beyond that of the written word would, at the very least, give all children more options. At its best, it could revolutionise our understanding of what real learning is all about!

ACTIVITY 1

Give your children a pencil and encourage them to draw. Who knows? You might still get a load of unintelligible splodges, but if you look hard enough you could find out a great deal more about their passions and what they think than you ever would by talking to them! (adapted from Campaign for Drawing)

ACTIVITY 2

Individually, make notes: 'Imagination to me is...?' Then, in groups, discuss and give feedback on the proposition 'Imagination is more important than knowledge...'

Part 4

Working in Early Years Teams: Developing Empowering Communities

11 Leadership in early childhood settings

Jan Savage and Caroline Leeson

Introduction

Leadership has emerged as an important issue for all early childhood professionals, not just for those who hold leadership or management positions within a whole range of provision and services. It will be argued that developing leadership skills is an important part of any early years practitioner's responsibility, no matter what stage they are at in their career.

The context within which services for children and families currently operate can be characterised as one of change in a fast-moving world with ever-shifting goalposts. Change is the name of the game. There has been a constant stream of national strategies, government initiatives and related policies since the Labour government took office in 1997. These have been introduced at national level and are gradually being implemented and interpreted at local level, impacting upon provision and services. Many of these initiatives have signalled a move towards a multidisciplinary approach to delivering *integrated* services for children and families, at least in theory, although it can be debated as to how effective this is currently in practice. This has, in its turn, created a demand for debate on the most appropriate leadership styles and tone for these new ways of leading, managing and developing services for young children.

The idea of flexible, co-ordinated services is, however, not a new one. For example, a number of nursery centres were set up in London and other cities in the late 1970s, which offered state nursery education with wrap-around daycare facilities and often a range of other services to meet the needs of their local communities. These centres did not become a widespread phenomenon and the staff working in them were definitely challenged to find new ways of working in partnership across different services such as education, social services and health. Individual practitioners today are certainly attempting to communicate and resolve issues starting from very different backgrounds and perspectives. The significance of the implications of 'integration' for leadership in current early childhood practice will be highlighted throughout this chapter. It is the context of 'integrated services' that sets the challenges for leaders in the early years apart from those in other sectors of public services, let alone the business world. Helping everyone involved to 'think outside the box' or developing a box big enough or flexible enough for everyone to think inside will be a major challenge.

'Moving towards integration' – an overview of current initiatives

Several sections of the National Childcare Strategy (DfEE, 1998b), including the setting up of Early Excellence Centres, Sure Start programmes and Neighbourhood Nurseries, have given the impetus for settings to become multidisciplinary and multifunctional. This has precipitated an expansion of functions, roles and responsibilities that early childhood professionals undertake. In the Early Excellence Centre pilot programme's second annual evaluation report 2000 (DfEE, 2001) it was suggested that Early Excellence Centre heads have to develop their management and organisational skills to manage the diverse range of services within their settings. The report highlighted that already these heads were under significant pressure and finding their role extremely complex and demanding, trying to deal with increasing management responsibilities and competing demands from parents, children, community and LEA.

In the government's Green Paper, *Every child matters* (DfES, 2003) a key strategy involves plans to establish children's centres in each of the 20 per cent most deprived neighbourhoods in the country by 2006. This continues the push towards integrated services. The intention is that these centres will 'combine nursery education, family support, employment advice, childcare and health services on one site' to provide integrated care and education for young children (p.7).

Similarly, one of the keys to early intervention and effective protection for 'disadvantaged' children will be 'on the spot service delivery':

> *Professionals will be encouraged to work in multi-disciplinary teams based in and around schools and Children's Centres. They will provide a rapid response to the concerns of frontline teachers, childcare workers and others in universal services.*
>
> (ibid. p.9)

This will require strong leadership with powerful, motivating vision, a type of leadership perhaps not always in evidence.

Lord Laming's report into the case of Victoria Climbie (Department of Health, 2003) was one of the first inquiries into the death of a child to criticise the calibre and expertise of leaders and managers in all services for young children rather than placing the blame on frontline staff. The collective failure of leaders to lead with vision and to take responsibility for managing their staff was seen as a major contributory factor in the events leading to Victoria's death. The Green Paper picks up these criticisms and explores requirements for leaders and managers to be better trained and to attend to the training and development of their staff.

Underpinning both Lord Laming's report and the Green Paper is the belief that managers should manage more effectively, accept accountability and be more proactive in developing multidisciplinary training opportunities for all frontline staff and that this will take place in a multiprofessional context. However, there may be difficulties to overcome, some of which are referred to in the Laming Report, for example, how do individual professions work together and how can this collaborative practice be effectively led? Anxieties had already been expressed about the ability of agencies to collaborate under the Children Act of 1989 (Department of Health, 1999).

'The experience has highlighted again the difficulties of achieving joint vision, priority and ownership across organisations' (Glennie, 2003, p.183). A recent report by the Audit Commission (2003b) is highly critical of the failure of local government to grasp the nettle of corporate governance, suggesting that, even at the highest levels, leaders are poor at communicating their vision and promoting their services effectively. So it would appear to be an elusive ideal, this visionary leader who will effectively promote the needs and aspirations of young children and their families.

One of the difficulties for leadership in the early years is the lack of theory to assist with the understanding and practice of leadership. Rodd (1994, 1998) has argued that, although there is 'an abundance of literature on leadership as it pertains to business, industry, human services and education in general, little has been written specifically for the early childhood profession'(1998, p.xi). This is still, sadly, the case a decade later. Two key questions throughout this discussion must be:

- How helpful is this other literature or do we also need to consider different frameworks when discussing early childhood settings?

- Are there values underpinning all work with young children and their families that provide guidance and define elements of what constitutes effective leadership?

What might being a leader in a multidisciplinary, multifunctional setting mean in practice?

In discussions nationally about support and training for leaders of children's centres there appears to be some acknowledgment that the role is complex and that they would not be expected to perform as functional managers. The key focus would be bringing together the skills, expertise and experience of a multidisciplinary team for the benefit of families, children and communities to help everyone 'to think outside the box'.

This might involve:

- developing a 'new' team out of two teams or more with very different philosophies and practice;

- sometimes promoting radically different ways of working with both children and their families;

- the challenge of reaching all parents, getting them on board and developing effective partnerships.

Much of the theory and literature on the management of organisations is currently drawn from the world of business and is often of only limited usefulness in illuminating work in early years settings, which are less goal-orientated and more person-centred. This means that we need to rethink some of the models of leadership and management that already exist within local authority bureaucracies and establish new ones that reflect the aspirations of recent reports and recommendations and facilitate working together with the child at the centre of practice.

Values

Workers in the early years need to think clearly about the values that underpin their work – how do they view small children, their families and the wider community? In the Laming Report this was examined in some detail. The report was highly critical of the increasingly service-led, as opposed to needs-led, approach adopted by many services which would normally be regarded as keen advocates for children. It was concluded that this attitude was largely to blame for the final outcome of Victoria's death.

We would argue that the following principles should underpin all effective services for young children and should be encapsulated in any vision promulgated by leaders in the early years:

- respect for young children as powerful people, who have ideas and thoughts that need taking seriously;
- children as co-constructors of knowledge;
- a real commitment to social inclusion;
- the provision of holistic services to children and families;
- professional learning communities of children/staff/parents.

A crucial question posed by the current debate on leadership and the development of services has to be, do we want leaders 'to fix things' in early childhood settings or is there a different way forward? We would argue that more emphasis needs to be placed on a collegial approach with a focus on distributive leadership, that requires an approach to lifelong learning by all with development of leadership skills as an important aspect. An important task for all practitioners at whatever stage in their careers is, therefore, to develop theoretical and practical frameworks on leadership and management appropriate to contemporary early years provision based upon knowledge of relevant theory and research.

What is leadership?

Leading and managing in the context of early childhood settings is, if nothing else, extremely complex. In this section we will explore some aspects of the question – what is leadership? Like the wind, it seems to be one of those things you know when you experience it, but which is often difficult to define precisely. There are possibly as many definitions of leadership as there are those who wish to write about it. We have had a fascination with leaders for centuries, attempting to establish and understand what defines the leader as opposed to the led, gaining insight and trying to encapsulate strong and weak characteristics in order to test/predict or seek for those who may lead in whatever field we are engaged in. Leaders are seen as having a profound effect on whatever organisation they are in charge of, sometimes beneficial and sometimes detrimental. Leadership is often considered to involve influencing the behaviour of others, often to persuade them to follow a path defined by the leader. Thinking about 'best' leaders and 'worst' leaders in history is an absorbing occupation and often used by those attempting to make sense of the phenomenon.

In order to begin to understand how leaders function and to draw some conclusions about the implications for early childhood, we will examine some theories that are already in existence, their roots and development. No theory exists in isolation. It is often through writers disagreeing with aspects of past theory that new and different ones emerge. Figure 2 shows diagrammatically some of the connections between the theories that we are considering. We will offer a critique of those theories and begin to outline the development of new ideas relevant to early childhood.

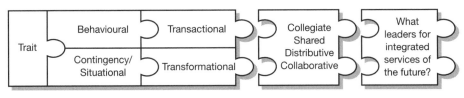

Figure 2 Some theories of leadership

Leadership theories have come, predominantly, from the field of industry. Throughout the twentieth century studies have focused on contributing to a body of knowledge in order to give the world of business an understanding of what to look for and enhance in the leaders they employ. These theories have increasingly been used in other fields, and during the last 20 years in particular, have been scrutinised and developed within the areas of education and social welfare.

Leadership theories can be broadly divided into the following categories: trait theories; behavioural or style theories; contingency or best-fit theories; and transformational theories. They are not necessarily exclusive, as van Maurik (2001, p.3) explains:

> *Although it is true that the progression of thinking tends to follow a sequential path, it is quite possible for elements of one generation to crop up much later in the writings of someone who would not normally think of himself or herself as being of that school. Consequently, it is fair to say that each generation has added something to the overall debate on leadership and that debate continues.*

We will examine each of these categories in turn, identifying any movement from one to the other and discussing their efficacy in early years education.

Trait theory

Trait theory formed the basis of most leadership research up until the 1940s. Attempts were made to identify various personality traits or personal characteristics, which, if present in an individual, would indicate his or her suitability as a leader. Key traits were usually identified by studying successful leaders in history, e.g. Julius Caesar, Alexander the Great, Mahatma Ghandi, Martin Luther King. Workers in this field developed tests to attempt to predict which people applying for a leadership position possessed these traits and, therefore, were the most employable.

For example, Cattell (1968) used a statistical procedure called factor analysis to discover what he considered to be the most important underlying traits. He identified 16 'personality' factors using what he called 'L data' or 'life records', systematically identifying those traits that he felt were core. Psychometric testing began to be developed around this idea, using questionnaires and 'objective' tests. Qualities such as emotional stability, extraversion, conscientiousness, have all been identified as desirable traits in a leader (Cattell, 1968). Using tests to establish whether people have particular identified qualities proved attractive to the business world for two reasons. Firstly, the predictive quality supposedly promised less risk of employing the wrong person. Secondly, the innateness of trait theory suggested that money need not be spent on training leaders to do their job as eventually their skills would shine through.

Although as a theory there have been many criticisms, aspects of trait theory are still incorporated in training to support leaders (headteachers) in education today. Psychologist David McLelland's seminal work on human motivation (see, e.g., McClelland, 1987) is currently used by the National College of School Leadership (NCSL) where traits are described as 'non-conscious drivers', i.e. they influence our behaviour throughout many aspects of our lives including our working lives and leaders' working lives.

In summary, trait theory is based on an assumption that traits are innate rather than learned, that leaders are born rather than made. Experience, however, shows us that this is not the case: not all leaders are born leaders. Studies of successful leaders show different qualities; not all have identical qualities. Most of the early research focused on male leaders in history. What does this say about women leaders, particularly pertinent in the early childhood context, where the vast majority of leaders are women?

The main criticism of trait theory is that it is too simplistic, that other factors also need to be taken into account. So researchers began to focus on leaders' actions rather than their attributes, the situations that leaders find themselves in and how these may predict the traits or qualities required for that particular situation. Gradually the focus shifted from thinking about the leaders themselves to issues of leadership and what styles of leadership can be identified and described.

Behavioural theories of leadership

Dissatisfaction with trait theory led to the development (again in industry) of descriptions of leadership styles and the identification of a typology as an attempt to establish predictable tests on which people's ability or lack of ability to lead and manage specific teams of people in organisations could be judged. The focus was now on how leaders behaved. Dozens of leadership styles were identified by a whole range of different writers using different words to describe essentially similar behaviours. Influential writers such as Blake and Moulton (1964), for example, developed a Managerial Grid to assist in this identification process with the assumption that there is a best style of leadership. Likert (1967), another key writer in the field, suggested four different styles which incorporate some of the main ideas around at the time. These were:

- *exploitative/authoritarian*, where leaders manipulate their subordinates and are used to prescribing tasks without question from their staff;
- *benevolent/authoritarian*, where leaders are used to being in charge and have a paternalistic approach to their employees;

- *consultative*, where employees are asked their opinion prior to leaders making decisions;

- *participative*, where employees are involved in the decision-making processes.

Likert's typology, however, was based on the assumption that individuals are fixed with a particular style and are, therefore, unable to shift from one style to another when the task and/or personnel change.

In the 1930s, Lewin identified three different leadership styles: autocratic, *laissez-faire* and democratic. Autocratically-led teams were those where the physical presence of the leader was required in order to get the work done. 'Follow me, I am right behind you' summarises a *laissez-faire* approach to leadership. Democratically-led teams were those who could be given autonomy and responsibility and could be trusted to do their work without being constantly overseen. In order to be successful the leader would need to possess the appropriate style. Style theories, therefore, did offer the opportunity to begin to understand what has happened when leadership appears to go wrong, i.e. a particular style has been used that was inappropriate for the team or the task that was being carried out.

Tannenbaum and Schmidt (1973) were interested in the processes of decision-making and continued work defining the autocratic–democratic continuum. They outlined a continuum of situations and styles that could be used to identify the leadership requirements at any one time. Context was beginning to be recognised as important. This proved useful as it began to show that, over time, leaders may need to move from one style to another as teams developed in competence and that an autocratic leader would not be successful with a team of capable people who would wish to develop their own autonomy.

Neugebauer (1985, cited in Rodd, 1994, 1998) related styles of leadership specifically to early childhood contexts with typologies of the Task Master, the Comrade, the Motivator and the Unleader, suggesting that the third was the most effective in these contexts. Again, this was a useful thought as we see a move towards an increasingly autonomous workforce in early years with higher expectations regarding qualifications/experience and calibre of personnel.

To summarise, criticisms of style theories include the point that people rarely lead using one style all the time. The influence of the context and situation in which leaders may find themselves may not be fully acknowledged. Frequently leaders have a variety of styles available to them that they feel comfortable with and are able to use; hence the development of contingency theories.

Contingency or situational theories of leadership

So what becomes interesting to researchers here is how leaders are effective in particular contexts. Contingency or situational leadership theories were developed, therefore, with the idea of 'best fit': an effective leader will choose a leadership style that is appropriate to the task at hand and the calibre of staff. Effective leaders will use their professional judgement, maturity, experience and preferred leadership style to determine how they are going to lead in a particular situation. Fiedler (1978), a leading exponent of contingency theory, argued that successful leadership is contingent upon the situation leaders find themselves in, the structure of the task, the characteristics of all the people involved, both leaders and led, and the nature and quality of the relationship between them. Hersey and Blanchard (1977) identified four styles that leaders could call upon to lead in different situations taking account both of tasks to be done and the relationships between the leader and others in the organisation. These were:

- *telling* – a style often required in situations where the task is repetitive or needs doing quickly;
- *selling* – a style that encourages and motivates people to do the tasks required;
- *participating* – a style required when the competence of staff is high, but unacknowledged by them so tasks still need facilitation, supervision and support by the leader;
- *delegating* – a style used where high staff motivation and competence means they are able to get on with the task without supervision or direct support.

In order to be successful according to contingency or situational leadership theory, leaders need to be skilful at reading the requirements of the context in which they work (Telford, 1996). A key question, therefore, is what style and traits can be utilised so that the best will be achieved out of given situations.

Criticisms of contingency theory include the view that it mainly comes from American theorists and may not transfer readily across the Atlantic and, once again, it is heavily dependent on research on male leaders.

Transactional and transformational theories

Burns (1978) developed another set of ideas by distinguishing between transactional leadership (getting things done) and transformational (visionary) leadership. According to Burns, *transactional* leadership, the primary focus of management literature, can best be described as the deployment of what are now recognised as effective, good and proper management techniques. It is, therefore, about the use of negotiation with the led, an exchange of services for various kinds of rewards (both extrinsic and intrinsic) in order to reach a point of mutual satisfaction from which the work will ensue. Important aspects include setting up procedures, clear job descriptions, appraisal of performance, management by clarifying objectives, etc. The effectiveness of and, therefore, the importance and use of praise, recognition and the delegation of responsibility are also acknowledged in this style of leadership.

Transactional leadership can still be seen as working in a top-down rather than a bottom-up model of leadership. *Transformational* leadership is defined by Burns as moving beyond this. In transformational or visionary leadership, the leader and led work together on common objectives towards common aims.

Bass (1985), however, was critical of Burns' view that the two theories were oppositional. He preferred to see them as complementary and useful to each other and expanded and refined ideas about transformational leadership. Van Maurik (2001) suggests that the two should be looked upon as progression from one to the other as demands upon leaders were becoming increasingly complex towards the end of the twentieth century. Working from transactional towards transformational leadership helps and enables both leaders and led to navigate around high levels of uncertainty in unstable and uncertain times. It is hardly surprising with constant and rapid change being a key characteristic of life through the 1980s and 1990s that interest in transformational leadership rose to the fore at that time.

To summarise, some key aspects of transformational leadership are as follows. It is about hearts and minds, about empowering people to learn and to seek change and improvement, not about controlling them. Links can be made here to Maslow's (1943) hierarchy of needs. It is a people-oriented approach rather than being focused mainly on tasks or products. It is about trusting those with whom you work, transforming feelings, attitudes and beliefs and having an impact on the culture of the organisation. The view is espoused that anyone should be able to lead (Owen, 2000).

Leadership today

As we move into the twenty-first century, effective leadership is described in a multitude of ways as being about 'shared', 'distributive', 'collaborative', 'invitational', 'collegiate' leadership, to name but a few. All of these build on aspects of transformational leadership. Rodd (1994), Owen (2000) and Telford (1996) all advocate that anyone can take on a leadership role, given the right context and opportunity: 'Leadership, at its best, is a shared venture engaged in by the many' (Telford, 1996, p.9).

Nias *et al.* (1989) were among the first to develop ideas about collaborative leadership within the school context, where leaders and led have shared values, beliefs and attitudes which assist them in working towards the overt goals of the organisation. Continuing in the context of schools, Southworth (1998) argues that as there is much to manage and less time for any individual to lead, schools actually need many leaders, who take and share leadership roles. He argues that this has implications regarding shared headship; otherwise there will just be a redistribution of management tasks rather than shared leadership. This may well be pertinent to leadership in multidisciplinary and multifunctional integrated early childhood settings.

Owen (2000) takes the view that it is an important part of the human spirit to wish to lead and to be able to do so. She identifies leaders as only being successful if they have effective structures around them; a relevant point, when we consider the anxieties surrounding multidisciplinary working in child protection. Bolman and Deal (1991, in Telford, 1996) consider transformational leadership in four contexts or frames in order to help us understand the theoretical underpinning of all leadership theories:

- *structural*, which includes the formal roles and relationships of the workplace;
- *human resource*, which focuses on the needs of the individuals within the workplace;
- *political*, described as the internal politics and power struggles;
- *symbolic*, or the culture of the workplace.

Again from within the world of education, Telford (1996) argues that 'collaborative' leadership takes from all four frames, using them to analyse the tasks and to work towards the vision of the school.

There is the sense that leadership theory has moved from the 'hard' world of industry and business towards a more 'touchy/feely' world where people are valued for themselves, not just the work they do. This is perhaps vital and maybe inevitable as we have developed complex working worlds, trained and developed staff to higher competencies and created more service-oriented business as opposed to ones dealing in inanimate products.

Throughout the 1990s writers considering leadership in education, often in discussions of managing change through school improvement and school effectiveness, have argued that much of past theory on leaders and leadership is redundant today. Stoll and Fink (1996, p.101) argue that: 'traditional descriptions of leadership which tend to sort leaders into categories or typologies are inappropriate for the postmodern age and the challenges it brings educational leaders'.

The old paradigm of leading from the front is no longer applicable. The concept of head-teacher as a 'leader among leaders' as exemplified by Day et al (1998) is a further example of the paradigm shift. In the literature a clear focus on leadership rather than management emerges in the 1990s with leadership being seen as the responsibility of the whole team, a shared and collaborative process.

Another argument has been that often rationalist models deny the complexities of human behaviour, hence an interest in applications of both inter and intra-personal intelligences (Gardner, 1984) and emotional intelligence (Goleman, 1998; Goleman *et al.*, 2002).

Emotional intelligence

Emotional intelligence has stepped into the world of leadership to provide a further dimension to transformational leaders. Goleman *et al.* (2002) set out why it is imperative to have emotionally literate leaders. These are leaders who are aware of their own emotions, are committed to the professional development of themselves and others, are empowering, trusting, optimistic, have a life outside the working environment and look after their own physical and emotional well-being (McBride and Maitland, 2002, pp.198–9).

Ethical leadership

Ethical leadership, as espoused by Bottery (1992), looks at the responsibility of the leader to think about how their setting fulfils its purpose. Bottery argues that the legislation that encapsulates the setting and its task is highly relevant and needs to be taken into consideration when embarking on any leadership decision making. What is the setting for? Ethical leadership is, therefore, seen as acting with moral purpose.

Leadership in general must maintain an ethical focus which is oriented towards democratic values within a community. This has to do with the meaning of ethics historically – as a search for the good life of the community … ethics here refers to a more comprehensive construct than just individual behaviour; rather it implicates us and how we as a moral community live our communal lives.

(Foster, 1989, p.55)

How does this manifest itself in action? The answer to this question is particularly relevant to early childhood services where the interrelatedness of working with people for people is paramount for success. Rodd (1998) for example, identifies four key areas within ethical leadership. These include the:

- promotion and protection of children's rights;
- provision of a high-quality and economically viable service which does not compromise children's rights;
- administration of services in accordance with the profession's ethical principles;
- employment of an early childhood code of ethics to guide the resolution of ethical dilemmas.

Interestingly, we still do not have written codes of ethics in the UK to inform workers in all early childhood settings.

Conclusion

We consider the following to be key issues to debate in order to clarify the position of leadership in early childhood services:

1. The debate about the relevance of building on past theories of leadership continues today. The Hay Group, for example, who have worked with the NCSL to further develop the Leadership Programme for Serving Heads (LPSH) starting in 2003, still work with leadership styles as a central concept. They suggest that there are six styles that can be used in the context of education as well as other business contexts all over the world. These styles are coercive, authoritative, democratic, pace-setting, affiliative and coaching. Authoritative and coaching styles are deemed to be of great significance for head teachers. It can be argued that this also has relevance to the complexity of the world of early childhood services.

2. The role of gender – how does gender affect leadership? As previously identified, most leadership traits have been based on male leaders. In a female-dominated profession, what traits are valued? Is it helpful to argue that women feel more comfortable empowering others and encouraging team decision-making than instructing or directing others? Have men been so socialised to compete as individuals, to see a direct connection between effort and reward, that they are, as a result, much more comfortable using direct control in leadership? The waters are certainly muddy in this respect.

Kagan certainly presents the argument that women leaders prefer multiple, shared and joint styles of leadership within an ethos of collaboration (Kagan and Bowman, 1997). Do female leaders, therefore, move naturally towards transformational styles of leadership? It is perhaps noteworthy that key advocates of this style, Rodd (1994, 1998), Hall (1996), Telford (1996) and Owen (2000), are all women writers. Hall (1996), in her study of six women managers in education, suggested that their leadership had roots in their childhood and life experiences that could not be divorced from their gender identity. She argues that:

in order to understand them as heads it is necessary to understand them as women ... in order to understand men as heads, it is necessary to understand them as men. In order to understand leaders and managers in education, we must also understand them as people.

(Hall, 1996, p.184)

3. What is the government's agenda? It would appear that the role of chief executive is in ascendancy as opposed to the role of leading professional and this seems to be promoted by many government reforms and policies. Leaders are expected to manage targets, budgets and staff. The requirement to balance the books is taking precedence over the inspirational aspects of leadership. This can clearly be seen in the policy of allowing business to take over so-called 'failing' schools, hospitals and other public services, where they have no intrinsic understanding of the setting, but know how to make the books balance. Is it possible or feasible for leaders to also be managers? Does this result in job overload? We are already seeing evidence of this within education and within the first cohort of Early Excellence Centres.

4. What is the moral and ethical purpose of provision in early childhood? What are we trying to achieve? Are services designed to allow today's workforce to go about their business knowing their children are being cared for, or is it about enhancing children's experiences in the here and now, or is it about assisting their progression towards adulthood? Moss and Petrie (2002) present a cogent argument that 'childhood is an important stage of the life course in its own right, which leaves traces on later stages' (p.101). If we believe this, then there are huge implications in terms of new sorts of relationships between children, between adults and between children and adults. Clear statements about our philosophy need to be central to the debate on what sorts of leaders we want.

We would argue that leadership in early childhood services should be inclusive for all participants: staff, children, parents and leaders. Leadership is about learning, becoming wiser and more knowledgeable. This does not necessarily mean knowing a lot of things, but is more to do with knowing about self and acting in the right way given particular situations, developing learning cultures for staff and parents as well as children.

We can certainly suggest that we do not need only superhuman, charismatic leaders as they cannot be emulated by the many. We leave the final comment to Fullan (2001, pp.136–7), who has written extensively about managing change in a complex world and who argues that the chief role of leadership is:

to mobilise the collective capacity to challenge difficult circumstances … ultimately your leadership in a culture of change will be judged as effective or ineffective not by who you are as a leader but by what leadership you produce in others.

ACTIVITY *1*

During the next few weeks read a variety of national and local newspapers and collect articles that demonstrate aspects of leadership. These could include references to politicians, football managers, celebrities, local initiatives, businesses, public services, etc.

Try to identify for yourself components of successful leadership to discuss in a small group.

ACTIVITY *2*

In a small group, plan an early years setting of your choice. Consider the following aspects:

1. Outline the vision, purposes and aim of your particular setting.

2. Describe, in detail, the services you will offer, the market you seek to serve and the premises you will require.

3. Identify the staffing implications of your plan, in terms of numbers, roles, qualifications, terms and conditions.

4. Identify how your setting will meet the needs of you, your staff, the children, their families and the wider community.

5. Develop a short-term and a long-term plan of what steps would need to be taken to create your setting.

This could form the context for an assignment discussing key leadership issues related to your particular setting.

12 Working with colleagues

Caroline Leeson and Lesley Griffiths

Introduction

Effective professionals working in the field of early years need to be skilled in, and to understand the nature of, collaborative practice – the ability to work with others from different professions and perspectives, often in difficult circumstances. Recent government policy initiatives, such as the Children Bill 2004, emphasise the necessity for agencies to work together in order to safeguard children and to be more effective in their work with families. In order to work in this way, practitioners need to have a panoply of skills at their disposal: communication, negotiation, team working, reflection and evaluation. In this chapter, we will explore some of the key issues for effective practice and seek to demonstrate the interrelatedness of the core skills of communication, team working and emotional literacy. We will also be arguing that the concept of 'colleagues' should be taken in its widest sense, encompassing friends, clients and family, as well as professional and work colleagues. It is important that, throughout this debate on working together, we do not lose sight of in our own attitudes towards children, which may prevent us from including them in our list of colleagues. Seeing the child as 'victim' or the child as 'threat' (Hendrick, 1994) will interfere with our ability to see the child as a colleague. This should be addressed because no amount of policy or political encouragement will further the interests of children until our beliefs about their abilities and status are examined and challenged. We would argue that young children are capable of participating in simple and complex decision-making and should be actively involved. We will consider how understanding the theory of the psychological processes involved in making relationships and interacting with others can enable each of us to work more effectively within our teams and to work collaboratively with members of other teams.

The early years context

In early years work, a wide range of organisations and individuals is involved in working with, and on behalf of, young children. Let us consider for a moment a young child whose parents may be experiencing difficulties at home. The child and her family may, during the course of a week, see different people from many different agencies, all of whom will be offering some sort of expertise and support to the family. A child of another family may communicate with a childcare team, an after-school care team, a childminder, maybe a speech therapist, health visitor or doctor; perhaps even more people could be added to the list. It may be that circumstances dictate that the same person does not necessarily visit the family each week and this situation increases the need for collaborative practices.

Working with colleagues – some definitions

For the purposes of this chapter, we are taking 'colleagues' to mean people who interact and work together towards a common, identified goal. We are not thinking of colleagues purely in the professional work situation. In fact we would argue quite strongly that working with our professional colleagues would and should spill over into our interactions with them outside work and that we ignore the holistic aspects of the people we come into contact with at our peril. People come to work with a wide range of emotions, motivations and priorities. To know and understand these will help us to work more effectively together. We therefore see colleagues in the widest sense of the word and would prefer to look at a collegiate manner of operating at all levels of our interactions with others. We would promote a 'supportive collegiality' (Kydd *et al.*, 2003, p.162) where people are working together pooling their strengths, giving each other support and helping with individual weaknesses. Nias *et al.* (1989) identify such a model as one where there is a high dependence on the relationships between people and where time and priority are given to ensure that this is promoted.

In order to be clear as to what we mean by 'work', we need to look at the social psychology of work and the values attached to it, to begin to identify the cultural positions people start from when viewing working with colleagues. We need to be mindful of the sense of duty attached to work and the issues of power that can affect the decisions that are made and the actions that are taken. Early years work is people-based, highly dependent on interpersonal relationships and on understanding how people operate and how they think about their work. Nias *et al.* (1989) explore organisational culture, identifying five key factors: beliefs and values; understandings; attitudes; meanings and norms; symbols rituals and ceremonies (p.11). They also go on to explore factors that get in the way of creating an effective working culture: the building that people work in; the organisational arrangements; the time given for working and communicating together; the personal inclinations of the individuals involved; and the traditions attached to ways of working. One of us once worked in a family centre where there were no meetings to share ideas, thoughts and developments and no time given to exploring strengths and weaknesses and thereby developing a sense of identity. This group of people (it could not be called a team) fell apart in a very short period of time, with long-term sickness and new jobs being the practically convenient, but emotionally costly, way out for many members. A recent study undertaken by Carlyle and Woods (2002, p.1) identified that one of the key causes of stress was seen by some teachers as follows:

> As far as school is concerned, much of the problem was seen to reside in negative emotional structures, inadequate and ill-designed to cope with the vast changes of the late 1980s and 1990s. These structures bred negative emotional climates, low levels of emotional literacy, and high levels of emotional labour.

The negative emotions within the schools were reported to be the result of:

> ...crisis management, poor communication systems, autocratic decision making, and bullying management styles.

Organisations that operate under these conditions may fail, as Carlyle and Woods suggest, because they do not see the importance of effective team working either for themselves or their individual team members.

Emotional literacy, developed from the work of Steiner (Weare, 2004), would help us to begin to identify emotional strengths and weaknesses within such a team and thus within the organisation. These ideas are becoming more widely used on an individual basis, within schools and other organisations. We would argue that organisations which do not work towards emotional literacy might only be working in the interests of a few members, at the expense of the emotional well-being of others.

Working together in partnership

Partnership is a term that has been a key word for policymakers since the late 1980s (Hornby, 2000) to mean the increased involvement and sharing of power with families, children and carers. As early as the 1960s, the need for strong links between home and school was highlighted by Plowden (Central Advisory Council for Education, 1967, p.37). In 1989, the Children Act required professionals to work in partnership with children and their families to design effective care packages based on co-operation and building on considerable evidence that such collaboration assists in keeping children considered 'at risk', with their families. The Education Reform Act 1988 gave parents the right to be consulted over whether or not schools should remain in local authority control, the underlying belief being one of giving power to parents in a situation where they had none.

We see this trend continuing, with the recent proposals in the Children Bill (2004) signalling government plans to make agencies work in partnership to improve services and communication between them. This desire to have agencies working together has the laudable aim of improving services and communication, but appears to have grown out of the ideology of managerialism: the expectation that the books will be balanced, that a minimum amount of public money will be used. This creeping managerialism in public services began with the 1974 National Health Service reorganisation, with a focus on the greater centralisation of resources, managerial efficiency, co-ordination of services and corporate management across the whole organisation. This was further developed in the 1990s with the purchaser/provider split in health services. Social services have followed a similar path with the introduction of the concept of corporate parenting (making decisions for all children in care rather than looking at individual cases) and the buying in of services that offer best value (Community Care and NHS Act, 1990). In education, schools manage their own budgets and opt in or out of services provided by the local education authority depending on any identified financial benefit. Centralised planning and budgetary awareness are at the core of this model and the expectation is that there will be measurable and cost-effective outcomes that can be audited. It remains to be seen whether or not this model can be usefully applied to early years services. It is very difficult to put a price on providing stable foundations for vulnerable children, or on raising the aspirations of families whose expectations are low, or on compensating for a poor start in life. We would argue that failing to assist the most vulnerable children in society will have financial implications – unsupported children may, in adulthood, fail to take a productive part in society and may go on to need more expensive and long-term support services.

Effective partnership

For partnership to be maintained it is vital that there are effective strategies in place to facilitate two-directional communication and support.

(Fitzgerald, 2004, p.21)

But what are these effective strategies? Let us start with names. How do we define our partners? As clients, service-users, patients, mums and dads, cases ... colleagues? All of these terms are value-laden; some have negative connotations, implying a weaker or inferior position to the 'professional'.

So we need to think very carefully about the labels we place on people and how we promote partnership and collegiality.

To work together all parties need to have a shared sense of what partnership means to them all.

(Fitzgerald, 2004, p.7)

Defining what partnership means to us will affect the way we work – and will inform our attitudes and our policies. Miell and Dallos (1996, p.299) suggest that partnership may be difficult because of the perceived status of professionals who come from privileged backgrounds in terms of class, race, education and, frequently, gender. This is a key point – when dealing with a social worker, for instance, one isn't dealing with a person, one is dealing with the whole edifice of the social services that stands behind (and will back up) that person.

In entering into a relationship with a professional body, individuals appear to be negotiating from a position of disadvantage and they are, to some extent, obliged to comply with the professionals definition of their needs.

Since the Education Act of 1944, parents have been required to send their children to school (unless they can show they are being educated 'otherwise'). There has been a move to encourage schools to work in partnership with parents and to increase opportunities for parental involvement. The Curriculum Guidance for the Foundation Stage (QCA/DfEE, 2000, p.9) asserts that: 'When parents and practitioners work together in early years settings, the results have a positive impact on the child's development and learning'.

The Education Act (2002) picks up this point and emphasises the importance of setting up home–school agreements as a way of forging partnerships with parents. Scourfield (2003) argues that this could be seen as control rather than partnership, suggesting that some partnership ideologies may be control mechanisms in disguise.

There are various frameworks for developing partnership. In education, Holt (cited in Fitzgerald, 2004) devised a 'ladder of empowerment' that agencies can use to identify an appropriate level and type of partnership. In social welfare, the 'continuum of service user participation' (Martin and Henderson, 2001, p.162) serves a similar function. Both frameworks measure how meaningful and genuine the partnership is for both the professional and the families involved. They demand that we look at any situation and ask whether the plan we are developing is one of genuine empowerment and autonomy or one of lip service to an ideal. For a partnership to be effective, everyone needs to see how they fit into the partnership and what they bring to it in terms of an agenda, motivation, emotion, information and ways of working.

Obstacles to effective partnership

The dangers of not working in partnership were highlighted by the inquiry into the death of Jasmine Beckford (London Borough of Brent, 1985). There was found to be serious collusion between the parents and the social workers that led to an over-identification with the family and a lack of appreciation of Jasmine's position. Similarly, the Ainlee Walker inquiry (Newham Area Child Protection Committee, 2002) showed how professionals became frightened of the parents' aggression and concerned for their own safety. This resulted in them withdrawing and leaving the child without support, demonstrating the need to keep focused both on the issues in a case, and on the processes of working in partnership.

What about families that do not wish to be involved in partnerships? Some families expect the professionals to get on with their job without involving them – either because they are not interested or do not have the time or the skills, or because they feel intimidated or unworthy. Some families, for example, in child protection work, are afraid of becoming involved with professionals because of the possibility that their children might be taken away from them. However, there are clear duties for all professionals to ensure that parents are informed and have real opportunities to be involved with the decisions being made in their children's lives. It is not good enough for parents to say that they do not wish to be involved, or for professionals to say that they will not offer a partnership in certain cases. The Children Act 1989 makes it clear that social workers have a duty to ensure that parents are invited to become involved and that every effort is made to include them (ss 22; 23; 24; Sch 2 paragraph 15, 1989). However, research by Farmer and Owen (1995, in Leathard, 2003) found that those families who were under-confident in their role, or had difficulties articulating their position, found it hard to fulfil their role in the partnership with the professionals working with them. Practitioners should therefore think very carefully about how they enable parents to participate – perhaps choosing neutral territory for meetings, providing opportunities for rehearsals and offering refreshments. One of the authors ran a family centre and worked closely with parents who used the service to rehearse case conferences, providing pads and pens for use in meetings (one parent pointed out that lack of these 'props' served to underline the differences in status of the participants).

In education, the Curriculum Guidance for the Foundation Stage (QCA/DfEE, 2000) advocates that all parents should be involved in their child's learning and outlines various strategies to encourage practitioners to develop an effective partnership by showing respect, understanding the role of the parents, listening, being flexible, giving time, valuing different perspectives and collaborating in a genuine way. Again, holding meetings at appropriate and convenient times and places and ensuring that any consultation is a genuine process can all help towards partnership working. This can be difficult to achieve, especially if families have had bad experiences with other professionals. Managing conflict and facilitating a more collegiate way of working, is the goal of partnership. Even the most difficult of parents want the best for their children and instead of abandoning the idea of partnership, we should ask instead why anger and mistrust are making the partnership so difficult to maintain.

Children as colleagues

We often overlook the children themselves when we talk of partnership. Too often we take a paternalistic approach to children, seeing them as helpless and incapable of making decisions for themselves. Knutsson (1997, p.37) says this is all too often an approach taken towards both children and the elderly:

> *Age segregated social patterns ensure that contradictory information from human development research about unused human capacity in the earliest and latest years of life do not penetrate to policymaking circles. What began as a humanitarian concern for the weak has resulted in a depersonalizing and devaluing of individual capacity through a doctrine of concern that has converted people from subjects to objects of social concern.*

Children can feel a sense of powerlessness when they are not party to decisions that affect them and this may have serious repercussions throughout their lives. It is reported that adults who find it difficult to make relationships often reveal that they were not involved in even the smallest decisions as children and the resultant self-doubt has left them unable to make choices for themselves (Dallos, in John, 1996). Decision-making has implications for building resilience – the way in which a situation is dealt with, the impact of the situation and the degree to which the child is involved, can have lifelong implications (Daniel *et al.*, 1999). The need to practise and become competent in decision-making is crucial to emotional well-being and the development of integrated persons (Clarke and Clarke, 2003). Research into school councils (John, 2003), children experiencing divorce (Neale, 2002) and children being involved in decisions about their health (Thurston and Church, 2001) all point to children's ability to discuss objectively and appropriately the important decisions that have to be made about their environment and their lives.

There is a tendency for professionals to believe that children are dependent on their parents and that parents will act as responsible advocates for them. This may not always be the case – the child abuse enquiries mentioned above show how children can get lost in adult agendas and are no longer seen as separate beings with their own story to tell. In the Climbie Report (Department of Health, 2003), Lord Laming observed how little time was spent on asking Victoria what her views were. She was always interviewed in the presence of her aunt who, it transpired, was one of the perpetrators of her abuse (DfES, 2003). The argument is often made that children cannot be involved in discussions as they are not fully cognizant of all the facts. But how often do adults have all the necessary information? People make decisions, plan and act according to their beliefs at the time. We would argue that children should have the same opportunity. When children are involved in working together, the high degree of competence and the richness of decision-making and action can be astounding (John, 2003).

Sometimes our underlying attitudes towards children prevent us from viewing them as valued members of the community and therefore as colleagues. It may be an anxiety about relinquishing power and control; it may be about pressure of time, or poor skills or limited resources. Some might argue that we need to address the 'child' in ourselves before we can see children as co-constructors of our world (see Chapter 2, 'Becoming a person').

A recent piece of work by the Blueprint Project demonstrated the very real ability of children to work with adults to create a policy document about how children experience the care system. The subsequent launch of the report (February 2004) saw young people interviewing politicians and civil servants raising important questions about the work being done by adults for children.

Viewing children as colleagues and co-constructors of our world has repercussions for the way we work together as adults, the way we shape our work and the way we maintain relationships with one another.

Working and communicating together

Within the early years context, people work together in a variety of situations, teams and frameworks: multiagency projects; care management teams and strategic decision-making groups (Atkinson *et al.*, 2002). At the heart of the Children Bill (2004) is a desire to establish new forms of multidisciplinary work to improve services to those families identified as needing intervention and assistance. However, there is evidence that professionals are defending their specialisms for fear of becoming deskilled and jockeying for their own power bases (in *Community Care*, April 2004). As a consequence, people are failing to see the potential available for collaborative work where all positions and perspectives are valued.

Jenny Lindon (2000) suggests there are risks involved in being open and honest with each other. She identifies different forms of communication and the risks associated with them. She points out that ritual and commonplace communications (such as about the weather or holidays) are relatively risk-free and these are the ones we engage in most frequently. On the other hand, thoughts and opinions are fairly high-risk because we worry about what people will think of us. Peak intimate experiences are full of risk and rarely engaged in except with people we trust. From this we would argue that it is important to allow time to develop relationships and to build trust before we can expect partnerships to be close enough to encourage a free and open exchange of conversation and information (see Chapter 3, 'Developing communication').

Weisenger (1998, cited in Sharp, 2001, p.93) suggests ways in which individuals can work at facilitating effective communication at an emotionally literate level.

- *be inclusive;*

- *discourage dominance;*

- *be supportive;*

- *keep emotional tenor at a manageable level;*

- *invite disagreement;*

- *be aware of how each member participates and responds.*

McQuail and Windahl (1981) suggest that context and motivation are extremely important and that 'co-communicators' not only have to interpret what is being communicated, but also have to work out the motivations and personal agendas that form the subtext. At the same time, they must begin to construct a reply that will in turn be similarly translated and interpreted.

So we can begin to see that underpinning the idea of working together is a network of connections from the emotional level of individuals through to the culture of an institution. In early years childcare and education, it is important to be aware of how these private agendas of personal or organisational power and supremacy can take hold.

Fostering good communication

Each participant and each organisation involved in the care of a particular child needs to work towards an understanding of the others' points of view, to respect and value the differences and the similarities between those views, and to work with the assumption that everyone is working together for the good of the child and their family. Good communicators express their meaning in all sorts of ways – through body language, through 'paralanguage' (the way we say things and the way we listen), through appropriate choice of vocabulary, through the medium they choose to communicate in and by using their own experience to encourage and promote dialogue.

Successive child abuse inquiries report a failure among agencies to communicate effectively. Most recently, the Laming Report into the death of Victoria Climbie (Department of Health, 2003) highlighted how differing jargon, cultures and motivations prevented agencies from working together in meaningful ways. Leiba (2003) talks about the 'codification of communication' between professionals, where conditions and significances in a professional code can exclude others. This 'gang membership' creates barriers and confusions and harks back to the difficulties that Nias *et al.* (1989) talk about when looking at organisational culture. New members need to understand the codes and what they imply before they can participate effectively. Brechin (2000) writes about the challenge of co-ordination in communication, the need to identify points of contact, to negotiate meanings and assumptions, constraints and demands – effective communicators are open to other people's assumptions as well as their own.

One of the authors can still remember the first multiagency meeting she attended and her feeling of inadequacy as she struggled to get to grips with someone else's acronyms.

Interagency working

Links between agencies and participants need to be developed in such a way that everyone is valued and respected – this includes children and their families. We cannot assume that all stakeholders share the same view; therefore respect for all points of view is paramount (Fitzgerald, 2004).

One other point needs to be made here, and that is about consistency. We would advocate that as far as possible there is a need within multidisciplinary work at all levels for members of each team to work alongside familiar people from other teams. Consistency of personnel is vital to allow trust and respect to build and to nurture shared understandings, developing a kind of multidisciplinary attachment! This can be very difficult and needs careful management: sometimes a range of team members need to know about the work being undertaken so that they can be part of a pool of familiar faces. The new Children's Trusts will need to work towards this goal and take seriously the need for participants to know and trust each other fully.

Conclusion

Increasingly, vocational training (for doctors, nurses, social workers and teachers) is concerned with effective communication and working in partnership in all its different forms. In the future, all these professionals will be expected to liaise closely with one another for the benefit of the children in their care. Interagency team building and team building within early years settings all depend on a willingness to listen and a willingness to change. We would like to suggest some key factors that need to be taken into consideration:

- Challenging the models of working together that do not enhance communication between disciplines (Glendinning *et al.*, 2002).
- Raising the quality of the relationship between the team members (Ellis and Fisher, 1994); see also Chapter 3, 'Developing communication'.
- Strengthening the emotional content of relationships and interactions, both inside and outside the working environment.
- Improving management support for good communication through training.
- Increasing opportunities to influence and challenge decision-making processes.
- Working to break down stereotypes and power struggles among professions.
- Improving knowledge and understanding of communication theory, relationship theory and relevant skills (Ellis and Fisher, 1994).

- Encouraging professionals to reflect on their own practice and to become self-aware (Gould and Taylor, 1996); see also Chapter 13, 'In praise of reflective practice'.

- Raising motivation and fostering attitudes needed to work in true partnership.

- Developing professionalism, including conscientiousness and integrity.

As practitioners working with young children and their families, we need to challenge ourselves, our assumptions and our ways of working if we are to achieve effective working relationships. Most importantly, we need to address how we interact and communicate with others. We need to promote the importance of working together and to improve our ability to do so. Some of us may need to reconceptualise the way we regard young children. We need to be aware of how we renegotiate the roles and relationships we have with existing partners and how we integrate new ones. Most importantly of all, we need to develop trust between all who are working together for young children.

ACTIVITY 1

Over the next month, look through newspapers, journals and periodicals for coverage on health, education, police and welfare issues. Identify the following:

- *political bias;*
- *examples of good and bad practice;*
- *involvement of family and child in decision-making;*
- *quality of the working relationship between agencies;*
- *any communication issues highlighted.*

From this, begin to develop your own idea of what constitutes an effective early years practitioner and how government policy helps or hinders.

ACTIVITY 2

Compile a portfolio of your own experiences of the following:

- *communication;*
- *teamwork;*
- *partnership;*
- *emotional literacy.*

Examples of your own practice could come from work situations, group living, leisure activities or study experiences. What do these experiences tell you about these topics and your own skills? How have your experiences shaped your attitude towards working with others? What will you now seek to change?

ACTIVITY 3

Prepare for a presentation of information and a meaningful discussion with colleagues by finding out the following:

- *The history of a chosen profession; when were they first created, developed. What training did they initially have, if any and what historical developments are helpful to understand their identity and nature? Are there any key people who have pioneered the service creation or development?*
- *What laws underpin the expectations placed on this group of professionals?*
- *The current situation with this profession in terms of training, numbers, work details, ideologies.*
- *Are there any professional bodies to support, monitor or police the actions of their members?*
- *What role does this profession have in helping care for young children and their families? How is this role manifested?*
- *What responsibilities does this profession have? Who do they report to? Are there any specific duties they have to perform?*
- *What developments are in the pipeline for this profession?*
- *Any other information that you feel it would be useful for the group to have.*

Part 5

Researching Practice: Developing a Critical Mindset

13 In praise of reflective practice

Caroline Leeson

Introduction

An early years practitioner is helping children get changed for a gym session in the hall. She helps them get out of their everyday clothes, helping with zips and buttons, and into shorts, t-shirts and plimsolls. Afterwards, a colleague points out that she has helped the boys far more than the girls and that she actively encouraged the girls to manage themselves. Both practitioners pause to think about what that means, why it might be, what had been in her mind, what messages she was giving to the children and whether they had noticed. They decide to observe their own behaviour and that of other colleagues over the next few days and try to understand what was going on and what the implications were.

The case for reflective practice

> *Tell me and I will forget, show me and I may remember. Involve me and I will understand.*
> (Confucius, 450 BC in Pickles, 2004)

Reflective practice, or the importance of thinking over one's actions past and present and identifying the lessons learnt for future action, should be a crucial aspect of professional work and lifelong learning. The practitioners in the above example will learn far more about their behaviour, their underlying values and their impact on children from reflecting on their own practice than from anything they read in a book. This will then help them in future practice to be more confident, more responsive and ultimately more creative in their work, leading in turn to a positive influence on the world around them. Donald Schon (1983) suggests that one's ability to reflect on action and thereby engage in a personal journey of lifelong learning is a defining characteristic of professional practice. Schon argues that education is not like filling a glass and then expecting knowledge to simply spill over into practice. Rather, it is about the creation of opportunities to link theory to practice, to develop understanding about actions, assessing the impact of those actions, and it is about developing enhanced knowledge and skills that can be taken forward to bear on new situations. Increasingly, however, we appear to see a diminishing emphasis on these skills in the workplace. Instead we have policies and codes of practice which define the parameters of fact-based, routine responses to situations. Many writers warn that these are leading practitioners to experience greater anxiety and uncertainty (Ruch, 2002) and providing a poorer experience for the families with whom they are working (Saltiel, 2003).

This chapter seeks to explore the different models offered by theorists and to discuss how reflective skills may be taught, encouraged, achieved and maintained and to show why reflective practice should be seen as an integral part of developing competent professionals in early years care and education. In attempting to make sense of the topic for the reader, I have asked myself a series of questions. What is reflective practice? Why should we engage in it? How do we actually do it? Who can help with the process? What are the obstacles and opportunities that it offers us? I offer the reader an account of my own voyage around these issues and hope to persuade many of you to become reflective practitioners yourselves.

What is reflective practice?

Reflective practice is taking the opportunity to think about the work that we are doing, either as we are doing it or after we have done it, attempting to draw the lessons we can learn from it in terms of how that work has impacted upon us and others and how it made or makes us feel about ourselves.

Schon (1983) distinguishes between reflection *in* action, reflecting while doing something; and reflection *on* action, reflecting following the action. These critical skills of reflection help to develop insight and understanding, especially in those professionals such as social workers, teachers and healthcare workers who have a substantial impact upon the lives of others. I would suggest that, unless we engage in this process, the work we do has the potential to be ill informed and possibly dangerous because we may perpetuate practice that is no longer relevant, simply because that is the way it has always been done and no one has questioned whether it is still appropriate.

A scenario comes to mind of a nursery which offered the children Duplo bricks that had been disinfected in boiling water. The bricks had lost their shape and would not click together anymore. The fact that the bricks were useless escaped attention for several years and practitioners continued to be surprised that the children did not play with them. A practitioner who took time to notice what was going on around them and thought about the implications would have seen and questioned the practice and maybe used an alternative way of ensuring the bricks were clean!

Similarly, within my own field of child protection, a past colleague showed herself to be unduly keen to remove a child from an abusive household before she had fully engaged with the parent, establishing what might be done to remedy the situation. When encouraged to reflect on her actions, it became apparent that her own abusive background had allowed her to over-identify with the child and she failed to see the many positive signs that suggested that the family would benefit from active help rather than removal of the child. Very often, decisions made to remove a child from a dangerous situation reflect an underlying corporate anxiety about failing to protect rather than anything to do with the best interests of the child. A reflective practitioner can begin to attempt to make these decisions openly and honestly, questioning the influence of personal prejudice, social policy or current trends and examining the issue more objectively and more sensitively.

> *The challenge is the integration of theoretical knowledge with practical experience so that practice is ethically grounded and skilled enough to respond to the complex demands which society places upon them.*
>
> (Dempsey *et al.*, 2001, p.632)

This integration of knowledge and practice, using the theories available to us, is a crucial aspect of reflective practice. Research has shown (Eraut, 1994; Saltiel, 2003; Ruch, 2002) that practitioners do not always see theory as related to real experience. They feel that it may be interesting, but not necessarily applicable to the situations that they work in and they therefore dismiss it as remote and unusable.

Schon (1983) talks about 'technical rationality', where knowledge is divorced from experience, where values underpinning practice are never questioned or may not even be identified, leaving the practitioner unaware of how the context they work in, both locally and nationally, may liberate or constrain the decisions and actions they take.

Frequently the way reflective skills are taught fails to integrate the meaning of the experience with personal feelings and intuition, leaving people feeling that all they have engaged in is a pointless process of 'navel gazing'. Reflective practice should actually promote the use of theory and a greater understanding of the impact of one's work. Schon would argue that reflection enables one to develop one's own theory that then needs to be articulated and explored with others in order to become mutual understanding.

Reflection is not just thinking about what you do. Ghaye and Ghaye (1998, p.3) define it as 'practice with principle': 'Being professionally self critical without being destructive and overly negative'. It is not about denigrating our actions and doubting our practice, which can be personally damaging. Rather it should be a positive experience which enables practitioners to 'feel' their work, in contrast to the current, insistent belief that we should concentrate on and value hard facts rather than soft intuition. Reflective practice works with the rational and the emotional as it strives to move us to a place of shared understanding, acknowledging that every experience and every relationship is unique and therefore worthy of reflection.

Why should we engage in reflective practice?

When considering why we should engage in reflective practice, we need to establish what it means to be professional, what it means to make professional decisions and how that will be improved or developed by becoming reflective. Within the early years field, a professional is, increasingly, seen as someone in a position of power or authority over others. This authority is embedded in the way they think, make decisions and act upon those decisions in their work with children and their families. Practitioners engaged in working with young children and their families have a powerful impact on the lives of those they care for and this needs to be recognised. Practitioners' personal attributes, attitudes and methods of engaging will help to inform the people they work with about their own self-worth and how they in their turn could engage with others. In other words, if children and their parents/carers are treated as unique and valued individuals, they will be encouraged to develop strong resilience and self-esteem, which will have a powerful impact on their lives and the lives of those they come into contact with.

By virtue of their role, practitioners are often seen as experts in childcare and education and therefore a valuable source of knowledge and information on how to bring up children and how to behave in relation to them (Devereux and Miller, 2003). In education, the manner in which children are taught will affect their eventual educational outcome, the strength of their self-esteem and their ongoing engagement with the world around them. In the field of early years, practitioners are similarly powerful and have an increasing responsibility to maximise the potential of the children in their care (Department for Education and Skills, 2003). Reflective practice may help practitioners to think about the activities they provide and the quality of the interaction, learning and emotional content that they and the children have experienced (Department for Education and Employment, 2000).

Practitioners also have considerable power derived from the legislation they work under. For example, under the Children Act 1989, social workers have the power to remove children (section 44); and the right to intervene in the way family members seek to conduct themselves (section 47).

Gould and Taylor (1996) identify the following reasons for professionals to engage in reflective practice:

- to reduce uncertainty in practice;

- to enable competent transference of knowledge and skills between situations;

- to generate creative as opposed to programmed responses to the demands of the families we are working with.

In this way, they argue, we can begin to meet the requirements of our different disciplines and remain alive to possibilities in our practice.

We are also called upon to make difficult professional judgements. Eraut (1994) defined a professional judgement as 'the interpretive use of knowledge'. This 'also involves practical wisdom, a sense of purpose, appropriateness and feasibility' (Horwath and Thurlow, 2004, p.9). In order to make professional judgements, it is vital to use systematic processes of collecting information that show the steps taken to reach and later act upon the decisions made. Reflective practice is one of the ways in which this can happen.

If practitioners engage in reflective practice in this way, there are considerable benefits: a greater understanding of self and one's own motivations; an opportunity to begin to work on one's own life script and need for strokes (see Chapter 2, 'Becoming a person'); a chance to resolve past conflicts and to develop new skills, knowledge and understanding in the workplace and to begin to question why we do things the way we do.

There are also considerable benefits for the children and adults that practitioners come into contact with, because we are: 'dealing with both the cognitive and the emotional understanding of the client, valuing both as informative to the process' (Gould and Taylor, 1996, p.59).

Decisions and actions are considered creative and acknowledge the relationship and interaction with each person as a unique experience with a unique individual.

How do we do it?

In order for reflective practice to happen effectively, we need to adopt a model or structure that gives a meaning to the process and guides practitioners. There are several possible models available for developing the skills of reflective practice.

A number of writers on reflective practice identify cyclical models which proceed through stages frequently described as: having an experience, reflecting on this experience, taking learning from that reflection and using it to inform future practice (Kolb, 1984). Then the process begins again through another cycle. These stages are worked through systematically with equal importance given to each and the practitioner gradually acquires the habit of reflecting on things that go on in the workplace and learning to identify what is significant.

These early models of 'experiential learning', a term used by Kolb, have been criticised for failing to emphasise the centrality of reflection in the second stage, and Pickles (2004) argues that the steps identified do not always fit with the ways in which people think.

Seidel (1996, in Dempsey *et al.*, 2001) has similar stages defined as *looking backwards, looking inwards, looking outwards and looking forwards*. This model promotes deeper introspection and thought and has been used to great effect on social work training courses (Dempsey, *et al.*, 2001), improving the confidence and skills of many practitioners.

For me, the model that offers the greatest potential is that developed by Ghaye and Ghaye (1998) which recommends opportunities for reflection at different levels to help practitioners to improve and deepen their knowledge, skills and understanding as they become more reflective. Their model sees reflection, not as a closed circle, but as a spiral of action, thought and understanding which allows practitioners to revisit the different steps and develop ideas as they progress from one cycle to another. Ghaye and Ghaye emphasise both the individual and the organisational context of reflection, identifying how the workplace or society in which a practitioner operates affects their actions and values and has the potential to exert power and influence over them. The underlying premise of this model is that, at all times, practice is value-laden and that effective, reflective practitioners need to make clear links between their own values and practice, and the values and practice of the organisation they work for. For instance, in the example at the start of the chapter, the practitioner may have had an unconscious set of values about the respective positions of men and women in society.

Ghaye and Ghaye suggest various stages of reflection:

- *descriptive – giving an account of the incident under scrutiny;*
- *perceptive – making links between the description and our own feelings;*
- *receptive – allowing oneself to be open to different perspectives on the incident described;*
- *interactive – creating links between learning and any future action;*
- *critical – questioning accepted practice in a creative and constructive manner, developing new theories and ways of working for oneself and others.*

Reflection, then, requires hard, systematic thinking (and soft, intuitive insight), leading to a plan of action based on a critical evaluation of all the available evidence.

How do we actually do this in practice?

We have already seen the difficulties of practitioners not always appreciating the signifi-cance of the activity and how this leads to a failure to create a culture of reflection in and on action. I have identified a potentially useful model, but how do we actually get people to do it?

First of all we need to create the right conditions, the atmosphere, an ethos in which reflective practice can flourish. It requires a culture of trust, of working together, before people feel safe about opening up and examining their practice. It requires a culture that recognises the intrinsic value of each individual and which promotes an ethos where everyone believes they have something worthwhile to say.

Ruch (2003) investigated what made a successful reflective workplace:

> *The potential for reflective practice is greater in work contexts which afford containing, reflective spaces in which practitioners have the opportunity to think, feel and talk about their work. Team structures and practices and team managers are identified as pivotal in determining the existence and effectiveness of these reflective, containing spaces.*

So time, space and the value placed on the activity are all important. Secondly, we also need to think about the practical strategies available to us. Reflective journals are a popu-lar choice, where practitioners are encouraged to write down the general and particular experiences they have had throughout their day, reflecting on their emotional and intellec-tual impact (Gould and Taylor, 1996). Another strategy is to write things down, think about actions for oneself and then share those thoughts and analyses with others both on paper and verbally, offering one's experience to an individual or a group to be unpacked and investigated (Stefani *et al.*, 2000; Dempsey *et al.*, 2001; Boud *et al.*, 1985; Schon, 1983). A further strategy is storytelling, where people narrate a story of their experience and others comment on it (McDrury and Alterio, 2000). McDrury and Alterio identify eight different storytelling methods and feel that an informal setting where there is only one lis-tener and the story is spontaneous, i.e. not prepared and probably appearing as if out of nowhere, offers the most learning and a sense of catharsis for the narrator. A student recently came for tutorial and as we talked she began to relate an experience the previous day where she had been involved with a child playing with a marble run. Other children had come to join in, moving in and out of the action, demanding different things of them-selves, the toy and the student. As the student talked, her face began to light up as she identified where she had taken a back seat, where she had seen genuine co-operation between the children and where they had solved a problem on their own and taught her something. By the end of the tutorial, I had a student before me who was filled with awe at what she had learned from a seemingly trivial encounter and excitement at what she could now understand about her role in children's lives.

> *One listener can provide undivided attention to the story and is more likely to focus on the affective domain. This pathway may also provide greater freedom for the teller to express unedited ideas, concerns and feelings.*
>
> (McDrury and Alterio, 2000, p.66)

Another strategy is 'critical incident analysis' (Chambers *et al.*, 2003). This is where people work on their own, reflecting on a specific event, thinking about what has happened and how they feel about it, then sharing this with others to deepen their own understanding through discussion.

A further strategy involves making 'statements of relevance' where people are encouraged to think about any learning event they have participated in and write down not only what they have learned, but also how they may use that learning in the future (Bourner *et al.*, 2002). This is then shared with others for deeper learning and understanding to take place. Statements of relevance are not simply descriptions and evaluations of the learning event, they are accounts investigating feelings, current knowledge and procedures, which are similar to the critical reflective stage of Ghaye and Ghaye's model. A central element running through all these strategies is the need for communication or discourse, a 'reflective conversation' (Schon, 1983; Kolb, 1984) to make explicit what had previously been implicit.

Who can help?

We can reflect alone, we can have an inner discussion setting out the dilemma and considering alternative courses of action, but it is sometimes better to talk things over with colleagues. It may be that we can only reflect so far on our own: we need other, like-minded people to give us the opportunity to co-reflect, to think about what we are looking at, to challenge our assumptions and prejudices and to look at the things we are avoiding because they tell us things about ourselves we would rather not face. Reflective practice is, potentially, a risky business and some people may be reluctant to engage – not everyone is prepared to challenge himself or herself, to demand answers from themselves or to look critically at parts of themselves that they take for granted. Dewey (1933, p.151) wrote:

> *One can think reflectively only when one is willing to endure suspense and to undergo the trouble of searching. To many persons, both suspense of judgement and intellectual search are disagreeable, they want them to be ended as soon as possible. They cultivate an over positive and dogmatic habit of mind, or feel, perhaps, that a condition of doubt will be regarded as evidence of mental inferiority. We must be willing to sustain and protract that state of doubt which is the stimulus to thorough enquiry.*

Ruch (2002) talks about a state of confusion and anxiety that often prevents practitioners from taking these risky steps in analysis and reflection. She cites Papell (1996):

> *Social work learners must perceive the human situation which they confront in their practice and recognise that their perceptions are filtered through their own thinking and knowing processes, through their own emotions and feeling processes and through the way they themselves integrate and regulate their own doing and behaving. Knowing the self is more than knowing how one feels. It is knowing how one thinks and acts.*

> (in Ruch, 2002, p.203)

This raises considerable anxiety around the amount of personal exposure that may be required. Lindon (2000) explores how much personal risk is attached to different levels of communication and sees personal, peak experiences as the most risky of all. There is a danger that people will be less than honest if they perceive a risk they are not prepared to take, that there are considerable demands placed on them to cope with uncertainty, to deal with grey areas.

Gould and Taylor (1996) argue that those moments are the best opportunities for reflection, giving chances to develop self-knowledge as well as to reconsider decision-making, interventions and actions taken.

A supervisor or mentor who will promote and encourage this risk-taking can also be helpful. Hobbs (1992) suggests that an effective mentor:

- is able to give away control;

- can negotiate structure;

- can allow mistakes;

- is able to cope with becoming redundant as the group develop their own way of working.

Any techniques used in the classroom to assist the learning of reflective practice need to be directed at the constructions of the students rather than those in the tutor's head or agenda (Boud et al., 1985). This is a challenge to the best of us. Who can resist evangelising about their own viewpoint, so that students and practitioners can develop their own theory and question that of their supervisor or mentor? It is hard to permit mistakes and allow the agenda to apparently slip away out of your control. Schon (1983) feels that, nevertheless, this is what must happen in a learning community of reflective practitioners; the balance of power must shift away from the teacher (or employer) towards the practitioners themselves, as they pursue meaning and challenge accepted practice and thought. He talks about a 'practicum', a group-learning environment where high levels of anxiety are acknowledged, allowed and supported:

> *A practicum is a setting designed for the task of learning practice. In a context, which approximates a practice world, students learn by doing, although their doing falls short of real world work ... it is a virtual world relatively free of the pressures, distractions and risks of the real one, to which, nevertheless, it refers. It stands in an intermediary space between the practice world, the 'lay' world of ordinary life and the esoteric world of the academy.*
>
> (Schon, 1983, p.37, cited in Dempsey et al., 2001, p.634)

This may be easy to establish in a university or college, but what about the workplace? A colleague or a group of colleagues must be identified to assist with reflective practice. Knight (in Boud et al., 1985) talks about people being paired together and forming a 'buddy' system to talk about their ongoing practice.

Smith and Halton (1993, in Gould and Taylor, 1996) talk about the use of a critical friend in much the same way, encouraging the reflector to look beyond the superficial and think about their feelings and deeper learning. Their research showed that far more reflection occurred through the use of a critical friend than through any other medium, including interaction with other members of staff.

> *Meaningful, reflective conversations can sustain and nourish us. They can raise individual and collective consciousness. Above all else they involve a discussion of values. This is at the heart of the improvement process.*
>
> (Ghaye and Ghaye, 1998, p.122)

What are the obstacles?

But there are problems and obstacles to overcome before this can happen, not least of which is the current climate of anxiety about the dangers of taking risks, the risks inherent in responding to needs creatively in a culture that sees expertise as the ability to assess a situation quickly and to plan and implement appropriate action almost instantaneously (Fook, 1997; Saltiel, 2003). In social work, for example, research by Ruch (2003) identifies: 'A steady increase in risk averse bureaucratic responses to the uncertainty, ambiguity and risk inherent in childcare social work'.

There is a danger of failing to look in depth and work on issues, within our practice and ourselves, and move forward. Beck (1996) argues that we need to ensure that our reflective practice means 'critical appraisal and change' as opposed to reflexivity, which he feels allows practitioners to deny that which challenges the ways in which we normally perceive the world, our workplace norms and culture (Scourfield and Welsh, 2003, p.403).

There is also the problem that reflective practice is not taken seriously enough. Gould and Taylor (1996, p.74) suggest that there is: 'A real danger of reflective learning becoming a populist bandwagon which legitimates the abandonment of academic rigour'.

Reflection may be seen as navel-gazing and practitioners need to provide clear arguments to justify it and to ensure that it is given the priority it deserves. Students and tutors, practitioners and managers, need to see reflective practice as an opportunity to put academic theory into a real context for developing learning, rather than as a soft option that encourages people to talk about their work in unstructured, incoherent ways. This is no easy task in a world that seems to value convergent knowledge (fact gathering) as opposed to divergent knowledge that is more creative and experiential, seeing this latter as difficult to judge in terms of quality and relevance. We need to ask whether tutors and managers can do what Hobbs requires of them as identified above, to let go and facilitate the development of the individual rather than to constrain them within a dogmatic set of procedures.

Stefani *et al.* (2000), in their work on college cultures, identify the obstacles to reflective practice where students are encouraged to get good marks for what amounts to little more than rote learning rather than for developing their own learning goals, taking risks, failing at certain tasks and relearning from their own errors. We need to look carefully at all our procedures and routines to ensure we promote rather than discourage the practices we value.

What opportunities does reflective practice offer us?

I feel there are many opportunities that will render the obstacles worth overcoming. There is the rich quality that deep learning adds to our practice (Boud *et al.*, 1985), offering us the opportunity to develop more creative answers to difficulties (Gould and Taylor, 1986), enhancing our problem-solving skills and moving into a world that recognises the needs of individuals and devises individual solutions to meet them.

> *Reflective learning only has value if its effect is to deepen the complexity of practice; rather than rejecting the sphere of the intellect, the reflective paradigm actually requires an engagement with some of the particularly difficult debates within social theory.*
>
> (Gould and Taylor, 1986, p.74)

Accomplished reflectors can begin to challenge political and philosophical aspects of procedures and policies (Gould and Taylor, 1986) and attempt to shape future policy and practice.

As reflectors, we are also offered an opportunity to know ourselves, study our motivations, needs, hopes and aspirations, leading us to explore the deeper depths of our innermost being and bring it into the light for systematic observation and thought, allowing us to become rounded individuals, thoughtful, engaged practitioners and true advocates for those with whom we work.

There is the opportunity to widen our scope: current literature and research on involving children (Lancaster and Broadbent, 2003; Broadhead, 2004) has begun a dialogue on the value of engaging children in reflecting on their own experiences and actions, helping them, their families and the practitioners around them to develop a unique insight into their world – a skill that will be invaluable throughout their lives. As we begin to take seriously the rights of young children, so should we value their ability to reflect.

The current political focus on a holistic definition of childhood offers us the chance to develop early years communities where practitioners from different disciplines can come together and reflect on the work they do, both separately and together, constructing a widely applicable theory of good practice that all can relate to. Government departments have sought to encourage and promote the development of reflective skills in practice (Department for Education and Employment, 2000; SCIE, 2003). We should accept this invitation and take it forward.

ACTIVITY 1

Think of a recent experience in your placement/workplace that caught your interest. Describe the situation as fully as you can and then work through the other steps as outlined by Ghaye and Ghaye: perceptive, receptive, interactive and critical. Share your thoughts with a friend or colleague and get them to question your initial responses. In this way try to deepen your understanding of the original situation. Then ask yourself why were you originally interested in it – what does that say about you and your own learning characteristics? How might all of this introspection and examination affect your future practice? How else might you begin to collect evidence to refine the personal theory you are beginning to develop?

ACTIVITY 2

Following your next learning experience, either in the classroom or the workplace, attempt to make a statement of relevance as described by Bourner et al. (2002). You will need to write approximately 500–1000 words looking at the relationship between theory and practice, demonstrating a good understanding of the main ideas and showing your own feelings regarding relevance to you and your practice or to the work situation in general, i.e. that what you have learned is important for all teachers. Do not simply describe or evaluate the learning. Share with someone else who experienced the same workshop/event and see what he or she feels.

14 Research projects in early childhood studies: students' active explorations of childrens' worlds

Jenny Willan

Introduction

Early childhood practitioners are frequently required to make important professional judgements on behalf of the children in their care. The judgements may be about a particular child's needs, or a course of action in the child's best interests, or about the best provision for children in a setting. Good professional judgements rely in large part on the systematic collection and recording of information and the thoughtful sifting of evidence from wider reading. This chapter sets out to introduce you to the process of research which you will need both as a student and as a professional practitioner in your chosen field within early childhood.

What do we mean by research?

The word 'research' has a daunting ring about it. It conjures up images of white-coated scientists and learned professors earnestly discussing esoteric topics in impenetrable language. But we are all researchers. We all gather information and make observations and build theories as part of our day-to-day interactions in our jobs, in our families and in our social lives. It is a necessary part of living. It is part of a process of constructing the world view that helps us to operate on a daily basis.

The distinction between everyday research and the research we need in our professional lives is one of degree. For instance, we might note that a child in our care is hostile with his peers and destructive of his environment. If we know him well, we may know that there has been a recent bereavement in the family and we would take this into account in assessing how best to interact with him. But if the behaviour was a complete puzzle, we might want to investigate further to see what might be causing it. We might suspect bullying perhaps, or disaffection with school, or a parental attachment problem, or abuse, or perhaps a hearing impairment or a learning disability that is making him frustrated and confused. In a situation like this, we would need to be more systematic in our approach in order to get at the root cause of the difficulty. We would need to ask questions, make observations and gather evidence to build a picture that best accounted for his behaviour. This is the kind of research this chapter is concerned with.

Research approaches and perspectives

There is no set recipe covering the techniques and procedures of research. There are many ways of investigating a topic and the type of research you choose to do will depend on the topic you want to pursue. Research seeks to throw light on an issue, sometimes to improve practice, sometimes to clarify thought. Early childhood research seeks for evidence to inform understanding and practice with young children. According to Stenhouse (1975, p.142), research is 'systematic inquiry made public'. However, although all research is systematic, the degree to which it is made public will vary. Children engaged in discovering something new are researchers – they are systematic in their approach but they may only make their findings public in the sense of sharing their discoveries with a parent or another child. Students engaged in research projects may limit their audience to colleagues or tutors. Practitioners may produce research but only distribute it among the people or children in their workplace.

Research is sometimes described as 'conceptual' or 'empirical' but most research is a mixture of both. Broadly, *conceptual* researchers consider a puzzling phenomenon and try to *think* their way to a solution, perhaps involving others in a dialogue to test out the strength of their explanations. Socrates employed this method to analyse the great questions of his day and Rousseau used the method in building his theory of education in his book *Emile*. Purely conceptual research depends on the experience, imagination and intellectual vigour of a single person or a small group of people who meet to exchange ideas.

Empirical researchers operate differently. They collect evidence and then develop it into a theory. Empirical researchers may *start* with a concept, an idea, but they base their theories and recommendations on an analysis of real-world data. But just like conceptual researchers, they need to collaborate and talk things over with others to refute or confirm the reliability of their theories. Perhaps the most familiar empirical researcher in early childhood studies is Piaget. His explanations of the way in which young children actively construct their world according to their stage of maturation has had a lasting impact on our understanding of how children learn (Gardner *et al.*, 1996). Over the past half century, his studies have been replicated (repeated) and sometimes disputed by other empirical researchers who have gathered further evidence to support or contest his earlier explanations. This is part of the empirical process: slowly and gradually we build up more and more evidence to refine and strengthen our understanding of what is going on around us. The process continues until the weight of evidence pushes us into a new way of thinking or a 'paradigm shift' (Kuhn, 1970).

Many research projects in early childhood are empirical. The empirical approach to research is to gather evidence in a systematic way. This evidence or data is used to build up a model (or picture) of what researchers and researched understand about the topic under investigation. Empirical researchers try to take account of their own 'perspective' – the beliefs and assumptions that underpin the way they set about looking for evidence. For example, in attempting to explain the hostile and destructive child mentioned earlier, a psychologist, a medical practitioner, a teacher or a social worker would all approach their explanation or interpretation according to their particular professional theories and values. By comparing the evidence each systematically gathered, we might be able to decide if the child was bullied, suffering an attachment dysfunction, hearing impaired, learning disabled or abused, or a combination of any of these. If the tests for evidence were applied by other professional individuals, the interpretation would be similar. Of course, some research seeks to overthrow a shared interpretation, perhaps to bring about a change in thinking or practice, and here the researcher needs to marshall evidence in the same systematic way to counter prevailing points of view.

This brief introduction shows how empirical research combines theory and practice in order to improve understanding. The more evidence we gather, the more reflective we are, the more we discuss our theories with our colleagues, the better we can serve the children in our care. Research is a process which is never finished; it is always open to modification through reflection and discussion with others – in early childhood work, a willingness to learn through collaboration with children and colleagues can help to clarify our growing understanding of issues. Research is a state of mind, a way of staying curious about the world and the people in it – it is not over once the report is written.

So how do we go about doing a research project?

Finding a topic

The first step is to identify a problem, a puzzle, a conundrum, something that sits uneasily in your understanding. For instance, you may have a feeling of vague anxiety about all the government money being pumped into early years when at your own pre-school you see vast amounts of effort expended on jumble sales to raise a few pounds for a new climbing frame. Or you might have a worry about your own child who has not yet reached a particular developmental milestone – late talking perhaps, or mastery of the skill of riding a bicycle, or successfully making friends. It may be the rise of a new orthodoxy that bothers you – increased educational testing for young children, the removal of children from families where abuse is suspected, the adoption of 'no cuddling' policies in childcare settings for fear of litigation under child protection laws, the suitability of inclusion programmes for young children with special needs. Wherever there is disquiet, there is an issue for research.

Reading around the topic

Once you have identified an area that you would like to investigate, the next step is to find out what other people have said about it. You might start by talking to friends and colleagues, watching TV programmes, listening to radio coverage, reading newspapers and magazines. Or you might go straight to the internet or the library bookshelves and journals. You will gradually build a portfolio of ideas and opinions and information, a list of sources, a list of names and organisations that have something to say on the topic. You will know who tends to take which position in a debate, who the key thinkers and researchers are, who are the mavericks and iconoclasts. Through your reading and discussion you will gradually refine your own viewpoint until you have reached the stage where you can formulate a research question.

Coming up with the research question

This is the point at which you ask yourself what exactly it is that you wa
What is the question you want to investigate? Is the question manageable
lect evidence about it? Can you find out enough in the time available? D
contacts, the money, a suitable group or individual that could help answer

Does the question lend itself to empirical study? Can you collect data on it in a live setting? Are you being realistic about your limitations? For instance, if you live in a rural
village in England, it would be very difficult to design an empirical study to evaluate the
relative merits of Sure Start, Reggio Emilia and Te Whariki. However, if you were an Italian
speaker with contacts in New Zealand, you might manage, via email and internet, to
gather teachers' views of childhood or education from practitioners in each system that
you could then compare with local teachers' views. Be as ambitious as you like but be
aware that you need to find a match between your skills and your aspirations, your
resources and the time available.

Reaching your target group

Opportunity might be the constraining factor in choosing your target group for a small-
scale research project. Ask yourself which group of people will provide you with the most
useful information. Can you access them easily? Do you need to write a letter of introduction requesting permission from someone in authority to approach the group? Can you
find a mutually convenient date to meet? If you are going to include children in your data
gathering, do you need to know term and holiday dates?

Risk assessment and health and safety issues

Now do a quick mental risk assessment. If you embark on this investigation, does it carry
any risks or threats to your proposed target group, the subjects of your study? Will you be
putting yourself at any personal risk? Are there any issues such as being alone with a participant? What about health and safety? Does the investigation leave you open to
litigation? For example, would you need special insurance cover you if you wanted to conduct research into children's ability to manage themselves in a challenging environment?
Once you have satisfied yourself that you have covered all the wider risks, you can begin
to think about the detail.

Ethics

As your research questions crystallise and you identify the people you want to study, you
will need to think about the ethical issues involved in human research. At all points you
need to act with integrity. You will already have considered this in broad terms when you
thought about a risk assessment and considered aspects of health and safety. Now and
throughout the study, you need to think about the detail – your research project should be
an ethical process at every stage. There may be issues of access to your research group,

ues of confidentiality and of your own accountability that may arise at any point during the investigation. It is your duty as a researcher to take responsibility for the well-being of the people who take part in your research – they are the collaborators in your research enterprise, not the objects of your study. You also need to remember that all participants in your research are bound by the same rules of confidentiality as you are.

There are published guidelines spelling out the issues researchers need to consider, to ensure that the subjects in a study are protected (e.g. British Psychological Society (1997) Code of conduct, ethical principles and guidelines). The following list of points should help to keep you on track. You should:

- provide a clear statement of the purpose of your research;
- obtain the informed consent of all participants;
- ensure that you are not deceiving or misleading participants;
- offer a debriefing after the study;
- allow participants to withdraw at any stage if they wish;
- guarantee confidentiality of information gathered in the course of the study;
- protect participants from physical and mental harm;
- observe without infringing privacy during your research;
- give advice to participants if results show up information that might cause harm if withheld;
- be accountable for the fairness and accuracy of your written report;
- be aware of the cultural sensitivities of the participants.

All the participants in your study should have a written copy of the ethical guidelines relating to your particular research, spelling out their rights and your guarantees, before they embark on the study. You should keep a copy for your own research report and include it as an appendix to your study.

Reviewing the literature

As you work on your research you will begin to identify specific areas of concern. As your focus becomes clearer you will need to do a systematic review of the literature relating specifically to your topic. Start with recently written articles and books and check the bibliographies for the most frequently cited articles and try to read as many of them as you can. Reading the literature is an interactive process involving both your own ideas and those of the writers you are reading. List the strands of thinking represented by the various writers you discover. Critically review the research; as you read, keep asking questions about what you are reading – is it fact, is it opinion, is it merely assertion? Monitor your own response – what do you tend to agree with? What strikes you as odd, unreasonable or challenging? As you study, talk with colleagues and tutors, debate the issues, share ideas, discuss concepts, co-operate over difficulties, refining and clarifying your understanding as you go. To keep you on track and to give you ideas about approaches to your own investigation, keep a list of points, such as:

- Is this study empirical?

- How did the researchers arrive at the research question(s)?

- Were the ethical issues of the research addressed?

- How did they investigate the questions? Can you summarise their approach?

- Why did they do it this way?

- What did the participants in the study have to do in order to provide information?

- How did the researchers justify their methods?

- How did they represent their data?

- How did they interpret what they found?

- Were there any aspects you wanted more information on or were there questions raised that you couldn't answer?

- How valid is it (i.e. did it measure what it set out to measure)?

- How reliable is it (i.e. would it yield a similar result if it was repeated under similar circumstances)?

- What perspectives (paradigm, mind set, underlying assumptions) underlie the study?

- If you were asked to investigate the same questions, would you follow the pattern of this piece of research?

- Could lessons learned from this approach inform your own investigation?

A useful way to keep track of what you are reading is to use Endnote, or a similar referencing software, which follows the conventions of the Harvard citation system and guides you through recording the information you need to build a bibliography. This is essential. There is nothing more frustrating than to copy down a relevant quote without the reference and finding, when you come to write up, that the book you used has been borrowed by someone else! If you don't want to use referencing software, use a card index or notebook. But be systematic and always write the whole reference down. Look at the references in this and other chapters for examples of what information you will need for your references – and don't forget to note the page number for direct quotations.

As you read, you may want to refine the focus of your investigation, so that it concentrates on a particular aspect of the research question you first thought of – this isn't a change of mind, it is a focusing of mind, a familiar part of the process of research. Keep talking to your colleagues, bounce ideas off them; you will find they have a lot to offer, things that might not have occurred to you.

Research approaches

Your path will largely be determined by the topic you want to investigate but it will also depend on how you see the world yourself. The kind of empirical research that has been done in the social sciences over the past century has been subject to various fashions and political influences. Sometimes scientific experiments have been in vogue, sometimes surveys of large populations, sometimes case studies with 'neutral' observers, sometimes case studies with participating observers. More recently, case studies rooted in action research (where practitioners study and develop the effectiveness of their own practice) have been popular. Currently, in early years there is a concern with children's rights issues and many case studies involve listening to children's own voices. Whatever approach you use, the key point is that you should choose an approach that is fit for your purpose. An essential point about doing empirical research is that it needs to be systematic. Any data you collect will only be as good as the research design that produced it. Whichever methods you choose for your research you must plan meticulously and keep careful records.

Look at your topic and ask how best you can gather evidence to address its concerns. Let the topic lead your design. You can gather evidence through both qualitative and quantitative approaches. The methods associated with each approach are different but most investigations involve both.

The qualitative approach

Qualitative data are produced when you gather information in a continuous form – interviews, observations, video text, reflective diaries, written accounts, focus group transcripts, tape recordings, language analyses, document analyses. Qualitative data are bulky and difficult to manage. The data can be reduced to a manageable size by summarising and generalising, by coding and clustering, by searching for underlying patterns. The validity depends on the integrity of the researcher to honestly represent the ideas that form the core of the data collected. Generally, qualitative research is illustrated by *verbatim* quotations or detailed descriptions of occurrences as they were recorded in the field and give the reader a sense of the authentic voice of the children and adults involved.

The quantitative approach

Quantitative data are produced when you reduce information – for example, from checklists, question responses, coded observations, scores, test results – to a numerical form. Reducing data into a quantitative form may not be the most appropriate for a small-scale study – there is a danger of generalising from small numbers. Numbers and statistics are notoriously slippery, especially when the sample being studied is small. Patterns can only be found in large samples – think of comparing the average height of three people against the average height of 1000 people. However, you may well be using some quantitative data, either from your literature review or in your own study. You need to look at the figures with a critical eye. In particular, you need to distinguish between correlation (a link between two or more factors) and *causation* (one factor affecting another) – many things can be linked or correlated by chance without being in any way causally related. You need to look carefully at the figures and ask what it means to say something is 'statistically significant'. For example, we might find that Key Stage 1 maths results in a school show that boys are lagging behind girls. Could it be explained by random chance or is there a strong relationship between one factor and another? Is the relationship between boys and maths, or is it between the particular cohort of boys in that class and their ability to do maths? Would the result be different with another year group?

Many small-scale empirical investigations are necessarily qualitative in nature because they are often limited to individual case studies, but they may have some quantitative elements and you will almost certainly come across quantitative data during your reading around your topic, so you need to be aware of both elements.

Collecting data

There are many ways of collecting data. You may even want to invent your own. One student observed three-year-olds spontaneously interviewing one another with a hairbrush that doubled as a microphone. The results were fascinating and prompted her into thinking of ways of using children as researchers rather than as subjects of research. The following selection of methods is not exhaustive but is intended to give you a flavour of what is possible.

You will probably choose a single case study or limited study of a few cases for comparison, rather than a larger survey for your research. These may involve a particular individual, a group, an event or perhaps an institution. Whichever you choose, you will need to design a method of collecting qualitative and/or quantitative evidence that will give you the best information to fit your purpose. Below is a selection of some common methods for collecting data – you may want to use one or several methods in your own study. For more detailed information on each method you might like to consult one of the many books devoted to research design, some of which are included in the further reading section at the end of this chapter.

Observation

You may want to do observations as part of your data gathering – for example, to study a physical setting, or a group, or an individual, or an event. You need to think about how you will position yourself to do your observation, both physically and metaphorically, depending on how involved you want to be with what you are observing. There are degrees of participation in observational approaches – at one end of the scale is the detached observer behind a two-way mirror, at the other end is the participant observer making covert notes or recordings alongside the people being studied. You may want to be somewhere in between. Generally, the tools for observation are pencil and paper, supplemented by observation schedules, tape recordings, video taping or photography (see Chapter 8, 'Observing children', for more details about observational methods). The box below shows some of the observational methods you might use.

Narrative observation – this is a naturalistic record taken *in situ*, using everyday language, picking out points that seem particularly salient at the time.

Focused observation – this is targeted on a particular child or children. It might entail making detailed notes of everything that happens in a short burst of time – perhaps five minutes. You could use this to focus on a particular child at regular intervals over time, to record changes in behaviour or development.

Timed observations – you might make notes on an activity, a particular child, or a group, timing your observations according to a predetermined interval. Or you might make detailed notes on how much time is actually spent on an activity or piece of behaviour, recording who, what, where, when and how.

Incident observation – you might choose to record the frequency with which a particular event or behaviour occurs and make detailed notes of each occurrence.

Observations are a useful source of information for many situations but they don't let the researcher get below the surface to probe the motives and understandings of the participants themselves. For this, some of the other methods are more suitable.

Questionnaires

Questionnaires are easy to send out and difficult to get back! They are also difficult to get right. If you are sure that a questionnaire will answer your purposes better than any other method, you will need to think very hard about the questions and you will need to try them out on several people before you use them for real.

There are some common pitfalls in writing questions for questionnaires. The following list might help you avoid some of them.

Ambiguity – where respondents don't know exactly what you mean. For example, 'How many places do you have at your nursery?' The nursery may have 25 places in the morning, 25 in the afternoon, and different children attending full- or part-time throughout the week. Do you want to know about full-time and part-time places or full-time equivalents? Or do you want to know how many different children attend each week?

Loose wording – where you don't know exactly what you mean. For example, 'Are the recent government policies on young children helpful?' Helpful for whom? Which policies do you mean?

Insensitivity – where you fail to take account of your respondents' possible circumstances. For example, asking of someone over 50 'Would you agree that the quality of the workforce is improving as more young people with better qualifications join?'

Double questions – where you expect people to answer both halves of the question in the same way. For example, 'Are you a regular visitor to nurseries and reception classes?' They could be a visitor to only one of these.

Hypothetical questions – where you ask an 'if' question and only elicit a meaningless answer. For example, 'If you had a child in your class suffering from separation anxiety, what would you do?' They might do any one of a hundred things, depending on the child.

Leading questions – where you imply within the question which answer you expect to get. Sometimes these questions contain assumptions – where you think you know all the possible answers but in reality you don't. For example, 'Do you agree or disagree with the proposition that teenage mothers are irresponsible?' Some may be, others may not. Sometimes they contain presumptions – where you think that there is only one way of looking at something but there are many. For example, 'How far do you think poor results in your school are due to the number of children from single parent households?' There may be no connection at all.

Overlapping categories – where you offer overlapping alternatives that can be misinterpreted. For example, 'How many children do you look after aged 0–2, aged 2–5, aged 5–8?' A child aged two and a half could go into either of the first two categories.

(adapted from Bell, 1999, pp.121–5)

There are many ways of asking questions in a questionnaire; you will have come across them many times and probably never given a thought to how they were constructed. The answers you get will depend partly on the wording you use but also on the way you frame the question. As you write your questions, try to imagine the sort of answers you might get and how you will deal with the information they elicit.

You could ask an *open-ended question*, such as 'How do you feel about the present management structure?', and then group your responses under headings. You could ask people to tick items in a list of alternatives, such as 'Which of the following apply to you?', and then summarise the number of responses in a chart or graph. You could provide a list of categories, such as 'Tick one of the following to show which best describes your job – Professional, Managerial, Skilled, Semi-skilled, Manual'. You may want respondents to indicate a rank order of preference, such as 'Put the following in order of importance ...', or to use a *rating scale* such as 'On a five-point scale, rate how useful you found the management training session on child protection'. Both rank order and rating scale questions express mathematical relationships and require careful use. As you write your questions, try them out on colleagues so that you cover as many eventualities as you can to iron out any difficulties in the design. Most importantly, ensure that your final draft questionnaire gets a thorough tryout before you use it for real. You will be surprised how differently people can read the same straightforward question!

Interviews

You may decide that questionnaires are too limiting and that an interview or series of interviews would serve your purpose better. Interviews depend for their success on achieving a rapport between interviewer and interviewee – quick-fire questions without any personal dimension are unlikely to yield any more than a postal questionnaire would. Face-to-face interviews are usually more successful at getting people talking than telephone interviews. A comfortable seat, a cup of tea, some small talk, all help to put you and your interviewee at ease – if you are doing an interview by telephone these will have to be metaphorical. But remember, interviews are time consuming to conduct and even more time consuming to analyse, so allow yourself plenty of leeway. An interview requires much the same thoughtful preparation as a questionnaire but unlike a questionnaire it has the advantage of allowing the interviewer to ask for further clarification, or to pursue an interesting line of thought, or to probe into motives and feelings. However, interviews are open to data 'corruption' through mis-hearing, misunderstanding, questioner bias, or a too cosy or too hostile relationship between interviewer and interviewee – so think carefully about every part of the process.

There are several ways to conduct your interview.

- *Structured interviews* are really verbally administered questionnaires, useful for collecting specific information which can be quickly categorised but not at all useful for probing.

- *Semi-structured interviews* are based on written questions or topics for discussion. They allow for a good deal of exploration but minimise the risk of straying away from the central purpose of the investigation. The interviewer can note down responses briefly and write up fuller notes immediately after the interview. It is useful to make a tape recording of the interview to check against your field notes. Transcribing tapes is a slow process and it may be better only to transcribe verbatim those parts of the tape that illustrate the argument most succinctly and those parts that do not fit your expectations.

- *Unstructured interviews* are not usually scripted and generally lead to wide-ranging discussion, much like a conversation. They are rather difficult to control but are very good if you want to analyse people's perspectives to try to find out what they consider to be the important aspects of the topic under discussion. They can also be useful as preparatory interviews when you are trying to get a sense of the area you want to investigate.

At the end of each question or topic during semi-structured and non-structured interviews, it is a good idea to check with your interviewee that you have correctly identified the main gist of the argument. You should keep all your field notes and tapes to check the reliability of your interpretations – as long as they are anonymous, or you have permission from participants, you can include them in your appendices.

Documentary evidence

Documents can be anything from film, radio, emails, pictures, government policies, minutes of a meeting, letters, diaries, even inscriptions on gravestones. They can cast light on present practice or through historical research show how the preoccupations of the past shaped emergent thinking in the present. Documentary evidence comes in two forms – primary and secondary. Primary sources generally relate directly and contemporaneously to the event being studied, while secondary sources are further removed. For you, doing your small-scale research project, the documents you are most likely to use are primary sources that flag up a contradiction for you. They could be contemporaneous accounts – of punishment, perhaps, in an investigation into views on smacking, or government policies on the Foundation Stage Curriculum in a study of reading, or children's drawings, letters and diaries in an investigation into the experience of hospitalisation.

If you use documentary evidence, you should ensure its authenticity by providing full details of its source. For example, if you asked someone to write about their early childhood experience of being evacuated during the Second World War, you would need to record their name (or initials) and the date of their account. If you make inferences from the documents, you should back up your statements with evidence from the text and ensure, as far as you can, that your reading of the meaning is consistent with the tone of the whole. For instance, you may believe that evacuation was probably a 'damaging' experience for the children involved. Your interviewee might have recounted one unhappy memory in an otherwise positive account – but you would not be justified in concluding from this one memory that evacuation had been a negative experience. The main danger, in using documentary (or any) evidence, is to select only those parts which best support your argument and to ignore the rest.

Logs and reflective diaries

Logs and reflective diaries are mainly used as a data source in action research studies where practitioners want to observe the effect of changes in their work practices or to follow their own development or learning curve over a period of time. An action research log or reflective diary follows a cyclical path of initial observation, a plan of campaign to effect a change in behaviour or practice, implementation of the plan, reflection on the outcome of the action, modification of the plan in the light of reflection, implementation, and so on. You might use it in helping a mother deal with 'the terrible twos', for example. You might discuss her reaction to her child's problematic behaviour and suggest an alternative approach. You would then note the effect of the new approach and reflect alongside her whether the new approach was having the desired effect or whether further modification was needed. Your log or reflective diary provides a record of the evolution of your thinking as you work through a process towards a deeper understanding.

Stories

Stories, both written and oral, can be particularly useful in early years research. Understanding how a child (or adult) represents his or her version of reality through the stories they tell can give us an insight into the way they think. There are several ways of using stories in research. You could look at the stories themselves – for instance, if you wanted to investigate what sort of choices adults make on children's behalf when they select books for them. You could look at children's relationships to the stories they choose – for example, you could investigate the fairy tales particular children ask for most often and relate their choice to their current concerns. You could look at the way people tell stories about their own experiences – for example, you could compare and contrast different people's versions of an event. Or you could ask a group of teachers to describe a 'challenging' child and relate their stories to constructs of childhood. You could even investigate the ways in which your own investigation is a form of storytelling! You might ask yourself how you make a 'story' out of your research, or how you tell yourself the story of your research experience. Using stories in your investigation involves you in thinking about intention and interpretation, about meaning systems, about the dynamics of an unfolding narrative and about the nature of 'truth' and 'reality'.

Analysing and interpreting data

As you collect your data – your questionnaires, your interviews, field notes, tape transcripts, video material, children's work, accounts or stories – try to see what is emerging. Your purpose at this stage is to discover patterns in the data. Patterns depend for their authenticity on your integrity as a witness to your data – it is your duty to be truthful. Be systematic. Make your data more manageable by using grids for questionnaire responses, highlighter pens for transcripts, line numbering for interview data, time indications for video and tape, charts to map the ebb and flow of dialogue. It is worth spending time on this at the outset, to find a system that works best for you. Begin your analysis by looking at surface features – sample size, number of responses, frequencies of response, common concerns, patterns of behaviour, different points of view – and move on to an evaluation of the relative importance of those. Your interpretation will rest on your understanding of the underlying patterns revealed through your analysis.

Use the following checklist to analyse and interpret your findings.

Sample size – How many people did you ask to take part?

Achieved sample – How many people actually took part?

Response rates – How many people answered each question?

Patterns – What are the most frequent and least frequent features?

Similarities and differences – Are there any differences or similarities? Are they related to any variables relevant to your research question – age, gender, ethnicity, attitude, likes and dislikes?

Clusters – Can you usefully group things together under a category? For instance, in interviews with childminders about smacking, you might want to cluster responses under headings such as 'child-centred', 'authoritarian', *'laissez-faire'*.

Themes – Are there common or contrasting themes running through the data?

Data that don't fit – Are there maverick responses? Remember, negative data are still data and worthy of comment because what is not there, or doesn't fit, can be revealing.

Dominant perspectives – Is there any evidence to show that your respondents subscribe to particular views that might account for their responses? Are there any counterexamples to help define the limits of your developing theory?

Testing propositions – Can you test the strength of evidence for your proposition/hypothesis/research question by collecting quotes, or examples or figures that illustrate or fail to illustrate it? (Remember your job is to provide a fair summary of your findings, not to sell your proposition or to talk it up to confirm it.)

Checking your interpretations – Can you check your interpretations with other viewpoints? (Social scientists test evidence through triangulation – interrogating it from at least two other viewpoints or through three techniques of investigation.)

Small-scale research studies are unlikely to produce conclusions that can be applied more widely to society at large; the purpose is more often to cast light on a quite specific situation or event or child or relationship. Students producing quantitative data in their investigations are sometimes tempted to make grand claims for their research with liberal sprinklings of percentages and pie charts to show their findings. By all means present your data in the form of a table or graph, but be very clear that the numbers involved are small and the effects you are describing are specific to your study. The best way to check that your analysis is sound and your interpretation fair, is to collaborate with other people – the people who were involved in your investigation and/or colleagues. Ask them to help you check the strength and accuracy of the evidence on which you base your arguments and conclusions, by reading it through and discussing it with you.

Writing up

Writing up can be fun; it is very satisfying to bring all that work and information neatly together in a spiral binding. But it can also be lonely and demoralising. Keep talking to friends and colleagues, understand that you will be your own fiercest critic, share your anxieties with other people who know how hard it is to write reports and take plenty of breaks!

Honesty is the key to writing a decent research report – honesty with the participants, honesty with the data and honesty with oneself. Don't worry if you haven't added to the store of human knowledge – it is more important that you acted with integrity and wrote up your report with due regard for the difficulties and rewards that you encountered on the way. Lots of research is inconclusive and many published research reports end with the words 'more research is needed…'. As long as you have collected your evidence fairly and thoroughly and considered the strengths and weaknesses of your methods and conclusions, you should have nothing to fear. However, you must avoid at all costs the two major crimes of research: fabricating evidence and plagiarising the words of others. Fabricating evidence means making up data or making claims that do not stand up to scrutiny. Plagiarising means using other people's ideas or words without acknowledging the source, whether that source is a book or the internet or any other medium. Both these misdemeanours can, and do, result in failed degrees and ruined reputations.

There are many different ways to write up your research. Your choice of model will depend on the kind of investigation you carry out and your intended audience. To give you an idea of the relative proportions of a report, you might like to look at the following guidance we give to undergraduates on an early childhood studies course.

Title page – a title to capture the spirit of your research question; author; date.

Acknowledgements – a courtesy page to thank all the participants and the other people who have given you support during the project.

Abstract – a one-page summary of your research topic, your methods, the data collected and the main findings.

Contents – main section headings with page numbers.

Introduction – 500–1000 words explaining what sparked your interest in your investigation and what each section of your report will cover.

Literature review – 1000–2000 words describing the main arguments around the topic.

Methodology and methods – 1000–2000 words explaining *why* you chose the methodological approach and what are the strengths and limitations of your methods in exploring your research question (some people include their questionnaires/interview schedules, etc., here; other people prefer to put them in an appendix).

Findings – as many words as it takes to present the results of your investigations. This may include charts and summaries of questionnaire responses, observations, interviews, documentary evidence, logs, reflective diaries, stories.

Discussion/analysis – 2000–3000 words explaining what your findings show and how they relate to previous studies.

Conclusions – 500–1000 words showing the implications of your study for further thinking and the recommendations you would make in the light of your findings.

Appendices – these should be numbered and should include your ethics protocol, permissions, any letters sent out to participants, raw scores and results, transcripts, copies of questionnaires or interview schedules, documentary evidence, logs, reflective diaries, stories.

Concluding remarks

Research is central to studying and working in early childhood – not only for adults but for children too. Children are little researchers, continually putting forward and testing theories as they build up a view of the world and their place in it. As students and practitioners, we need to keep this link between theory and practice alive in adulthood so that we can continue to develop our own understanding. As adults we can learn from investigating how things work in our own practice and relating our observations to the theories through which we operate. We can also learn through investigating the perspectives of those we work with – children's perspectives are just as worthy of investigation as those of the adults who work with them. Reflecting on people's behaviour, children's or adults', can inform understanding and improve practice and it is important that we make time to cultivate a habit of research and investigation as part of our thinking and working. This chapter has outlined some of the ways to do this.

Becoming a researcher and developing evidence-based practice is not just a question of a once-and-for-all training; it is about developing a research mindset. It is about an orientation towards continuing learning, a belief that every opportunity brings with it fresh opportunities for learning something new or understanding something differently. Research flourishes in an atmosphere of open enquiry where there is a will to share understanding and examine practice. It flourishes where there is a commitment to hearing and considering the views of everyone – children, colleagues, parents and students – in an honest spirit of open collaboration. If we fail to investigate our practice and interrogate our theories, we are in danger of simply perpetuating an uncritical repetition of doing things the way they have always been done.

ACTIVITY *1*

Choose a published research article which interests you and which describes an empirical piece of research.

Five key journals you might like to use are:

Early Years, An International Journal of Research and Development. *Stoke on Trent: Trentham.*

The European Early Childhood Education Research Journal. *Worcester: European Early Childhood Education Research Association.*

International Journal of Early Childhood. *Dublin: IUP for World Organisation for Early Childhood Education.*

British Educational Research Journal. *Oxford: Carfax.*

Children and Society. *Chichester, Sussex: John Wiley.*

Look at the section 'Reviewing the literature' in this chapter. Use the bullet points to help you read and analyse the journal article you have chosen.

FURTHER READING

Bell, J (1999) Doing your research project: a guide for first-time researchers in education and social science. 3rd edition. Buckingham: Open University Press.

Cohen, L, Manion, L and Morrison, K (2000) Research methods in education. 5th edition. London: Routledge/Falmer.

MacNaughton, G, Rolfe, SA and Siraj-Blatchford, I (eds) (2001) Doing early childhood research: international perspectives on theory and practice. Buckingham: Open University Press.

Robson, C (2002) Real world research: a resource for social scientists and practitioner-researchers. 2nd edition. Oxford: Blackwell.

Silverman, D (2000) Doing qualitative research: a practical handbook. London: Sage

References

Abbott, L and Nutbrown, C eds (2001) *Experiencing Reggio Emilia*. Buckingham: Open University Press.

Acredolo, L, Goodwyn, S and Abrams, D (2002) *Baby signs: how to talk with your baby before your baby can talk*. London: Contemporary.

Adams, S, Alexander, E and Drummond, MJ (2004) *Inside the Foundation Stage: recreating the reception year*. London: Association of Teachers and Lecturers.

Ainscow, M (1995) *Education for all: making it happen*. Support for Learning, 10 (4), 147–54.

Alanen, L (1992) *Modern childhood? Exploring the 'child question' in sociology*. Research Report 50. Finland: University of Jyvaskyla.

Alcock, P, Erskine, A and May, M (eds) (1998) *The student's companion to social policy*. Oxford: Blackwell.

Alcock, P, Erskine, A and May, M (eds) (2002) *The Blackwell dictionary of social policy*. Oxford: Blackwell.

Anning, A and Edwards, A (1999) *Promoting children's learning from birth to five – developing the new early years professional*. Buckingham: Open University Press.

Arnot, M, Gray, J, James, M and Rudduck, J (1998) *Recent research on gender and educational performance*. London: HMSO.

Atkinson, M, Wilkin, A, Stott, A, Doherty, P and Kinder, K (2002) *Multi-agency working: a detailed study*. Slough: National Foundation for Educational Research.

Audit Commission (2003a) *Services for disabled children: a review of services for disabled children and their families*. London: Audit Commission.

Audit Commission (2003b) *Corporate governance: improvement and trust in local public services*. London: HMSO.

Banton, M (1987) *Racial theories*. Cambridge: Cambridge University Press.

Barrett, GH (1986) *Starting school: an evaluation of the experience*. London: AMMA.

Bass, B (1985) *Leadership and performance beyond expectation*. New York: Free Press.

Beck (1996) in Scourfield, J and Welsh, I (2003) *Risk, reflexivity and social control in child protection: new times or same old story?* Critical Social Policy, 23(3). London: Sage.

Beetlestone, F (1998) *Creative children, imaginative teaching*. Buckingham: Open University Press.

Bekoff, M and Byers, J (1998) *Animal play*. Cambridge: Cambridge University Press.

Bell, J (1999) *Doing your research project: a guide for first-time researchers in education and social science*. 3rd edition. Buckingham: Open University Press, pp.121–5.

Bellamy, C (2002) *The state of the world's children 2003*: child participation. New York: UNICEF.

Bennett, N and Kell, J (1989) *A good start?: 4 year-olds in infant classes*. London: Blackwell.

Berne, E (1964) *Games people play*. London: Penguin.

Bertram, T and Pascal, C (2002) *Early years education: an international perspective*. London: Qualifications and Curriculum Authority.

Blake, R and Moulton, J (1964) *The managerial grid*. London: Bloomsbury.

Blakemore, K (2003) *Social policy: an introduction*. 2nd edition. Buckingham: Open University Press.

Blakemore, S, Wolpert, D and Frith, C (1998) *Central cancellation of self-produced tickle sensation. Nature Neuroscience*, 1 (7), 635–40.

Blueprint Project (2004) *Start with the child, stay with the child*. London: VCC.

Blunkett, D (2002) *Integration with diversity: globalisation and the renewal of democracy and civil society*, in Leonard, M (ed) Reclaiming Britishness. London: The Foreign Policy Centre.

Bottery, M (1992) *The ethics of education management*. London: Cassell Educational.

Boud, D, Keogh, R and Walker, D (1985) *Reflection: turning experience into learning*. Ipswich: Kogan Page.

Bourner, T, O'Hara, S and Barlow, J (2002) *Only connect: facilitating reflective learning with statements of relevance*. Innovations in Education and Teaching International, 37 (1).

Bowlby, J (1969) *Attachment and loss*: Vol. 1 Attachment. New York: Basic Books.

Bradbury, B and Jantti, M (1999) *Child poverty across industrialised nations*. Innocenti Occasional Papers, EPS 1971. Florence: UNICEF.

Bradshaw, J (2003) *Poor children*. Children and Society, 17, 162–72.

Bradshaw, J, Ditch, J, Holmes, H and Whiteford, P (1993) *Support for children: a comparison of arrangements in fifteen countries*. London: HMSO.

Brannen, J and O'Brien, M (eds) (1996) *Children in families: research and policy*. London: Falmer Press.

Brechin, A (2000) in Brechin, A, Brown, H and Eby, MA (eds) *Critical practice in health and social care*. Oxford: OUP.

Bridgeman, B (1992) *On the evolution of consciousness and language*, Psycoloquy 3 (15). **www.cogsci.ecs.soton.ac.uk/cgi/psyc/newpsy?** (accessed 3 January 2004)

British Psychological Society (1997) *Code of conduct, ethical principles and guidelines*. **www.bps.org.uk/documents/Code.pdf**

Broadhead, P (2004) *Early years play and learning: developing social skills and cooperation*. London: Routledge Falmer.

Bronfenbrenner, U (1979) *The ecology of human development*. Cambridge, MA: Harvard University Press.

Broström, S (1997) *Children's play: tools and symbols in frame play*. Early Years, 17 (2), 16–21.

Brown, B (1998) *Unlearning discrimination in the early years*. Stoke on Trent: Trentham.

Brown, S and Cleave, S (1994) *Four year olds in school: quality matters*. 2nd edition. London: NFER/QCA.

Bruce, T (1996) *Helping young children to learn through play*. London: Hodder and Stoughton.

Bruce, T and Meggitt, C (1999) *Child care and education*. 2nd edition. London: Hodder and Stoughton.

Bruner, JS (1966) *Toward a theory of instruction*. Cambridge, MA: Harvard University Press.

Bruner, J, Goodnow, J and Austin, J (1956) *A study of thinking*. New York: John Wiley and Sons.

Burke, C and Grosvenor, I (2003) *The school I'd like – children and young people's reflections on an education for the 21st century*. London: Routlege Falmer.

Burnett, J (ed) (1994) *Destiny obscure: autobiographies of childhood, education and family from the 1820s to the 1920s*. London: Routledge.

Burns, J (1978) *Leadership*. New York: Harper and Row.

Campaign for drawing. **www.drawingpower.org.uk**

Carlyle, D and Woods, P (2002) *Emotions of teacher stress*. Stoke on Trent: Trentham.

Carter, R (1999) *Mapping the mind*. London: Phoenix.

Cattell, R (1968) *Objective personality and motivation tests*. Illinois: University of Illinois Press.

Central Advisory Council for Education (England) (1967) *Children and their primary schools*. London: HMSO.

Chambers, P, Clarke, B, Colombo, M and Askland, L (2003) *Journal of In-Service Education*, 29 (1).

Christensen, P and James, A (eds) (2000) *Research with children: perspectives and practices*. London and New York: Falmer.

Claire, H, Maybin, J and Swann, J (eds) (1993) *Equality matters: case studies from the primary school*. Clevedon, Philadelphia, Adelaide: Multilingual Matters Ltd.

Clark, M (1988) *Children under five: educational research and evidence*. London: Gordon and Breach.

Clarke, A and Clarke, A (2003) *Human resilience; a fifty year quest*. London: Jessica Kingsley.

Claxton, G (1994) *Noises from the dark room: the science and mystery of the mind*. London: Aquarian/Harper Collins.

Cleave, S and Brown, S (1991) *Early to school: four year olds in infant classes*. London: NFER/Nelson.

Cockburn, T (1998) *Children and citizenship in Britain*. Childhood, 5 (1), 99–117.

Cohn, JF and Tronick, EZ (1987) *Mother–infant face-to-face interaction; the sequence of dyadic states at 3, 6, and 9 months*. Developmental Psychology, 23 (1), 68–77.

Cooley, CH (1902) *Human nature and the social order*. New York: Scribner.

Cotterill, R (1998) *Enchanted looms: conscious networks in brains and computers.* Cambridge: Cambridge University Press.

Cox, M (1997) *Drawings of people by the under-5s.* London: Falmer.

Cox, R (1995) *Shaping childhood: themes of uncertainty in the history of adult-child relationships.* London: Routledge.

Crace, J (2003) The *Guardian*, 15 July.

Craft, A (2002) *Creativity in early years education.* London: Continuum.

Craft, A (2003) *The limits to creativity in education: dilemmas for the educator.* British Journal of Educational Studies, 51 (2), June, 113–27.

Csikszentmihalyi, M (1992) *Flow: the psychology of happiness.* London: Rider Books.

Cummins, J (1984) *Bilingualism and special education: issues in assessment and pedagogy.* Clevedon: Multilingual Matters Ltd.

Cunningham, H (1991) *The children of the poor: representations of childhood since the seventeenth century.* Oxford: Blackwell.

Daniel, B, Wassel, S and Gilligan, R (1999) *Child development for child care and protection workers.* London: Jessica Kingsley.

Daniel, P and Ivatts, J (1998) *Children and social policy.* Basingstoke and London: Macmillan.

David, T (ed) (1993) *Educational provision for our youngest children*: European perspectives. London: Paul Chapman.

Davidoff, L, Doolittle, M, Fink, J and Holden, K (1999) *The family story – blood, contract and intimacy, 1830–1960.* London: Longman.

Davin, A (1990) *When is a child not a child,* in Corr, H and Jamieson, L (eds) *Politics of everyday life – continuity and change in work and the family.* London: Macmillan.

Davies, J and Brember, I (1999) *Reading and mathematics attainments and self-esteem in Years 2 and 6 – an eight-year cross-sectional study.* Educational Studies, 25 (2), 145–57.

Day, C , Hall, C and Whitaker, P (1998) *Developing leadership in primary schools.* London: Paul Chapman.

Daycare Trust (2003) *Parents need more help from government and employers as childcare bills rocket.* **www.daycaretrust.org.uk/article.php?sid=138** (accessed 31 August 2003)

Delhaxhe, A, Hindryckx, G, Olmsted, PP and Ma, Z (1995) *Study findings: children's daily routines,* in Olmsted, PP and Weikart, DP (eds) *The IEA preprimary study: early childhood care and education in 11 countries.* Oxford, New York, Tokyo: Pergamon Press.

Dempsey, M, Halton, C and Murphy, M (2001) *Reflective learning in social work education: scaffolding the process.* Social Work Education, 20 (6).

Department for Culture, Media and Sport (2001) *Culture and creativity: the next ten years.* **www.culture.gov.uk/global/publications/archive_2001/Creativity10yrs.htm**

Department for Education and Employment (1998a) *Meeting the childcare challenge*: a framework and consultation document. London: DfEE.

Department for Education and Employment (1998b) *National childcare strategy*. London: HMSO.

Department for Education and Employment (1999a) *All our futures: creativity, culture and education*. Suffolk: DfEE.

Department for Education and Employment (1999b) *The national curriculum handbook*. London: QCA.

Department for Education and Employment (2000) *Professional development: support for teaching and learning*. London: DfEE.

Department for Education and Employment (2001) *Early excellence centre pilot programme annual evaluation report 2000*. London: HMSO.

Department for Education and Skills (2001) *Special educational needs code of practice*. Nottingham: DfES.

Department for Education and Skills (2002) *Education Act*. London: HMSO.

Department for Education and Skills (2003) *Every child matters*. London: DfES.

Department for Education and Skills (2004a) *Provision for children under five years of age in England – January 2004* (provisional). **www.dfes.gov.uk/rsgateway/DB/SFR/s000464/sfr15-2004.pdf** (accessed 27 May 2004)

Department for Education and Skills (2004b) *Removing barriers to achievement: the government's strategy for SEN*. Nottingham: DfES.

Department for Education and Science (1967) *Children and their primary schools: a report of the central advisory council for education* (England) Volume 1. London: HMSO.

Department for Education and Science (1985) *Better schools*. London: DES.

Department for Education and Science (1990) *Starting with quality: the report of the committee of inquiry into the quality of the educational experience offered to 3 and 4 year olds*. London: HMSO.

Department for Work and Pensions (2002) *Households below average income 1994/5–2000/01*. Leeds: Corporate Document Services.

Department of Health (1989) *Children Act*. London: HMSO.

Department of Health (1990) *National Health Service and Community Care Act*. London: HMSO.

Department of Health (1999) *Working together under the Children Act 1989*. London: HMSO.

Department of Health (2003) *The Victoria Climbie inquiry report by Lord Laming*. London: HMSO.

Department of Health, Department for Education and Employment, Home Office (2000) *Framework for the assessment of children in need and their families*. London: The Stationery Office.

Derman-Sparks, L (1989) *Anti-bias curriculum: tools for empowering young children*. Washington, DC: National Association for the Education of Young Children.

Devereux, J and Miller, L (2003) *Working with children in the early years*. London: David Fulton.

Dewey, J (1933) *How we think*. Boston: D C Heath and Co.

Diamond, KE (2002) *Social competence in children with disabilities*, in Smith, PK and Hart, CH (eds) Blackwell handbook of childhood social development. Oxford: Blackwell.

Doherty-Sneddon, G (2004) *Don't look now … I'm trying to think*. The Psychologist, 17 (2), February 82–5.

Donald, M (1991) *Origins of the modern mind: three stages in the evolution of culture and cognition*. Cambridge, MA: Harvard University Press.

Dowling, M (1995) *Starting school at four: a joint endeavour*. London: Paul Chapman.

Downie, L (2003) *Visit report #1: my visit to Finland*. OMEP Newsletter, Autumn, 3–4.

Downing, B (2003) *'Fontanelle', The New Criterion*, 21 (8), 2003. **www.newcriterion.com/archive/21/apr03/down.htm** (accessed 3 May 2004)

Drummond, M (2001) *In my view. National Early Years Network Journal* 'Co-ordinate', 81, Summer.

Drummond, M (2003) *Breathe life into childhood*. Times Education Supplement, 28 November 2003.

Duffy, B (1998) *Supporting creativity and imagination in the early years*. Buckingham: Open University Press.

Dunbar, R (1998) *Grooming, gossip and the evolution of language*. Cambridge, MA: Harvard University Press.

Early Childhood Education Forum (1998) *Quality in diversity in early learning: A framework for early childhood practitioners*. London: National Children's Bureau.

Early Years Curriculum Group (1995) *Four year olds in school: myths and realities*. Action paper no. 2. Oldham: Madeleine Lindley Ltd.

Edwards, A (1999) *Research and practice: is there a dialogue?*, in Penn, H (ed) Theory, policy and practice in early childhood services. Buckingham: Open University Press.

Edwards, C, Gandini, L and Forman, G (eds) (1998) *The hundred languages of children: the Reggio Emilia approach – advanced reflections*. London: Ablex.

Elias, N (1969) *Sociology and psychiatry*, in Foulkes, SH and Steward Prince, G (eds) Psychiatry in a changing society. London: Tavistock.

Elias, N (1983) *The court society*. London: Blackwell.

Elias, N (1994) *The civilizing process*. London: Blackwell.

Elias, N (1998) *The civilizing of parents*, in Goudsblom, J and Mennell, S (eds) The Norbert Elias reader. London: Blackwell.

Ellis, DG and Fisher, BA (1994) *Small group decision-making: communication and the group process*. Singapore: McGraw-Hill.

Equal Opportunities Commission (2004) *It's time to get even*. **www.eoc.org.uk/cseng/ policyandcampaigns/timetogeteven.asp#_More_on_the** (accessed 5 May 2004)

Eraut, M (1994) *Developing professional knowledge and competence.* London: Falmer.

European Commission (2003) *Education across Europe. Luxembourg*: Office of Official Publications of the European Communities.

European Commission Childcare Network (1996) *A review of services for young children in the European Union, 1990–1995.* Brussels: European Commission.

Eurydice (2001) *The information network on education in Europe.* **www.nfer.ac.uk/eurydice/ about_us/about.asp**

Farrell, P (2001) *Special education in the last 20 years: have things really got better?* British Journal of Special Education, 28 (1), 3–9.

Fiedler, F (1978) *Situational control and a dynamic theory of leadership,* in Pugh, D (ed) Organisational theory: selected readings. Harmondsworth: Penguin Business.

Fisher, J (2002) *The foundations of learning.* Buckingham: Open University Press.

Fisher, R (1990) *Teaching children to think.* Cheltenham: Stanley Thornes.

Fitzgerald, D (2004) *Parent partnership in the early years.* London: Continuum.

Fogel, A (1997) *Developing through relationships: origins of communication, self and culture.* Chicago: University of Chicago Press.

Fook, J (1997) *The reflective researcher.* London: Allen and Unwin.

Ford, B (ed) (1982) *From Blake to Byron,* Vol. 5 of the New Pelican guide to English literature. Harmondsworth: Penguin.

Forman, G and Fyfe, B (1998) *Negotiated learning through design, documentation and discourse,* in Edwards, C, Gandini, L and Forman, G (eds) The hundred languages of children: the Reggio Emilia approach – advanced reflections. London: Ablex.

Foster, W (1989) *Towards a critical practice of leadership,* in Smyth, J (ed) Critical perspectives of educational leadership. London: Falmer Press.

Fullan, M (2001) *Leading in a culture of change.* San Francisco: Jossey-Bass.

Gaine, C (1995) *Still no problem here.* Stoke-on-Trent: Trentham Books.

Garcia, J (2002) *Sign with your baby: how to communicate with infants before they can speak.* Seattle: Northlight Communications.

Gardner, H (1984) *Frames of mind.* New York: Basic Books.

Gardner, H, Torff, B and Hatch, T (1996) *The age of innocence reconsidered: preserving the best of the progressive traditions in psychology and education,* in Olson, D and Torrance, N (eds) The handbook of education and human development. Oxford: Blackwell.

Gauvain, M (2001) *The social context of cognitive development.* New York: Guilford Publications.

Gelder, U (2003) *Carving out a niche? The work of Tagesmütter in the new Germany,* in Mooney, A and Statham, J (eds) Family day care: international perspectives on policy, practice and quality. London: Jessica Kingsley.

Ghaye, A and Ghaye, K (1998) *Teaching and learning through critical reflective practice*. London: David Fulton.

Gittins, D (1998) *The child in question*. London: Macmillan.

Glass, N (1999) *Origins of the Sure Start programme*. Children and Society, 13 (4), 257–64.

Glendinning, C, Powell, M and Rummery, K (eds) (2002) *Partnerships, New Labour and the governance of welfare*. Southampton: Policy Press.

Glennie, S (2003) *Safeguarding children together,* in Leathard, A (ed) Interprofessional collaboration: from policy to practice in health and social care. London: Brunner-Routledge.

Goldschmied, E and Hughes, A (1986) *Infants at work: babies of 6–9 months exploring everyday objects* (videocassette). London: NCB Books.

Goleman, D (1996) *Emotional intelligence*. London: Bloomsbury.

Goleman, D (1998) *Working with emotional intelligence*. London: Bloomsbury.

Goleman, D, Boyatzis, R and McKee, A (2002) *The new leaders*. London: Little Brown.

Gould, N and Taylor, I (1996) *Reflective learning for social work: research theory and practice*. Bodmin: Arena.

Graue, ME and Walsh, DJ (1998) *Studying children in context; theories, methods and ethics*. Thousand Oaks: Sage.

Hall, V (1996) *Dancing on the ceiling*. London: Paul Chapman.

Hatten, W, Vinter, L and Williams, R (2003) *Dads on dads: needs and expectations at home and at work*. London: MORI.

Hayes, D (2004) *Social services directors fear merged services will compromise child safety*. Community Care 22–28/04/04. Reed Business Information.

Head, J (1999) *Understanding the boys*. London: Falmer.

Hendrick, H (1990) *Constructions and reconstructions of British childhood: an interpretative survey, 1800 to the present, in* Constructing and reconstructing childhood: contemporary issues in the sociological study of childhood. London: Falmer.

Hendrick, H (1994) *Child welfare: 1870–1989*. London: Routledge.

Hendrick, H (1996) *Child welfare, historical dimensions, contemporary debate*. Bristol: Policy Press.

Hendrick, H (1997) *Children, childhood and English society, 1880–1890*. Cambridge: Cambridge University Press.

Hepper, P (2003) *Prenatal psychological and behavioral development*, in Valsiner, J and Connolly, KJ (eds) Handbook of developmental psychology. London: Sage.

Hersey, P and Blanchard, K (1977) *Management of organizational behavior: utilizing human resources*. Englewood Cliffs: Prentice Hall.

Heywood, C (2001) *A history of childhood – children and childhood in the West from medieval to modern times*. Cambridge: Polity.

Hill, M (2003) *Understanding social policy*. 7th edition. Oxford: Blackwell.

Hill, M and Jenkins, S (2001) *Poverty among British children: chronic or transitory?*, in Bradbury, B, Jenkins, S and Micklewright, J (eds) The dynamics of child poverty in industrialised countries. Cambridge: Cambridge University Press.

Hobbs, T (1992) *Experiential training: practice guidelines*. Chatham: Tavistock/Routledge.

Holden, J, Timms, C and Wright, S (2003) *Creative partnerships: exciting minds.* Draft Demos report, unpublished.

Hornby, G (2000) *Improving parental involvement*. London: Cassell.

Houlton, D (1986) *Cultural diversity in the primary school*. London: BT Batsford.

Horwath, J and Thurlow, C (2004) *Preparing students for evidence based child and family social work: an experiential learning approach*. Social Work Education, 23 (1).

House of Commons Select Committee (1989) *Children 3–5*. London: HMSO.

Hyder, T and Kenway, P (1995) *An equal future: a guide to anti-sexist practice in the early years*. London: the National Early Years Network in partnership with Save the Children/Equality Learning Centre.

INCA (2003) *International review of curriculum and assessment frameworks archive*. London: QCA. **www.inca.org.uk/**

Inoyatova, M (2002) *Tajikistan Global Education Workshop opening address*, 9 December 2002, from the Prologue to the UNICEF CARK (Central Asian Countries and Kazakhstan) Global Education Project Report (mimeo).

Inside Science 143 (2001) *The great escape*. New Scientist, 171, 2308, 15 September 2001.

Isaacs, S (1932) *The nursery years*. London: Routledge and Kegan Paul.

Isenberg, J and Jalongo, M (1997) *Creative expression and play in early childhood*. New Jersey: Merrill.

Iwaniuk, A, Nelson, J and Pellis, S (2001) *Do big-brained animals play more?* Journal of Comparative Psychology, 115, 29–41.

James, A and Prout, A (eds) (1990) *A new paradigm for the sociology of childhood?* Provenance, promise and problems, in Constructing and reconstructing childhood. Basingstoke: Falmer.

James, A and Prout, A (1997) *Constructing and reconstructing childhood*. 2nd edition. London: Falmer.

James, A, Jenks, C, and Prout, A (1998) *Theorising childhood*. Cambridge: Polity.

Janeway, J (1830) *A token for children*. London: Religious Tract Society.

Jeffrey, B and Woods, P (2003) *The creative school*. London: Routledge Falmer.

John, M (1996) *A child's right to a fair hearing*. London: Jessica Kingsley.

John, M (2003) *Children's rights and power; gearing up for a new century*. London: Jessica Kingsley.

Johnson, J (2002) *'The African spider cures'*. **www.art-galleries-**

schubert.com.au/www/Annual_Prizes/Poetry/winning_poem2002.htm (accessed 3 May 2004)

Jones, E and Reynolds, G (1992) *The play's the thing: teachers' roles in children's play*. New York: Teachers' College Press.

Jordanova, L (1989) *Children in history: concepts of nature and society*, in Scarre, G (ed) Children, parents and politics. Cambridge: Cambridge University Press.

Joseph Rowntree Foundation (1999) *Findings. March 1999*. York: Joseph Rowntree Foundation.

Kagan, SL and Bowman, BT (eds) (1997) *Leadership in early care and education*. Washington, DC: National Association for the Education of Young Children.

Katz, L and Chard, S (1996) *The contribution of documentation to the quality of early childhood education*. ERIC/EECE Digest: EDO-PS-96-2.
http://ecap.crc.uiuc.edu/eecearchive/digests/1996/lkchar96.html (accessed 13 June 2004)

Keenan, T (2002) *An introduction to child development*. London: Sage.

Knutsson, KE (1997) *Children: noble causes or worthy citizens*. Aldershot: Arena.

Kolb, DA (1984) *Experiential learning: experience as the source of learning and development*. Englewood Cliffs: Prentice Hall.

Kuhn, TS (1970) *The structure of scientific revolutions*. 2nd edition. Chicago: University of Chicago Press, pp.43–51.

Kydd, L, Anderson, L and Newton, W (2003) *Leading people and teams in education*. Buckingham: Open University Press.

Lancaster, P and Broadbent, V (2003) *Listening to children*. Buckingham: Open University Press.

Langan, M and Ostner, I (1991) *Gender and welfare*, in Room, G (ed) Towards a European welfare state? Bristol: School for Advanced Urban Studies.

Lave, J and Wenger, E (1991) *Situated learning: legitimate peripheral participation*. Cambridge: Cambridge University Press.

Law, S and Glover, D (2000) *Educational leadership and learning; practice, policy and research*. Oxford: OUP.

Leathard, A (2003) *Interprofessional collaboration; from policy to practice in health and social care*. London: Brunner-Routledge.

Leiba, T (2003) in Weinstein, J, Whittington, C and Leiba, T (eds) *Collaboration in social work practice*. London: Jessica Kingsley.

Lewis, J (1992) *Gender and the development of welfare regimes*. Journal of European Social Policy, 2 (3), 159–73.

Liddiard, M (1928) *The mothercraft manual*. London: Churchill.

Likert, R (1967) *The human organisation: its management and value*. New York: McGraw-Hill.

Lindon, J (2000) *Early years care and education in Europe*. Oxford: Hodder and Stoughton.

Lindon, J and Lindon, L (2000) *Mastering counselling skills*. Basingstoke: Macmillan.

Liu, S (2001) *The autonomous state of childcare: policy and the policy process in Britain*, Aldershot: Ashgate.

London Borough of Brent (1985) *A child in trust: the report of the panel of inquiry into the circumstances surrounding the death of Jasmine Beckford*. London Borough of Brent.

McBride, P and Maitland, S (2002) *Putting emotional intelligence into practice*. London: McGraw-Hill.

McCail, G (1986) *The 4 year old in the classroom*. London: British Association for Early Childhood Education.

McClelland, DC (1987) *Human motivation*. Cambridge: Cambridge University Press.

McDrury, J and Alterio, M (2000) *Achieving reflective learning using storytelling pathways*. Innovations in Education and Teaching International, 38 (1).

McQuail, D and Windahl, S (1981) *Communication models for the study of mass communication*. London: Longman.

Mannheim, K (1952) *The problem of generations, in Essays on the sociology of knowledge*. London: Routledge and Kegan Paul.

Martin, V and Henderson, E (2001) *Managing in health and social care*. London: Routledge.

Martini, M, and Kirkpatrick, J (1981) *Early interactions in Marquesas islands*, in Field, TM, Sostek, AM, Vietze, P and Leiderman, PH (eds) Culture and early interactions. Hillsdale, NJ: Erlbaum.

Maslak, M (2003) *Daughters of Tharu: gender, ethnicity, religion and the education of Nepali girls*. London: Routledge Falmer.

Maslow, AH (1943) *A theory of human motivation*. Psychological Review, 50, 370–96.

May, T (2001) *Social research: issues, methods and process*. Buckingham: Open University Press.

Mayall, B (2002) *Towards a sociology for childhood – thinking from children's lives*. Buckingham: Open University Press.

Meltzoff, AN and Moore, MK (1977) *Imitation of facial and manual gestures by human neonates*. Science, 198, 75–8. (Also in Slater, A and Muir, D (eds) (1999) The Blackwell reader in developmental psychology. Oxford: Blackwell.)

Miell, D and Dallos, R (1996) *Social interaction and personal relationships*. Buckingham: Open University Press.

Miller, A (1987) *Thou shalt not be aware: society's betrayal of the child*. London: Pluto.

Miller, L, Rustin, M, Rustin, M and Shuttleworth, J (eds) (1989) *Closely observed infants*. London: Duckworth.

Milner, D (1983) *Children and race: ten years on*. Beverly Hills: Sage.

Moore, M, Sixsmith, J and Knowles, K (1996) *Children's reflections on family life*. London: Falmer.

Moss, P and Petrie, P (2002) *From children's services to children's spaces: public policy, children and childhood*. London: Routledge.

Motluk, A (2001) *Read my mind*. New Scientist, 169, 2275, 27 January 2001, p.22.

Moyles, JR (1994) *The excellence of play*. Buckingham: Open University Press.

Murray, L, and Cooper, PJ (eds) (1997) *Postpartum depression and child development*. New York: Guilford Press.

Murray, L and Trevarthen, C (1985) *Emotional regulation of interactions between two-month-olds and their mothers*, in Field, T and Fox, N (eds) Social perception in infants. Norwood, NJ: Ablex.

NACCCE (1999) *All our futures: creativity, culture and education*. Sudbury: DfEE.

National Audit Office (2004) *Early years: progress in developing high quality childcare and early education accessible to all*. London: The Stationery Office.

National Families Network www.westcoastfamilies.com/htm/0208n_learningwomb.html (accessed 11 June 2004)

National Research Council Institute of Medicine (2000) *From neurons to neighborhoods: the science of early childhood development*. Washington, DC: National Academy Press.

Neale, B (2002) *Dialogues with children: children, divorce and citizenship*. Childhood, 9 (4), 455–75.

New, R (2000) *Reggio Emilia: catalyst for change and conversation*. ERIC Digest.

New Zealand Ministry of Education (1996) *Te Whariki: early childhood curriculum*. Wellington: Learning Media.

Newham Area Child Protection Committee (2002) *Report into the death of Ainlee Walker*. London: Newham Council.

Newson, J and Newson, E (1974) *Cultural aspects of childrearing in the English-speaking world*, in Richards, MPM (ed) The integration of a child into a social world. Cambridge: Cambridge University Press.

Nias, J, Southworth, G and Yeomans, R (1989) *Staff relationships in the primary school*. London: Cassell Educational.

Noddings, N (1991) *Stories in dialogue: caring and interpersonal reasoning*, in Witherell, C and Noddings, N (eds) Stories lives tell: narrative and dialogue in education. New York: Teachers' College Press.

Oates, J (1994) *The foundations of child development*. Oxford: Open University in association with Blackwell.

Oberhuemer, P and Ulich, M (1997) *Working with young children in Europe: provision and staff training*. Weinheim and Basel: Beltz.

OECD (2001) *Starting strong: early childhood education and care*. Paris: Organisation for Economic Co-operation and Development.

Office for National Statistics (1999) *Labour force survey*. London: HMSO.

Office for National Statistics (2001). *2001 Census*. London: HMSO.

Office for National Statistics (2003) *Social trends 33*. London: ONS.

Ofsted (2003a) *Creativity in the classroom*. **www/ofsted.gov.uk**

Ofsted (2003b) *Expecting the unexpected: developing creativity in the primary and secondary schools.* London: Ofsted.

Oliver, C (2003) *The care of the illegitimate child: the Coram experience 1900–1945*, in Brannen, J and Moss, P (eds) Rethinking children's care. Buckingham: Open University Press.

Olmsted, PP and Montie, J (eds) (2001) *Early childhood settings in 15 countries: what are their structural characteristics?* Ypsilanti, MI: High/Scope Press.

Olmsted, PP and Weikart, DP (eds) (1995) *The IEA preprimary study: early childhood care and education in 11 countries.* Oxford, New York, Tokyo: Pergamon Press.

Owen, H (2000) *In search of leaders.* Chichester: Wiley.

Øyen, E (1990) *The imperfection of comparisons*, in Øyen, E (ed) Comparative methodology: theory and practice in international social research. London: Sage.

Papworth, J (2004) *Parents pay as children play.* The *Guardian*, 7 February 2004.

Perner, J (1991) *Understanding the representational mind.* Cambridge, MA: MIT Press.

Petrie, P (2003) *Social pedagogy: an historical account of care and education as social control*, in Brannen, J and Moss, P (eds) Rethinking children's care. Buckingham: Open University Press.

Phillips, A (1998) *The beast in the nursery.* London: Faber and Faber.

Piaget, J (1952) *The origins of intelligence in children.* New York: Norton.

Piaget, J (1954) *The construction of reality in the child.* New York: Basic Books.

Piaget, J (1962) *Play, dreams and imitation in childhood.* New York: Norton.

Pickles, T (2004) *Experiential learning … on the web.* **http://reviewing.co.uk/research/experiential.learning.htm**

Pinker, S (2002) *The blank slate: the modern denial of human nature.* New York: Viking.

Pinkney, S (2000) *Children as welfare subjects in restructured social policy*, in Lewis, G, Gewirtz, S and Clarke, J (eds) Rethinking social policy. London, Thousand Oaks, New Delhi: Sage.

Plotz, J (2001) *Romanticism and the vocation of childhood.* New York: Palgrave.

Preschool Learning Alliance (2001) *Equal chances: eliminating discrimination and ensuring equality in pre-school settings.* London: Preschool Learning Alliance.

Qualifications and Curriculum Authority (2003) *Creativity; find it, promote it.* **www.ncaction.org.uk/creativity/**

Qualifications and Curriculum Authority/Department for Education and Employment (2000) *Curriculum guidance for the foundation stage.* London: QCA.

Qualifications and Curriculum Authority (2003) *Foundation Stage profile,* London: QCA Publications.

Qvortrup, J (1985) *Placing children in the division of labour*, in Close, P and Collins, R (eds) Family and economy in modern society. London: Macmillan.

Rake, K (2001) *Gender and New Labour's social policies.* Journal of Social Policy, 30 (2), 209–31.

Readings, B (1997) *The university in ruins*. Cambridge, MA: Harvard University Press.

Ribble, M (1943) *The rights of infants*. New York: Columbia University Press.

Rizzolatti, G, Fadiga, L, Gallese, V and Fogassi, L (1996) *Premotor cortex and the recognition of motor actions*. Cognitive Brain Research, 3 (1996), 131–41.

Rochat, P (2004) *Emerging co-awareness*, in Bremner, G and Slater, A (eds) Theories of infant development. Oxford: Blackwell.

Rodd, J (1994) *Leadership in early childhood*. 1st edition. Buckingham: Open University Press.

Rodd, J (1998) *Leadership in early childhood*. 2nd edition. Buckingham: Open University Press.

Rovee-Collier, C and Hayne, H (1987) *Reactivation of infant memory: implications for cognitive development*, in Reese, H (ed) Advances in child development and behavior, Vol. 20, pp.185–238. New York: Academic Press.

Ruch, G (2002) *From triangle to spiral: reflective practice in social work education, practice and research*. Social Work Education, 21 (2).

Ruch, G (2003) *Reflective practice in contemporary child care social work*. **www.hants.gov.uk/TC/ sspm/pi4.html**

Rusk, RR (1965) *Doctrines of the great educators*. London: Macmillan.

Saltiel, D (2003) *Teaching research and practice on a post qualifying child care programme*. Social Work Education, 22 (1).

Sawyer, RK (2001) *Creating conversations: improvisation in everyday discourse*. Cresskill, NJ: Hampton Press.

School Curriculum and Assessment Authority (1996) *Desirable outcomes for children's learning on entering compulsory education*. London: QCA/SCAA.

Schaffer, HR (1996) *Social development*. Oxford: Blackwell.

Schon, D (1983) *The reflective practitioner*. New York: Basic Books.

Social Care Institute for Excellence (2003) *Learning and teaching in social work education*. Southampton: Policy Press.

Scourfield, J (2003) *Gender and child protection*. Basingstoke: Palgrave Macmillan.

Scourfield, J and Welsh, I (2003) *Risk, reflexivity and social control in child protection: new times or same old story?* Critical Social Policy, 23(3). London: Sage.

Seltzer, K and Bentley, T (1999) *The creative age: knowledge and skills for the new economy*. London: Demos.

Shaffer, DR (1994) *Social and personality development*. Belmont: Brooks/Cole.

Sharp, C (2002) *School starting age: European policy and recent research*. Paper presented to the conference LGA seminar 'When should our children start school?', LGA Conference Centre, London.

Sharp, P (2001) *Nurturing emotional literacy*. London: David Fulton.

Shropshire, J and Middleton, S (1999) *Small expectations: learning to be poor*. York: York Publishing Services for the Joseph Rowntree Foundation.

Siraj-Blatchford, I (2001) *Diversity and learning in the early years*, in Pugh, G (ed) Contemporary issues in the early years. London: Paul Chapman.

Skelton, C (2001) *Schooling the boys: masculinities and primary education*. Buckingham: Open University Press.

Skelton, C and Hall, E (2001) *The development of gender roles in young children: a review of policy and literature*. Manchester: Research and Resources Unit, Equal Opportunities Commission.

Skevik, A (2003) *Children of the welfare state: individuals with entitlements, or hidden in the family?* Journal of Social Policy, 32, 423–40.

Smart, C, Neale, B and Wade, A (2001) *The changing experience of childhood – families and divorce*. Cambridge: Polity.

Smith, PK, Cowie, H and Blades, M (2003) *Understanding children's development*. 4th edition. Oxford: Blackwell.

Southworth (1998) *Leading improving primary schools; the work of headteachers and deputies*. London: Falmer Press.

Spock, B (1946) *Baby and child care*. New York: Duell, Sloan and Pearce.

Sroufe, LA (1995) *Emotional development: the organisation of emotional life in the early years*. Cambridge: Cambridge University Press.

Stainton Rogers, R and Stainton Rogers, W (1992) *Stories of childhood – shifting agendas of adult concern*. Hemel Hempstead: Harvester Wheatsheaf.

Steedman, C (1995) *Strange dislocations: childhood and the idea of human inferiority, 1780–1930*. Cambridge, MA: Harvard University Press.

Stefani, LAJ, Clarke, J and Littlejohn, AH (2000) *Developing a student-centred approach to reflecting on learning innovations*. Education and Training International, 37 (2), 163–71.

Stenhouse, L (1975) *An introduction to curriculum research and development*. London: Heinemann, p.142.

Stewart, I and Joines, V (1987) *TA today: a new approach to transactional analysis*. Nottingham: Lifespace Publishing.

Stoll, L and Fink, D (1996) *Changing our schools*. Buckingham: Open University Press.

Strategy Unit (2002) *Inter-departmental childcare review: delivering for children and families*. London: Prime Minister's Strategy Unit.

Sure Start www.surestart.gov.uk

Sutherland, P (1992) *Cognitive development today: Piaget and his critics*. London: Paul Chapman.

Tannenbaum, R and Schmidt, WH (1973) *How to choose a leadership pattern*. Harvard Business Review, May.

Telford, H (1996) *Transforming schools through collaborative leadership*. London: Falmer.

Thelen, E and Smith, LB (1994) *A dynamic systems approach to the development of cognition and action*. Cambridge, MA: MIT Press.

Thompson, N (2001) *Anti-discriminatory practice*. 3rd edition. Basingstoke: Palgrave.

Thompson, N (2003) in Harrison, R, Mann, G, Murphy, M, Taylor, A and Thompson, N (eds) *Partnership made painless; a joined up guide to working together*. Oxford: Russell House Publishing.

Thurston, C and Church, J (2001) in Foley, P, Roche, J and Tucker, S (eds) *Children in society, contemporary theory, policy and practice*. Buckingham: Open University.

Tipper, E (2003) *Visit report #3: my visit to the Czech Republic*. OMEP Newsletter, Autumn, 5–6.

Tizard, B (1988) *Early influences on later school attainment at age eight*. Paper presented to the conference NFER on four year olds in school: recent research, York.

Tozer, R (2003) *Visit report #2: my visit to Norway*. OMEP Newsletter, Autumn, 4–5.

Trevarthen, C (1979) *Communication and cooperation in early infancy: a description of primary intersubjectivity*, in Bullowa, MM (ed) Before speech: the beginning of interpersonal communication. New York: Cambridge University Press.

Trevarthen, C (2003) *Making sense of infants making sense. Intellectica* (Revue de l'Association pour la Recherche Cognitive), 2002/1, 34, 161–88, Paris. **www.psy.ed.ac.uk/Staff/staff/colwynt /papers/Intellectica%202003.htm** (accessed 25 May 2004)

Trevarthen, C and Hubley, P (1978) *Secondary intersubjectivity: confidence, confiding and acts of meaning in the first year*, in Lock, A (ed) Action, gesture and symbol: the emergence of language. London: Academic Press.

Truby King, F (1937) *Feeding and care of baby*. Revised edition. London: Oxford University Press.

UNESCO (2003) *Global monitoring report 2003/04*. **http://portal.unesco.org/education/ en/ev.php-URL_ID=25838andURL_DO=DO_TOPICandURL_SECTION=201.html** (accessed 11 June 2004)

UNICEF (2002) *Global education in the CARK region*, CARK (Central Asian Republics and Kazakhstan). Global Education Project.

Van Maurik, J (2001) *Writers on leadership*. London: Penguin.

Vygotsky, LS (1968) *Thought and language* (translated by E Hanfmann and G Vakar). Cambridge, MA: MIT Press.

Vygotsky, LS (1978) *The role of play in development*, in Cole, M, John-Steiner, V, Scribner, S and Souberman, E (eds) *Mind in society: the development of higher psychological functions*. Cambridge, MA: Harvard University Press.

Wall, K (2003) *Special needs and early years: a practitioner's guide*. London: Paul Chapman.

Weare, K (2004) *Developing the emotionally literate school*. London: Paul Chapman.

Wesley, J (1872) *Works*. London: Wesleyan Conference Office.

West, A and Varlaam, A (1990) *Does it matter when children start school?* Educational Research,

32 (3), 210–17.

White, B (1996) *Globalisation and the child labour problem*. Journal of International Development, 8 (6), 829–39.

White, J (2002) *The child's mind*. London: Routledge.

White, M (1999) *PM's 20-year target to end poverty*. The *Guardian*, 19 March.

White, M (2001) *Taking children seriously*. The *Guardian* and Save the Children supplementary publication for the UN Special Session (September 2001), withheld and issued May 2002.

Woodhead, M (1989) *School starts at five … or four years old?: the rationale for changing admission policies in England and Wales*. Journal of Educational Policy, 4 (1), 1–21.

Woodhead, M (1998) *Child work and child development in cultural context: a study of children's perspectives in selected countries in Asia, Africa and Central America*, in Johnson, V et al. (eds) Stepping forward, children's and young peoples's participation in the development process. London: Intermediate Technology Publications.

Woods, M (1998) *Early childhood education in preschool settings*, in Woods, M and Taylor, J (eds) Early childhood studies: an holistic introduction. London: Arnold.

Woods, M and Taylor, J (1998) *Early childhood studies: an holistic introduction*. London, Arnold.

Woods, P, Boyle, M and Hubbard, N (1999) *Multicultural children in the early years: creative teaching, meaningful learning*. Clevedon: Multilingual Matters.

Wordsworth, W (1888) *The complete poetical works*. London: Macmillan.

World Education Forum (2000) *The Dakar framework for action, education for all: meeting our collective commitments*. Paris: UNESCO.

Young, IM (1997) *Intersecting voices*. Princeton, NJ: Princeton University Press.

Young, M and Wilmott, P (1957) *Family and kinship in East London*. Harmondsworth: Penguin.

Zelizer, VA (1985) *Pricing the priceless child: the changing social value of children*. New York: Basic Books.

Index